| DATE | | | |
|------|------|------|------|
|  |  |  |  |
|  |  |  |  |
|  |  |  |  |
|  |  |  |  |
|  |  |  |  |
|  |  |  |  |
|  |  |  |  |
|  |  |  |  |
|  |  |  |  |
|  |  |  |  |
|  |  |  |  |
|  |  |  |  |
|  |  |  |  |

# Language Arts

## Arts

## And The Young Child

Thomas D. Yawkey
THE PENNSYLVANIA STATE UNIVERSITY

Eunice N. Askov
THE PENNSYLVANIA STATE UNIVERSITY

Carol A. Cartwright
THE PENNSYLVANIA STATE UNIVERSITY

Mary M. Dupuis
THE PENNSYLVANIA STATE UNIVERSITY

Steven Hunter Fairchild
JAMES MADISON UNIVERSITY

Margaret L. Yawkey
TYRONE (PENN.) AREA SCHOOL DISTRICT

F.E. PEACOCK PUBLISHERS, INC. ITASCA, ILLINOIS 60143

Copyright © 1981 by F. E. Peacock Publishers, Inc. All rights reserved
Library of Congress Catalog Card No. 80-52447
International Standard Book Number 0-87581-263-5
Printed in the United States of America

# DEDICATED TO

. . . . those preservice and inservice early childhood educators who continually seek and strive to improve their abilities to teach the language arts more effectively to those young children with whom they work. BEST WISHES!

## THE PEACOCK
## EARLY CHILDHOOD EDUCATION
## SERIES

### By Everett T. Keach, Jr.


**LANGUAGE ARTS AND THE YOUNG CHILD**

**A PRIMER ON TEACHING READING: Basic Concepts and Skills of The Early Elementary Years**

# FOREWORD

The Peacock Early Childhood Education Series evolved from the recurrent complaint from early childhood teachers that they needed, most of all, during their professional training sequence, a practical, relevant and concise treatment of methodology in their field-based experiences. This need extended into their entrance into the teaching profession.

As prospective teachers and beginning teachers, they understood the need for a broad foundation in child development, history of early childhood education and principles of learning. In numerous instances, however, this subject matter content overshadowed the treatment of classroom strategies to be used in teaching specific areas such as the language arts, social studies, and reading — strategies which are sorely needed in the field-based setting.

Related to the increasing emphasis upon field-related activities in the professional training sequence of the prospective teacher of young children is the need for classroom-tested activities that are functional in terms of: (1) the needs of the child and (2) the limited experiences of the prospective teacher.

In consideration of the above, the series is committed to provide — both in its current and in its future publications — viable activities for children in those subject areas normally introduced in an early childhood curriculum.

In addition, the series will provide bibliographies and other resources to extend the capabilities of a prospective or beginning teacher to arrange meaningful and productive learning experiences for the young child.

The concept of a methods text for students majoring in early childhood education is timely. In recent years, there has been a discernible move to separate the training of elementary teachers into two distinct programs — early childhood and middle school. Accompanying this trend has been a restructuring of syllabi in the professional training sequence resulting in a more definitive body of content to be studied in each program. There are, unfortunately, too few materials available for these emerging programs that have a sufficiently definitive focus to justify their use. Currently, elementary methods text are just that — textbooks that attempt to run the gamut from the kindergarten to the sixth or eighth level of schooling. These texts can only partially serve the needs of those specializing in early childhood education. What the Peacock Early Childhood Education Series has achieved is a series of texts tailored for the specific student population with whom the early childhood education major will be working.

The authors associated with the series have been chosen for their rich background in early childhood education as well as their proven ability to develop exciting, practical and clearly-delineated activities that can be implemented in the classroom. Their collective experiences base includes associations with Headstart and Follow-through programs, Right to Read projects, pioneering curriculum development projects in specific content areas such as social studies and the humanities, and curriculum development consultancies with international agencies and foreign governments.

Everett T. Keach, Jr., Editor
Early Childhood Education

Athens, Georgia

# PREFACE

This textbook covers the most relevant and meaningful areas of the language arts. These areas include: (a) spelling; (b) views of the young child's development and growth; (c) listening; and (d) imagination and creative expression. *Language Arts and the Young Child* is aimed at preservice and inservice educators in day care, nursery, kindergarten, and primary grades, and covers teaching and learning of the language arts in youngsters, ages two/three through age eight. Further, it can be used exclusively for early childhood language arts courses as well as for those courses on language arts that encompass *both* early childhood and elementary education. Finally, there are many benefits and special features of this textbook which make it useful to preservice and inservice educators and college instructors. They are: (a) showing the development and extensions of handwriting; (b) employing creative expression and imagination in language arts learning; (c) developing teaching ideas and strategies through an activity base; (d) identifying specific listening skills and spelling concepts that can be learned by the young child; (e) pinpointing child development approaches and language arts teaching strategies; and (f) developing oral language and composing. Thus, *Language Arts and the Young Child* is an effective tool for those adults desiring to work or those currently working with young children.

Thomas D. Yawkey
Eunice N. Askov
Carol A. Cartwright
Mary M. Dupuis
Steven H. Fairchild
Margaret L. Yawkey

University Park, Pennsylvania
Harrisonburg, Virginia
State College, Penn.

# ACKNOWLEDGMENTS

Many individuals and agencies contributed to the development of *Language Arts and the Young Child.* We owe debts of gratitude to F. Edward Peacock, President, and Thomas R. LaMarre, Vice-President, of F. E. Peacock Publishers, Inc., for their initial and continued support of this project and their belief in the contributions of this textbook to early education and to Peacock's Early Childhood Education Series. We would also like to express our particular appreciation to Professor Everett J. Keach, Jr., of The University of Georgia's College of Education and Editor of Peacock's Early Childhood Education Series for his thorough professional critique of and his supportive, personable, and reflective thoughts on the manuscript. To all those we are also grateful for their comments and reactions to earlier drafts of this textbook.

To Professor Fred H. Wood, Head, Division of Curriculum and Instruction, The Pennsylvania State University, University Park, we owe our thanks and gratitude for the continued support of this project since its inception and to his contributions to the authors' development of the manuscript for this book. We are also indebted to those undergraduate students in our Early Childhood and Elementary Education courses at The Pennsylvania State University and to the children and teaching adults in selected child care centers and elementary schools in the State College vicinity for enabling us to try our ideas with them. T. Yawkey, one of the authors, would like to express particular appreciation to: Ford C. Price, Jr., President; Jerome P. Welch, the Publisher; Barbara J. Frye, Field Editor — Research and Program Development in Oklahoma City, Oklahoma; and Richard R. Smith, Central Regional Manager, Colorado Springs, Colorado, all of The Economy Company Educational Publishers, Inc., for their continuing support of his writing and researching in language arts and reading which made possible the research constructs underlining Chapter 7 of this textbook. Without all of the professional assistance of the above individuals, this book would not have been possible.

In addition to individuals we would also like to thank the following agencies which gracefully permitted us to use some of their materials for this textbook. These agencies, organizations, and publishers are: Academic Press (New York); Charles E. Merrill Publishers (Ohio); Educational Products Information Exchange (New York); Ginn Publishers (Massachusetts); Harper and Row Publishers (New York); HICOMP Outreach Project (University Park, Pennsylvania); Macmillan Publishers (New York); Pennsylvania Department of Education (Harrisburg, Pennsylvania); University of Iowa Press (Iowa City, Iowa); and Viking Press (New York).

# CONTENTS

# CHAPTER 1
# VIEWS OF THE LANGUAGE ARTS: AN OVERVIEW

*A good teacher of young children is also a good teacher of the language arts.*

*The Authors*

As an early childhood teacher you hear Shanda say to Sally, "You can't play with me!" and watch Sally's smile disappear into a frown. In the corner of the classroom, Barton is smiling and patting Angelo on his back and he responds by brushing Barton's drooping locks across his forehead. You also note Elizabeth moving her arms up and down beneath a Superman cape and Beatrice, Judy, and Daniel stacking blocks — one object on top of the other — in the block corner. Meanwhile Elizabeth swoops alongside Kenneth and Ismil and with her Superman cape still flopping, states, "You are the bad guys and I will catch you and put you in jail!"

The youngsters are communicating their thoughts in verbal and nonverbal ways. Likewise, you also communicate to your children in verbal and nonverbal fashion. Your smile says to the youngsters, "I like you and what you are doing." Moving your forefinger down says to them, "Sit down!" Your voice tells the pupils, "It's time for lunch." Communication involves sharing thoughts and ideas between children and between you and the children. Language arts are the basic processes that help people send, receive, and understand messages in verbal and nonverbal ways.

Accordingly, the areas, or fields, of the language arts as defined in this book are speaking, listening, spelling, writing, and imaginative thought and creative expression. The primary goal of each of the areas comprising the language arts is communication. What you do and say and what children do and say in informal and formal settings at the preschool, kindergarten, or primary grades all has impact on the growth and learning of the language arts. Because the language arts and its various subcomponent areas stress communication in some form or fashion, they enable children to function effectively in the peer, classroom, family, and neighborhood groups.

Thus, the language arts are basic and crucial to all good school programs for the young child. In addition, they are a substantive part of every youngster's development and formal learning. As a teacher of young children, from two or three to eight years of age, you play a major part in determining what language arts content is taught and how it is taught. You have much to say in shaping and guiding youngsters in soundly developing and effectively learning these crucial and basic concepts. For example, the amount of time scheduled for language arts per classroom day, the use of incidental experiences for language arts instruction, the preparation, planning, and implementing of the instructional objectives of your language arts program, and their evaluation all help to shape the learning and development of language arts concepts and ultimately determine the effectiveness of your program.

This book is designed to develop, expand, and enrich your competencies as an early childhood teacher of the language arts. Whether you teach at day care, nursery, and other preschool levels or at the kindergarten and primary grade levels in public or private schools, the message of this book is clear and straightforward. As a teacher of young children you help, guide, and instruct children in their most formative years. In these early years, the concepts and skills in communication and the language arts become the bricks and mortar of present and future living, learning, and earning. Furthermore, since language, thinking, and socioemotional development and learning are all interrelated, the early childhood educator, working with young children in their formative years, is first of all a teacher of the language arts.

Although there are the Sallys, Bartons, Angelos, and Shandas in your classroom to guide through emotionally troubled times; mathematics, science, and other subject-matter disciplines to teach; theme-oriented units such as pets, families, and transportation to introduce and complete; and parents, peers and supervisors with whom to work, children's learning of language arts concepts is one of your primary responsibilities. Accordingly, the overriding message that flows throughout this book is that a good teacher of the young child is, in turn, a good teacher of the language arts in early childhood programs.

In the following section of this chapter we provide a rationale for the importance of the language arts to the development and learning of young children and to good programs in early childhood education. Next, the content of the language arts and its role or function in good schools for children are described. In turn, each of the six chapters in the book shows the importance of one of the various areas of the language arts to growth and learning, identifies appropriate strategies for teaching communication processes, and suggests additional resources that you can use to enrich and expand your repertoire of understandings, skills, and attitudes as an early childhood educator of the language arts.

## IMPORTANCE OF THE LANGUAGE ARTS

There are several reasons why the language arts are crucial to the growth and learning of children you teach and to your education and development program. These reasons are: (1) Language arts develop communication processes; (2) Language arts enable children to participate in vicarious experiences; (3) Language arts are language and thought; (4) Language arts are personality growth; and (5) Language arts assist the growth of bilingual-bicultural children. Each one of these reasons, viewed separately or taken as a group, points to the vital role played by the language arts for every child. Language arts reflect life itself (2).

## Communication

Language arts are important to the individual child and to your education and development program because they teach forms of communication. Communication uses language in nonverbal and verbal ways to transmit meaning from audible sounds and observable gestures. In early childhood, we think of language as both nonverbal and verbal, since both symbols represent and transmit meanings to others. The nonverbal symbols may be facial, arm, trunk, neck, and other body movements or part- and whole-body coordinations. At the same time, these nonverbal symbols represent meanings. For example, Sally's facial frowns represent "sadness" while Barton's smile shows "happiness" and Elizabeth's rapid arm and shoulder movements represent "Superman flying." The verbal symbols may be vocal such as audible sounds and combinations of sounds as well as graphic symbols such as intelligible drawings and pictures as well as letters and combinations of letters (2). These verbal symbols also transmit meanings to other people, for example, Shanda's statement, which excluded Sally from playing with her, and Elizabeth's, which included two members of her peer group in her make-believe activity.

The fact that the language arts teach, develop, and enhance forms of communication makes it primary to other subject and social living areas. Since almost all of the school day in early childhood involves some form or mode of verbal and nonverbal communication, the language arts become central to teaching and working with young children. In this context, the fifteen to twenty minutes at the preschool level or thirty to forty minutes in the primary grades that are scheduled for language arts activities are only a small part of the time per classroom day actually devoted to the language arts.

The fact that young children spend the majority of their time throughout the school day practicing, developing, and learning communication in formal and informal ways lends additional support to the importance of the language arts. Using verbal and nonverbal forms throughout the day, youngsters become immersed in a sea of communication about them. Whether performing receptive language activities of listening, reading readiness, formal reading or expanding expressive language actions such as speaking, nonverbal actions, writing readiness (for instance, drawing) and formal writing, children receive, send, and interpret the senses of seeing, listening, speaking, smelling, touching, and moving. You can insure that your language arts program contributes to the learning and growth processes of communication. To find out how much clocktime is really spent in the language arts, you can do a small survey. Visit an early childhood classroom and interview the teacher. Ask the teacher questions to help you estimate the amount of clocktime that is devoted to or used in the communication processes and determine the significant contributions that language arts make to formal and informal routines throughout the day. Some of these questions are:

1. How much time per day is alloted to the formal teaching of language arts in the classroom? The answers to this question clearly show the amount of formal time allocated to language arts learning and development.
2. How much time per day is allotted to teaching language arts in related content areas in the classroom? For example, if you observe the classroom teacher asking the children to name pictures of animals in pre-science or taking them on a field trip to a new shopping mall or fire station and having them talk about their experiences in social education, language arts are being used and taught. The first experience is teaching language memory through science readiness, and the latter is aural and oral language comprehension in social education.
3. How much time per day is allotted to the language arts in informal sessions, such as getting ready for the playground, going to the rest room, working on projects in individual or small-group settings, doing activities in free time, and sharing ideas through incidental experiences? The time allocated to these informal and constructive sessions involves various forms of communication, since receptive and expressive modes of the language arts are used to convey ideas and thoughts meaningfully.

After you complete your survey, you will be astonished at the amount of clock time per day used to teach the language arts formally or informally. As the hub of the developmental and educational wheel of early childhood programs, the language arts have a great impact on shaping whether or not young children succeed or fail in present and future living, learning, and earning.

## Vicarious Experiences

There are two types of experiences that are interrelated with the language arts, each in different and interesting ways. First, direct firsthand experiences are the bricks and mortar of the language arts' development and learning. From direct association with the environment of concrete objects and people, the very young child learns and models language and communication forms. For example, the infant learns the concepts of "bottle," "cat," or "spoon" only after having received direct experiences with these objects in the environment. Having associated the concrete physical object with the verbal symbol for it, the infant begins to use language symbols to communicate needs and desires. Accordingly, the young child requires direct sensory impressions from the surrounding physical world to develop language and conceptual processes. With each new firsthand experience the infant soaks up information like a sponge, adds novel vocabulary words, and learns new and deeper meanings to familiar words and previously acquired concepts. The initial and subsequent development of language and conceptual processes require firsthand experiences based on the use of the senses of seeing, listening, smelling, touching, tasting, and movement. Thus, direct experiences are interrelated with language because they provide the child with opportunities to develop representational concepts using the senses. They also enable the youngster to associate sounds, words, and sentences with concepts. Direct firsthand experiences contribute to the language arts by constructing a firm foundation of conceptual understandings, skills, and attitudes for further scaffolding of language learning and concept development.

The second type of experience which is interrelated with language arts is vicarious experience. Vicarious experiences are "secondhand" and enable the child to understand and relate new and unfamiliar information with past experiences and essentially comprehend new communicative and conceptual processes through the old ones. In this instance, the language arts transmit vicarious experiences that enable the child to develop, shape, and expand new understandings, skills, and attitudes.

Through hearing books and stories, seeing roles that are dramatized and television and motion pictures, the language arts can provide a rich source of vicarious experiences to expand the child's initial scaffolding. As the age of the child increases, he or she learns more and more concepts through vicarious experiences provided by language activities because he or she is already well grounded on firsthand experiences in the environment. Accordingly, vicarious experiences acquired through the language arts play a larger and larger role in the development and expansion of conceptual and communication processes. As children read more and more books, listen discriminatively to conversation between peers, and see more and more of their world through television and motion pictures, the language arts increase their contribution to growth through vicarious experiences.

## Language and Thought

The relationship between language and thought also shows the importance of language arts. Researchers generally consider, and their research results show, that the growth and functional use of language is interrelated with the development of thought. From the perspective of cognitive development, there are several major characteristics of thinking in young children from ages two or three through eight. Some of these characteristics of thought are: (1) egocentricism, (2) decentration, and (3) transformation.

Egocentric thought is the inability of young children to see or view themselves from another's perspective. Since they are unable to take the role of another person conceptually by "stepping inside their shoes," young children see the world, situations, events, and people only from their own concrete viewpoints. For example, one young child standing on a curb watches his friend ride by in a car. Although the child sees his friend moving by in the car, he cannot take the conceptual perspective of the other youngster in thinking about and seeing himself from that vantage point. Here, the child on the curb cannot see himself from his friend's perspective — as standing still. Young children have not yet developed abstract thought to put themselves in the place of others. Since they show egocentric thought, they cannot explain or describe themselves, people, events, or situations from the perspective of the other. Thus, language learning and use are both limited by the egocentric level of thought.

Decentration is an intellectual capacity of the youngster to attend and focus conceptually on superficial rather than salient characteristics of situations, events, and stimulus properties of objects. In decentering, the youngster attends to and conceptualizes in "specifics" rather than "wholes." For instance, a youngster is presented with two sets of four marbles each. The marbles are blue in color, and those in one set are aligned in a row three inches apart from one another. The members of the other set of marbles are all clumped together forming a square in shape, each placed five inches apart from the other. When asked whether each set contains the same number or whether one set has a greater number of marbles in it than the other set, the youngsters most likely respond with, "one set has a greater number." On being asked which set has the greater number, they most likely answer or point to the set whose numbers are aligned in a row. Even though the youngsters count and see the adult build the two sets or they construct the sets themselves, the children conceptualize and attend to specifics, in this instance, the spaces between the objects rather than the wholes, or cardinality. The youngsters show thought characterized as decentration. And, in turn, the language they use to explain, transmit, and communicate their thoughts reflects their level of thinking. Accordingly, the thought and language generated in this problem-solving situation, by adult standards at least, represent inaccurate mental and verbal pictures of real events and of reality.

The third characteristic of thought that also shows the interrelatedness of language and thought is transformation. Transformation is the conceptual ability to interrelate a series of successive events in time and space. However, the young child of three or four generally has not acquired thought transformations. Thus, instead of seeing relationships between successive events, the youngster views them as single events — with each one separate and independent of the other. For instance, the young child walking through a forest sees a rabbit as it dashes beneath a bush. A second or two later, this child comes across the same rabbit heading for its burrow. Because the child cannot conceptually transform events in this instance, he sees the same rabbit twice but thinks that there are two rabbits. Even though it is the same rabbit, the child explains there are two rabbits, reasoning that each was seen at a different time and place.

As the thought processes in the young child grow and nonegocentric thinking, centration, and transformation abilities develop, language abilities also increase in quality and quantity. Researchers point out that thinking and using language are interrelated and interdependent systems that benefit one another more and more as the child increases in conceptualization and age.

## Language and Personality

Just as language and thought are interrelated, language and personality are also interdependent. The language arts and communication processes, in general, can influence personality development and learning through self-concept and social group contacts. The language that young children use to express desires, wishes, concerns, and interests becomes a reflection of their social selves. Using communicative processes of the language arts, children interact with one another in their physical and social worlds. Young children who effectively communicate with one another act and react with language. In turn, they receive feedback that helps shape their self-image and self-esteem. For example, youngsters who have problems using communication find it difficult to have their ideas and thoughts understood in a clear and straightforward fashion. Because of these difficulties, the messages they send are not interpreted by another individual or a group, and the information they receive reflects confusion. Regardless of the way in which these children respond, the self-concept bears the brunt of uneasy or inadequate feelings that are generated. For example, through continual use of infantile expressions, preschoolers can be labeled by their peers and unfortunately in some cases by their teachers as "babies." The feedback these children receive because of their use of infantile expressions can affect the way they view themselves. They may actually begin to act like infants, perhaps becoming withdrawn or shy or aggressive. Youngsters' self-concept is molded by the language they use as they send, receive, and interpret communication from each other. The bilingual-bicultural child, who either partly or solely speaks a language other than English, can easily become the object of ridicule and criticism by the peer group. The self-concept in turn bears the brunt of this battering, and as the child internalizes this negative feedback, he or she begins to feel like a "bad" and unworthy individual compared to peer-group members. The youngster is extremely sensitive and vulnerable to the surrounding world. Language is one factor that helps shape and mold self-concept and the child's desire and interest in present and future learning and schooling.

Secondly, language can increase or decrease social group contacts. Language is developed and learned in social group contexts, and children use their fullest range of communication abilities when interacting with one another. Language, if used appropriately, can help develop social group contacts and contribute to constructive personality growth as well as generate situations that maximize potential for generative growth. The youngster who continually communicates to peers by using restrictive coding such as "You can't play with me!" reduces social group contacts and in turn decreases opportunities to share ideas meaningfully and expand language repertoire through interaction. With continual cues for exclusion, social isolation may effect personality development.

In social programs for the young child at the preschool-kindergarten and primary grade levels, you may experience a boy or girl who won't talk. Although, in this instance, the youngster may be passively and silently resisting excessive domination by significant adults, this situation is another example of the interrelationships between language and personality development. The personal and self-protection the child may be acquiring by not talking, in addition, show the effects of personality and language problems that may eventually become more serious. Although the situation of a child who "won't talk" may be overcome by arousing curiosity and immediate reinforcement for communicating interests, recognizing the interrelationships between language and personality is a necessary first step in working with young pupils as a teacher of the language arts.

## Bilingualism

The language arts are important to all pupils and especially to young bilingual-bicultural children, because through communication processes they can: (1) better understand their own native heritages; (2) develop positive attitudes about themselves; and (3) develop greater sensitivity toward others. There are thousands of bilingual-bicultural youngsters in our schools at early childhood levels, and more are entering schools daily.

These children may be Native American, Vietnamese-American, Hispanic-American, or others, and they may come into the classroom able to speak only their native languages or a combination of English and native languages with varying degrees of proficiency in both. Trying to eliminate or restrict the use of the native languages is neither beneficial to your language arts program nor helpful to these children's motivation, learning, self-concept, or school success. Eliminating or restricting the use of native languages is also not consistent with contemporary early childhood theory and practice, since the focus is on cultural pluralism and its contributions rather than an outdated and restrictive "melting pot" philosophy.

The language arts are especially significant to bilingual-bicultural programs for they have the potential to provide for the development of both English and the native languages. Being able to speak two languages in our present society is neither a handicap nor a barrier to these children's intellectual learning as we once thought, because cultures have intermeshed and we need to understand and communicate with each other across a pluralistically oriented society.

Having the language arts serve the child with divergent language patterns contributes to a better understanding of native heritages. Being able to show proficiency in the native and English languages, one of the goals of the contemporary language arts, means that the bilingual-bicultural child must first identify with the native heritage. Identifying with the native heritage, children with divergent language patterns feel that their cultures are important and contribute to themselves. Having your program in the language arts assist bilingual-bicultural children to understand their heritage means that their native language is welcome and used in the classroom. As a teacher you can facilitate understandings, beliefs, and attitudes of this heritage as well as encourage the growth of communication processes by learning to greet bilingual children in the native language, studying about the culture and introducing that content through the language arts, developing and using school word lists in the native language, making and using a home word list in that language, and inviting guests to the classroom from various cultures to present special programs or as resource people. In addition, there are numerous other opportunities for having the language arts contribute to a better understanding of the bilingual-bicultural child's heritage.

Secondly, through communication processes youngsters with divergent language patterns can develop positive attitudes about themselves. Your use of the native language in the classroom, support of native cultures, and treatment of bilingual-bicultural children like other children create positive attitudes toward learning in the bilingual-bicultural youngster. With such support, bilingual-bicultural children perform better in these endeavors and show confidence and stability in their lives at school and home. Using the language arts to contribute to the development of positive attitudes can be achieved in many ways. Supporting the use of the native language through role-play activities, songs, and fingerplay games are only some of many ways that create self-positivism in bilingual-bicultural youngsters.

The third way that the language arts contribute to communication processes of the bilingual-bicultural child is in building sensitivity to others. The use of native and English languages in early childhood classrooms assists all children to become more aware of various cultural values through communication processes. This understanding of cultural values and appreciation of cultural pluralism contributes to sensitivity to others. Language arts activities, aimed at developing sensitivity to others by understanding their own and other cultural patterns, provide greater potential for interaction among children in classroom settings. Thus, the language arts effectively contribute to children's learning and ultimately to their school success through communication processes aimed at understanding their heritages, developing positive attitudes about themselves, and learning greater sensitivity toward others.

The basic reasons for the importance of the language arts are that they are the foundation for learning and development of young children in early childhood education. Based on their contributions to communication processes, vicarious experiences, language and thought, language and personality, and bilingual-bicultural children, the language arts form the core of development and learning opportunities for school programs in early childhood. Whether you schedule the language arts as a separate subject-matter discipline along with mathematics, science, and others in your school program or as the core of your routines for other subjects and special thematic areas, they contribute greatly to intellectual, social, and motor growth and learning. Although the abilities among individual children vary widely, a program of understanding, encouraging, and helping them acquire the concepts and skills of the language arts assists them in leading productive and worthwhile lives. Good teachers of the language arts are guided by the deep concern that the potential for learning and developing communication processes belongs to all children (1).

## LANGUAGE ARTS CONTENT FIELDS

As previously described, the language arts content fields are defined as speaking, listening, spelling, writing, and imaginative thought and creative expression. Although not a content field, another area that is related to language arts learning is the view you have of the young child. Without an understanding of the views and beliefs you have about the young children in learning and development, each of the content fields of the language arts taken separately or as a group has only a small impact on them. Accordingly, the decisions you make about language arts programming in your classroom rest on your views and beliefs of how young children learn and develop. Thus, in this section, we summarize the areas of the language arts covered in the chapters of this text as well as provide a rationale for making important decisions in teaching these communication processes based on the views of how children learn and develop.

## Views of the Young Child in the Language Arts Program

Chapter 2 of this text explores in depth the bases for decision making in language arts programming in early childhood education. This section of this chapter briefly introduces the content presented in Chapter 2. The decisions you make in teaching the language arts and the communication activities you provide for children rest on your views of how young children learn and develop.

All views of how children learn and develop can be grouped into three categories. They are: (1) cognitive-interactionist, (2) behaviorist, and (3) maturationist. Regardless of which one or ones you may follow, it is important, first of all, to recognize your own orientation or orientations and systematically to put it (or them) into practice to help make decisions in working with young children in the language arts. Although understanding and viewing the child and making educational programming decisions in the language arts based on one or more categories of developmental and learning approaches may sound academic, theoretical, or dull, the fact is that you show your views of the young child. Just as you show certain attitudes in the clothing and cars you select, in similar fashion, you choose and make decisions about language arts programming based on your views and beliefs about yourself and about young children in planning and implementing communication experiences. Your views of how young children develop and learn, then, become road maps that permit you to make decisions about learning in systematic rather than haphazard fashion.

The behaviorist, maturationist, and cognitive-interactionist road maps explain how children learn and develop. They are briefly described here. The maturationist view regards biological or internal factors as primary causes of mental, physical, and personality growth. Accordingly, developmental growth proceeds as a function of age. New mental, physical, and personality concepts and skills emerge in the child at critical periods in the early and later years of the life span. The environment provides the nutrients that help enrich, sustain, and expand these new emerging concepts and skills. Using the maturationist road map in planning your teaching of the language arts suggests a number of practical applications. You would plan an enriched language arts program in which the child is immersed in a communication environment that would activate normal biological or innate capacity for language growth. Taking advantage of these critical periods of language growth, you play a supportive role in providing materials and experiences at the right time. You take the lead from the child and shape your language arts program and select materials and experiences based on the needs of the child and critical periods of development. Following the maturationist road map, your language arts program is totally child-centered. You do not push or rush children in developing communication progresses.

Using a cognitive-interactionist road map to describe the route children take to develop mental and related cognitive functions such as language leads you to chart your course in the language arts program around both the child and the environment. Here, children develop mental abilities such as language by what they do with language using their own physical and mental actions. The cognitive-interactionist view holds that development is a product of interactive forces between the child and the environment. Both the environment, made up of physical objects and ideas, and the child account for the present level of mental growth. The factors that help shape the intellectual development of the child are (1) direct experiences with the physical world, (2) social experiences and transmission of ideas through instructions such as the family, school, and religious organizations, (3) maturation, and (4) problem-solving experiences and processes. Development thus evolves as the child is challenged by experiential events. In turn, the child actively meets these experimental challenges through cognitive or intellectual self-reorganization and restructuring. As a result of this self-restructuring, the child's intellectual functions such as language proceed. The cognitive-interactionist perspective of how children develop has several implications that help shape your language arts program.

First, language ability is generally determined by the child's level of intellectual development. This idea suggests that the language arts program must nurture intellectual growth through a strong emphasis on manipulation, exploration, and active involvement with materials and in social peer group dialogues. Secondly, language abilities can stimulate intellectual growth in certain instances in which youngsters are required to represent absent objects and recall past events. Accordingly, your language arts program would have elements of dramatic and sociodramatic play. These elements or techniques provide children with opportunities to change themselves into others as shown by their verbal and motor actions. The conceptual ability to represent objects that are absent through dramatic and sociodramatic play places a heavy emphasis on communication processes to transmit meaning. Thirdly, developing cognitive functions such as language requires self-structuring and self-organization. In the language arts program, the teacher must largely follow a "wait-challenge-wait" procedure. In the "wait-challenge-wait" role, you arrange language arts materials for the children to challenge their mental functions. In turn, problem-solving interactions arise in which you guide children through inquiry processes to present them with ideas that help them restructure and reorganize their thinking. The integral relationships between thought and language are not clearly seen in the cognitive-interactionist perspective. Guided discovery, conceptually challenging materials, and peer group-teacher interaction are some of the hallmarks of language arts programs using a cognitive-interactionist perspective as a guidepost.

With the behaviorist road map, biological determinants of how children develop and learn play a much smaller role in shaping than in either maturationist and cognitive-interactionist views. The role of the environment is emphasized. Accordingly, learning in a young child is a product of special individual stimulus situations and reinforcing elements in that child's particular environment. The child's responses to learning must be observed and demonstrated in the environment. In turn, those responses become signals to a behaviorist that the youngster is acquiring skills. These visible acts or behaviors that show that youngsters have learned can be counted. They become the basis for measuring the amount of learning that has taken place through discriminative stimuli and reinforcing elements in the environment. The language arts, first of all, are seen as a series of academic skills that are crucial to the young child's learning. In this instance, behaviorists think that the child must use communication processes correctly. The quality and quantity of the youngster's language depend on success in school. Secondly, you as the teacher determine the language arts skills that children are to learn and master and identify appropriate stimuli and reinforcement. Accordingly, children do not fail to learn, but the teacher may have failed to determine the proper set of discriminative stimuli and reinforcement. Thirdly, the instructional objectives for each lesson are specific and show the conditions of behavior in which the children display the actions, the end or terminal skills you desire them to acquire, and the criterion you accept as evidence that they have mastered the skill. Finally, programmed materials for language arts learning are very useful and desirable, since they are skill-specific and have reinforcement and automatic feedback built into them. They have great utility, for they clearly show whether pupils have learned the skills and concepts.

The behaviorist, maturationist, and cognitive-interactionist road maps are very different views of how children learn and develop. Using these road maps for decision making helps you to determine how to teach and guide your children in developing and learning the communication concepts in the language arts.

## Listening

In Chapter 3 of this book, you will read about listening as a content field of the language arts. Chapter 3 identifies a series of key skills and concepts that can be effectively taught throughout the early childhood years. These selected skills and concepts, contributing to the listening act, help the child "tune in" to the auditory environment. They are (1) auditory perception skills, (2) following directions, (3) deriving word meanings from context, and (4) auditory communication. The key to successful mastery and use of these concepts and skills of listening is to teach them for their own value as well as with other subject fields such as in formal reading.

Very briefly, auditory perception is the ability to become aware of sounds from the auditory environment, discriminate between similar and different sounds, and repeat the sounds that are heard. As such, auditory perception is made up of a series of component processes: (a) auditory awareness, or the ability of the child to listen for sounds, (b) auditory discrimination, or the capacity to recognize sounds that are similar and different, and (c) auditory memory, or the ability to repeat those sounds heard in the environment.

Following directions means teaching the child to recognize, understand, and act on simple one-step and multiple-step directions. One-set directions simply give the children one item or bit of information on which to act at a time. Examples of one-step directions are "Put your crayolas away," "Hang up your coat, please," or "Please hand me that sock puppet." Multiple-step directions carry a series of actions to be completed or performed. Some examples of multiple step directions include "Please put your blocks away and go to the rest room," "Pick up the book on the floor, please, put it on the shelf, and continue adding the numerals on the board," and "Please hand this paper bag to Theo, return to your play group, and tell me about your construction play."

The third main concept and skill area of listening is "deriving word meaning from context." This one is also extremely important. It highlights the fact that when we listen, we do not really need to think about all the words spoken in order to understand them. Unless the word or sets of words are new to us, are unusual in sound, or arouse our interest in some fashion, we derive meaning of a series of spoken words from context, inferring meaning from of the entire set and understanding the words through context. Deriving word meanings from the context in which they are spoken is an effective tool for young children to acquire through planned experiences or incidental situations throughout the day.

Auditory comprehension is the fourth major concept and skill area in listening. It means the mental ability to understand and grasp the meaning of information presented orally. Using auditory comprehension, you might ask the child who has just heard a story to retell an event in it. Or, at a more advanced level of auditory comprehension, you might ask the youngster to retell the entire story from beginning to end and require some form of interpretation about the character's feelings or motives in the passage. Teaching auditory comprehension by asking children to retell events or the entire narrative from stories or asking for interpretation of story characters and situations requires the youngsters to listen for details as well as use varying levels of thinking. Accordingly, skills of auditory comprehension require pupils to understand and group meanings of oral material and expression at both literal and predictive levels.

At the literal level of auditory comprehension, the questions you ask youngsters based on stories, other oral material, and oral expression require simple recall of information. At the predictive level, a more conceptually advanced form of auditory comprehension, youngsters must not only recall information but also use it in a meaningful way. In teaching auditory comprehension at the predictive level, the children must use known factual information gleaned from content to arrive at novel solutions to more conceptually abstract questions.

Chapter 3 describes and explains the area of listening in more detail and provides additional insight into meaningful activities that help children learn these skills and concepts. Ways of evaluating listening performance are also examined. Giving full attention to teaching listening serves the best interests of young children as well as the vital area of language arts.

## Oral Language Development and Composing

Speaking, or oral language development and composing, is thoroughly described in Chapter 4. The section on speaking in this chapter briefly introduces you to this area of the language arts and summarizes some of the major points explained in Chapter 4. Oral language development and composing rest primarily on speaking or oral expression. As such, there are several characteristics of oral language.

First, children transmit ideas and thoughts to peers and adults using oral expression. They spontaneously compose and transmit these messages to enable others to understand and react to them. Secondly, the oral language transmits symbols that represent objects, people, and situations in our society. The spoken symbols vary from culture to culture. Although they vary from society to society and are arbitrarily determined by its members, all spoken symbols are representations of the real world. The third characteristic of oral language is that it has a system. *System* is grammar or an organized set of sounds, sound-word patterns, endings, and word order that are understood by users of the language. Speaking is also a learned habit, and this characteristic shows why it is so important to school and home settings.

The fifth characteristic of oral language is communication. It permits children and adults to understand one another and is only useful to the extent that it fulfills this objective. Because speaking is oral, arbitrary communication, is a learned habit, and has a system, it is extremely important to language arts and to children in their early years.

These characteristics vary in quality and quantity according to the age of the student. The child develops and learns several skills and concepts basic to speaking, including distinctive features, types of sentence patterns, vocabulary, and articulation. Distinctive features of the syntactic system used in oral language are (1) sentences with subjects and predicates, (2) noun phrases, (3) negative forms, and (4) past tense. Types of oral sentence patterns that can be taught and assessed are (1) declarative, (2) negative, (3) question, and (4) imperative.

Knowledge of vocabulary enables children to describe their own life and surroundings in words. One type of vocabulary learning stresses categories of words, such as those for people, objects, and situations; those indicating relations such as "under" and "over"; and descriptive words, for example, "big," "small," and "round." The second type of vocabulary teaching reflects aspects of the world that are not a part of the child's immediate environment. This type of oral vocabulary growth and learning occurs from vicarious or "secondhand" experiences. Children learn this type of vocabulary from favorite television shows, peer group discussions, and favorite stories heard or read.

The fourth aspect of oral language which can be taught to young children is called articulation. Articulation is the ability to pronounce speech sounds such as "b" in "baby" or "t" in "top." Distinctive features and sentence patterns as part of syntactic system in speaking, vocabulary, and articulation are all vital and important aspects of the development and learning of oral language in the language arts program in early childhood education.

Accordingly, we recommend several specific goals for oral language instruction. These important objectives, discussed in detail in Chapter 4, are: (1) developing fluency, (2) encouraging syntactic development, (3) facilitating vocabulary learning, (4) integrating oral language use with daily living and learning, (5) encouraging self-expression, and (6) teaching oral language as thinking. In addition, this chapter identifies activities and experiences that help you in developing oral language and composing and suggests ways to evaluate speaking processes. The more we examine oral language and composing, the more interesting and vital they become to our language arts program for children in their formative years.

## Handwriting

Handwriting, another area of the language arts, is explained in depth in Chapter 5. This chapter looks at handwriting as communication through graphic symbols rather than discussing cursive or manuscript forms.

There are three basic stages in the development and growth of handwriting readiness. Skills and concepts in these stages are taught and developed. The outcomes of learning these readiness skills are greater muscle control and perceptual growth that enable the child to master the actual writing process as we know it. Making arm and hand movements is stage one of handwriting readiness. Children push, pull, pound, roll, bounce, or move objects in play. As a direct outcome of using these and other movements, children learn motor actions and body coordinations of the shoulders and upper arms. The second stage begins when the child makes controlled motor actions and movements. These movements resemble the writing process. As children handle and use drawing and painting tools, their arm and hand movements are strengthened. Small and large muscles of the fingers, hands, and arms and those of body coordinations develop, and children learn how to control them. They learn and practice controlled straight, curved, and circular motions of shapes that later become letter and numeral symbols in cursive and manuscript forms.

The third stage of readiness for handwriting is called copying. After becoming aware of objects and people and developing mental images and movements characteristic of stages one and two, perceptual images and motor actions combine in the child's thought and action. The outcome is copying objects. With much practice, youngsters are able to move into the actual handwriting systems that form the bases for manuscript and cursive writing.

Beyond the readiness stages, the child formally learns skills of handwriting. These basic skills are (1) handwriting strokes, (2) letter formation, (3) size, (4) proportion, (5) spacing, (5) alignment, and (6) line quality. These skills are examined in depth in Chapter 5, which discusses the mastery of horizontals, verticals, diagonals, and circulars that are handwriting strokes to be mastered. Letter formation, size, proportion, alignment, and line quality skills also prepare children to produce and practice manuscript and cursive writing.

These skills and concepts contribute to legibility, the primary objective of handwriting instruction and an extremely important quality to observe and assess in children's acquisition of writing processes.

The handwriting area of the language arts is encouraged in preschool-kindergarten children by initially preparing the classroom environment. When handwriting materials of various types and varieties are placed in the classroom, youngsters are encouraged to use them and in turn to develop and learn major readiness and advanced concepts and skills in the writing process. Using a variety of handwriting materials facilitates reflexive, maturational, and learning actions and reactions. Whether practicing handwriting skills in individual or group settings, the youngsters master new motor movements. Along with writing movements, they acquire the new set of vocabulary terms in the process. These terms can be grouped into categories; very briefly these are (1) general, (2) directional, (3) visual discrimination, and (4) spatial relations. Terms from these categories, described in Chapter 5, can be introduced and mastered as the youngsters practice writing skills.

As children master readiness and more advanced skills in handwriting and understand some of the vocabulary, formal training in manuscript and cursive systems begin. The usual sequences of formal lessons in handwriting are (1) letter formation and required stroke and sequence patterns, (2) transition from writing on unlined to writing on lined paper, and (3) practice in the program components of writing as they relate to letters on lines. Attention should be given to assisting them to develop constructive attitudes toward this important language arts area. Accordingly, the youngsters should internalize the objective of legibility and the habit of analyzing and correcting their own works.

In addition to these concepts and skills, Chapter 5 develops additional insight into teaching handwriting at the preschool-kindergarten and primary grade levels through writing activities and evaluation procedures. Handwriting, a tool of communication, is a means of sharing thoughts, abilities, and ideas and is a vital area of the language arts, focusing on written messages, legibility, and efficient production of handwriting symbols.

## Spelling

This section briefly shows the importance of spelling to the language arts and summarizes some of the major points discussed in Chapter 6.

When the young child first recognizes that letter sounds combine to form words, while listening and observing mother or teacher write his name for example, he or she becomes aware of spelling and the need for it. Then youngsters slowly realize that they are immersed in a print world — an environment of printed symbols strung systematically together to transmit meaning. Without a conventional pattern for spelling words, there is no way in which meaning can possibly be derived from these symbols. Being immersed in a print world also makes youngsters more aware of the interrelationships between spelling and other areas of the language arts.

The relationship of spelling to speaking means that children who articulate and pronounce words clearly will likely become good spellers. Pronouncing sounds of letters and words incorrectly produces spelling problems because children (and adults) try to spell what they say. Spelling and writing processes are also linked. Young preschool-kindergarten children receive their first introduction to spelling on an informal basis. After drawing pictures, they ask the teacher to write their name on or label them in some fashion, and in turn, they copy the words. Primary grade children usually do not begin formal spelling lessons until second grade although they are well aware of the sounds of letters and words in written form. Additional relationships between spelling and other areas of the language arts are learned as children gain more experience and have increased needs to explore language in informal and formal settings.

Chapter 6 also emphasizes that regardless of the grade level in which spelling is formally introduced, teaching the child to spell large numbers of words is an unsound practice because children, in all likelihood, do not continually use all these words in their speaking, writing, or reading. It is also a well-known fact that both children and adults continually use a small number of words in their writing compared to the number they actually know. Accordingly, there is little gain from teaching children to spell many words. Thus, Strickland (3) recommends a basic spelling-word range of 2,000 to 2,500 for children in grades 1 through 6 of the elementary school. The same generalization about teaching "too many" also applies to teaching spelling rules. Thus, teach formally those spelling rules that have few exceptions and consistently apply to large numbers of words. Examples of relevant and basic spelling words for older children and several sound spelling rules are identified and explained in Chapter 6.

Essentially, there are two methods of teaching spelling commonly used in our primary grades. The first method is spelling as adult-prescribed, and the second is spelling as child-relevant. Briefly, the adult-prescribed method uses lists of words largely taken from commercially prepared spelling books or workbooks. These lists are developed by adults for children and are estimates, at best, of spelling words pupils should be taught. The second method is child-relevant with spelling lists developed from the pupils' own written compositions and oral expressions. The words that students need to use in their stories and creative expressions and endeavors become those that they learn to spell.

Regardless of whether you use either or both methods of teaching spelling, children learn to spell words that they use in writing and spelling activities and in school and home experiences. Accordingly, assigning and testing for spelling words per week as an independent language arts class is appropriate if the students also use these same spelling words in other communication activities and subject-matter experiences. Using these same words in application is a procedure that produces dividends for children's learning as well as focuses clearly on the purpose of spelling. Spelling through meaningful use ties together the areas of the language arts and integrates them with actual learning and living experiences.

In teaching children to spell words, you can effectively use several techniques. The success of these techniques with primary grade children has been successfully proven. Chapter 6 identifies and explains several of these approaches. It also stresses that these approaches must be systematically and consistently used if they are to work for you and your children. Each approach to the teaching of spelling has a sensory base. In other words, learning and developing abilities to spell, like acquiring other subject-matter skills and concepts, rest on the use of the senses. The more children see, hear, touch, smell, and use movement as a base for their learning to spell words, the more effectively and efficiently they acquire them. In addition, all approaches to spelling have a mastery step in which children repeat the spellings of the words, practice them, and then use them in actual written stories, activities, and experiences in oral expression. The wide range of individual differences in learning to spell can be accommodated by using approaches to teaching spelling, employing them systematically and consistently, and recognizing that the primary purpose of spelling is communication in written form.

Additional ideas presented in Chapter 6 on spelling include assessment instruments to evaluate children's performance, resources that you can employ to enrich your spelling programs, and activities to assist children further in learning to spell. Above all, spelling, taught and learned in informal and formal settings, is an essential element in all language arts programs in early childhood education.

## Imaginative Play and Creative Expression

Chapter 7 of this book addresses imaginative play and creative expression. Like any area of the language arts, this one also contributes to communication processes through growth in imaging, increased recall, discriminative listening, development of novel forms of communication, learning socially appropriate communication and motor actions. In Chapter 7 each of these contributions is explained in depth.

Like other areas of the language arts, the skills and concepts of imaginative play and creative expression are developed and learned through systematic attention and planned procedures at the preschool-kindergarten and primary grade levels. These important techniques used at the preschool-kindergarten level in promoting creative and expressive concepts include identifying goals for teaching creative processes, selecting and working with creative play materials, and guiding the growth of telling stories.

Identifying goals for teaching creative processes means recognizing and using the ingredients necessary to develop imaginative play activities. The greatest amount of imaginative thought and creative expression occurs when the children exercise self-direction, internal control, and self-motivation in deciding on and carrying out play activities.

Another technique to promote creative thought and expression is selecting appropriate classroom materials. This strategy facilitates imaginative processes by using a variety of play objects, permitting choices, and insuring a balance of materials in classroom environments for young children. A third technique is developing creative dramatics activities. Creative dramatics and its various forms are ways youngsters create impromptu drama. Examples are fingerplays and action games. Another technique is guiding the growth of telling stories, which is ideal for encouraging creative processes. Telling stories is natural and spontaneous, and youngsters use words and movements to explain characters and situations. Each of these, and others as well, is described in depth in Chapter 7.

For primary grade children, there are several other types of activities and techniques that require more abstract thinking and complex forms of language than those at the preschool-kindergarten level. Some of these are pantomime, directed role play, and mental imagining through games. Guiding pantomime provides opportunities for the youngsters to express themselves through gestures and body movements. The actors show movements and emotions as they imitate a person, situation, or object but may not speak or make sounds. Another technique is directed role play, with a set of ten steps used as a guide and tool. This technique, like the others, capitalizes on the relationship between learning role taking and developing creative thinking and expression. Mental imagining through gaming is another technique that is ideal for older children. In using it, the youngsters mentally project imaginative thoughts about people, animals, situations, and many other things and orally express them under your guidance. In addition, mental imagining through gaming provides opportunities to generate hypothetical events and practice productive thinking as facilitators of creative expression. Following these procedures and using the techniques with children at the preschool-kindergarten and primary grade levels will encourage the development and learning of creative thought and expression. By guiding the children in these techniques for creative thinking and expression, children model, practice, and use them in school and home settings.

Chapter 7 also provides ways to evaluate creative thought and expression. Encouraging and facilitating imaginative thought and expression in young children contribute to the language arts and to the development of creative processes.

This brief overview of the content areas of the language arts discussed in each chapter of the book has shown the importance of the language arts to you and to the children you teach in early childhood. Teaching the language arts in appropriate ways means that they will effectively serve you in developing your communication program at preschool-kindergarten and primary grade levels. Learning about and using the content ideas from the chapters on the views of the young child; listening, oral language development, and composing; handwriting; spelling; and imaginative play and creative expression can help you become a good teacher of the language arts and a good teacher of young children.

## REFERENCES

1. Barkan, Manuel. *Through Art to Creativity*. Boston: Allyn and Bacon, 1960.
2. Petty, Walter; Petty, Dorothy; and Becking, Marjorie. *Experiences in Language: Tools and Techniques for Language Arts Methods*. Boston: Allyn and Bacon, 1976.
3. Strickland, Ruth. *The Language Arts in the Elementary School*. Lexington, Mass.: D.C. Heath, 1969.

# CHAPTER 2
# VIEWS OF THE YOUNG CHILD

*Should I be doing more with the basic skills in the language program?*
*What do I really think about the value of learning centers?*
*Should I use some programmed instruction materials with some children?*
*Do I make good use of the language experience approach?*
*Does the DISTAR program have possibilities for my children?*
*Where do I stand on the skills vs. holistic debate?*
*Are language activities for young children primarily for enrichment?*
*Should I be more careful about stating behavioral objectives for lessons?*
*Should I use money from the materials budget for language development kits?*

Questions, questions, questions. Decisions, decisions, decisions. What's a teacher to think? What's a teacher to do? Whose advice should be followed? Is there one true view of language development? Is there a best way to teach language to young children? How does a teacher sort through the carnival-like brouhaha surrounding the announcement of any "new" approach or materials?

These are difficult, complex, and provocative questions. As you might expect, the answers are far from simple. The purpose of this chapter is to provide some foundation for decision making about language arts programs for young children. The idea that *we teach children, not content* is an important part of this chapter. We want you to go away from reading this chapter thoroughly convinced that *there is nothing so practical as good theory.* Some important learning and human development theories are described. Language development activities appropriate for young children are also included. But the activities themselves are not nearly so important as the linkages between the learning and developmental theories and the teaching practices. The major objective of this chapter is to persuade you of the validity of the following statement:

> Good theory is a blueprint for practice; if you understand which theory or viewpoint about how children learn and develop you believe in, the decisions you make about language arts teaching will be less complex and more consistent and logical.

A secondary objective is to provide information about the diversity of the clientele — the children — in early education programs. Of special interest is the impact of Public Law 94-142, the Education for All Handicapped Children Act. It is expected that there will be increasing integration of handicapped and nonhandicapped youngsters as a result of P.L. 94-142.

## THE VALUE OF THEORY

As you read the chapter, it will be very clear that we do not subscribe to the "wonderful things to do next Monday" or "bag of tricks" type of teaching young children, no matter which content area is involved. We do believe in theories of child development as valuable tools for making educational decisions. Moffett and Wagner state the case very well:

> Faced with thirty or so wrigglers in a room you may grow quickly impatient with theory. But good theory should serve as a blueprint for action so that you know what to do Monday and any other time. It should provide a basic framework that indicates what to do in any situation and why to do this rather than that. It does not guide, however, by spelling out action as specifically as a musical score or a recipe. It gives you a comprehensive and integrated perspective within which all problems can be placed, a consistent way of thinking so that you can think what to do as you go. This is critical, because all that you can plan definitely for a class is something general enough to encompass all students. Running a classroom cannot be like following a script. Panic comes from forgetting your lines and not being able to improvise. Trying to stick to a script causes more difficulty than playing by ear. But playing by ear works only when you have thought out well what you are about. If you understand deeply enough what you are doing, you don't need to keep asking, "What do I do Monday morning?" (15:2)

Most of you would probably readily agree on the general responsibilities of a teacher. You would no doubt agree that all teachers must:

1. Have objectives in mind
2. Arrange and manage the learning environment
3. Understand and attend to individual differences
4. Select teaching materials
5. Deliver instruction to children
6. Evaluate children's progress

These roles and expectations for teachers are generally agreed upon regardless of content and clientele. But there are considerable differences of opinion about the *specifics* involved in performing the roles. There are thousands of possible objectives, materials, and methods from which to choose. And there are no formulas to insure a perfect choice even though advocates of one method or another may claim they have the panacea for whatever it is that must be done.

How does a teacher make decisions about these important roles? Are the decisions different for children with different characteristics and needs?

This chapter is an attempt to answer these questions. The key to the answers lies in a consideration of the value of theory as a means of deriving program practices for young children.

Many benefits are likely to result from the careful and consistent application of theory. According to Peters,

> An explicit and solidly based theoretical stance is seen as critical to the improvement of early childhood programming. Theory provides a basis for planning and acting in consistent ways. Through recourse to theory the teacher can derive program goals, set priorities, develop appropriate teaching methods, select materials, deductively arrive at solutions to everyday problems, and predict appropriate responses to future situations. (16:9)

Theory allows us to make predictions about the outcome of actions and events. Use of a theory increases the chances that certain outcomes will occur in certain situations and under certain circumstances. For example, suppose a teacher plans to teach a small group of children to sort pictures of farm animals into one group and pictures of farm buildings into another group. The general objective is, of course, to develop classification ability. There are literally hundreds of ways a teacher could go about achieving this objective. Suppose, however, that the teacher believes in the ideas of Piaget and tries to use teaching strategies consistent with an interpretation of Piaget's ideas about cognitive development. The children are encouraged to manipulate the picture cards. The teacher asks, "Why did you put that one there? What could you call that pile? How will you know which pile to put this new card on?" The teacher asks questions that gradually lead the children to do the sorting. The children are asked to label the two different piles and state the rule for making the classification. Chances are that the children are more likely to achieve the objective under the Piagetian approach than they would if the teacher went about achieving the objective in trial and error, haphazard fashion. The example is analogous to the use of a road map when traveling to a new location. The chances of getting there directly are much greater if you follow the map than if you rely on your instinct and general sense of direction.

Teachers are continually bombarded with information and need a comprehensive framework to use in analyzing and evaluating educational methods and materials. No matter how many catalogs you browse through searching for information about educational materials, no matter how many teachers' magazines you read in hopes of locating a number of interesting teaching ideas, no matter how many language arts textbooks you study (including this one!), no matter how many courses and seminars you attend, the information is not helpful until you have a way to organize and make sense of it. You need to become an educated consumer of educational information and ideas.

Teaching cannot be based upon blind faith about the efficiency of an approach nor on intuition or the momentum of an idea currently on the bandwagon. While a large store of teaching ideas and techniques is an asset, teachers still must know which techniques to select and why. Developmental theories help us to understand and influence children's behaviors. They help us become educated educational consumers. They serve as the basis for selection, classification, and evaluation of teaching methods and activities. In short, developmental theories bring order to program design and teaching.

In a later section of this chapter we will consider which parts of any theory are most useful for deriving program practices and teaching ideas in the language arts for young children. But first, let's consider some general trends in the field of early childhood education. These trends highlight significant changes in the field since the 1960s and provide information about recent attempts to design programs for young children from an explicit theory foundation.

## TRENDS IN EARLY CHILDHOOD EDUCATION

The 1960s were a boom decade for early childhood education. There was enormous expansion of the number and types of services offered to children and families. Spurred by the acceptance of psychological research supporting the contention that intelligence was dynamic and educable, Head Start was born. It was intended as a means of serving young children and interrupting the poverty cycle for many families. In the private sector, nursery schools, play groups, and parent cooperatives increased in number as more and more parents became convinced of the value of early education, for the development of cognitive skills as well as for its socializing possibilities. The availability of public school kindergarten programs improved. Day care programs increased and moved from an emphasis on custodial care to developmental, educational care. Thus there emerged a variety of vehicles for delivering educational services to young children.

### Implications for Curriculum

A rich literature arose from the Head Start experience. There was a great deal of excitement and enthusiasm surrounding the development and implementation of the large variety of promising programs for young children associated with Head Start. In fact, at the point of evaluating the Head Start effort, the variety of programs presented problems. Early evaluation efforts were organized to compare certain Head Start program models systematically. Early interpretations of the program comparison studies were directed at identifying the "best" program model for young children. Subsequent, and perhaps more realistic, uses of the evaluation data were directed more at isolating and appreciating the unique contributions of model programs for the needs of the children to be served. What occurred was a movement toward acceptance of the idea that differences in programming practices were valuable. Researchers seemed less interested in searching for the "best" or universally appropriate method or approach for educating young children.

One approach to organizing and understanding the information arising from the various model programs of the Head Start era was to categorize programs according to the dominant theoretical view of human development underpinning the curriculum. Many researchers came to accept developmental theory as a major means of discriminating critical differences among early childhood programs. In other words, they discovered that one very helpful way of bringing order to the great mass of information about different model programs was to think of the programs as expressions of the application of different developmental theories.

As more and more researchers and program developmental specialists began to get into the act, it became clear that almost all model programs could be grouped into three major categories: (1) behaviorist, (2) cognitive-interactionist, and (3) maturationist. What's more, researchers gradually came to the conclusion (some of them reluctantly) that no one approach or program model was better than any other. What seems to be critical is that teachers have some program model (or approach, or theory) in mind when designing programs and delivering instruction (25). Simply stated, it doesn't much matter what you believe as long as you believe in something and can systematically put that something you believe in into practice with children in the classroom.

The state of knowledge in the early childhood education (ECE) field now is such that there are no crystal clear signals that would justify a recommendation for the adoption of any one of the developmental perspectives to the exclusion of the other two. We are taking a pluralistic view by telling you that all three are valuable, showing you how to derive language arts program practices for young children from all three perspectives, and encouraging you to make up your own mind about which perspective is right for you and for the children you teach.

We are convinced that teachers' beliefs about children, teaching, and learning make a difference in how they act on a day-to-day basis in the classroom. Even beliefs that are not yet out in the open influence teachers. You might be a behaviorist and not even know it! Or perhaps you are a Piagetian at heart and haven't yet identified yourself as such. Your personal belief system about children and learning is important. We will show you how this personal belief system can be identified with one of the three developmental perspectives mentioned earlier. Weikart sees a major role for the curriculum as a bridge between theory and practice for the teacher, not the children. He says,

> *The curriculum is for the teacher, not the child.* The primary role of curriculum is: (1) to focus the energy of the teacher on a systematic effort to help the individual child to learn; (2) to provide a rational and integrated base for deciding which activities to include and which to omit; and (3) to provide criteria for others to judge program effectiveness, so that the teacher may be adequately supervised. The successful curriculum is one that permits this structuring of the *teacher* to guide her in the task of adapting the theory she is applying to the actual behavior of the children. (25:40-41)

The identification of three groups of developmental theories is not as recent as Head Start, but we do have the Head Start literature to thank for renewing interest in the linkages between theory and practice. The three broad streams of educational and psychological thought can be traced back to the early Greek philosophers. The interpretation of basic ideas varies somewhat from generation to generation and from program to program, but the basic ideas have not changed dramatically since the times of Plato and Aristotle. Of course, there is continual refinement of the ideas, which comes from developmental psychologists thinking about the application of the theories and from educational practitioners thinking about the theories themselves. The relationship between theory and practice is like a two-way street, with each group constantly helping the other polish and hone their ideas, and with the information flowing back and forth across the street.

## More Programs for More Children

In addition to the resurgence of interest in the relationships between theory and practice, which is related to the Head Start program development efforts, another major trend has had considerable impact on early childhood curriculum, including language arts programs. Just as there is a great deal of diversity in programs, there is much variety in the clientele being served. As recently as the 1950s, early childhood programs were primarily reserved for the children of the well-to-do or the very poor. Those who came from poor families were sometimes served in custodial day care programs funded by welfare agencies. Children from more privileged families attended private nursery school programs for a few hours of play and social activity each day, primarily to give their mothers a break from child care and to provide socialization experiences for the children. Fewer than one-half of the five-year-olds in the nation had public school kindergarten programs available to them.

But all that has changed dramatically in the last twenty years. Child advocacy groups now lobby strenuously for the availability of early childhood programs for all young children, not just the rich or the poor or children with problems. The so-called culturally disadvantaged children served by early Head Start and other federally inspired efforts of the 1960s opened the floodgates for all children. Public school kindergarten programs are now available to a majority of the nation's five-year-olds. Handicapped and gifted children are included more and more often. The variety of needs that these children bring to the early childhood learning situation has had a major impact on early childhood curriculum.

## Integrating the Handicapped and the Gifted

Public Law 94-142, the Education for All Handicapped Children Act, was signed into law in 1975. The law speaks to the right of every child, including those with handicaps, to a free public education and mandates the increased participation of handicapped children in regular schooling. Education at the public expense for all handicapped children from five to eighteen years old is guaranteed by P.L. 94-142. In those states that provide public education to children younger than five and older than eighteen, the same public education services must be provided to handicapped children in these age ranges. Some states extend the components of the law to the gifted as well as the handicapped. Experts estimate that one out of every ten children (about 8 million) in the United States needs special education services as defined in P.L. 94-142.

Portions of the law that have major implications for curriculum are the individualized educational program (I.E.P.), the concept of least restrictive environments, and due process provisions. Education for each handicapped child is to be achieved by the preparation and use of an individualized educational program. The I.E.P. must include information about the child's present performance levels, descriptions of both long- and short-term goals, and a description of specific educational services that will be required in order for the child to achieve the goals. The I.E.P. must be prepared by the child's parents, teachers, qualified consulting professionals and, if possible, the child. Progress on the I.E.P. must be reviewed annually. Sample pages from an I.E.P. for a handicapped child are shown in Figure 2-1 (10:56 and 57).

The law specifies that handicapped and nonhandicapped children should be educated together, unless "the nature or severity of handicap is such that education in regular classrooms cannot be achieved satisfactorily." The provision in the law is sometimes referred to as "mainstreaming" and is often misunderstood. It is true that the typical pattern for dealing with the handicapped was to segregate them in special schools and classes. The intent of the new law is to bring the children more into the normal mainstream of life. While all handicapped children will not be able to participate fully in the mainstream of education as their nonhandicapped peers do, it is expected that many handicapped children can be moved from rather isolated settings into less restrictive settings where they can interact more freely and in more normal ways with their nonhandicapped

# INDIVIDUALIZED EDUCATIONAL PROGRAM FOR HANDICAPPED CHILD

Instructional Area: Communication Skills: Receptive Language

*Present Educational Levels: Receptive Language*
Sue Ellen attends to verbal stimuli. She has a receptive language age of 2 years, 4 months. She can carry out a two-step oral commission with real objects. Sue Ellen demonstrated knowledge of 12 to 27 pairs of adjectives or relationship concepts.
Annual Goal: Sue Ellen will learn new relationships and concepts.

| Short-Term Objective | Instructional Methods Media/Material Title(s) (Optional) | Evaluation of Instructional Objectives | |
|---|---|---|---|
| | | Tests, Materials Evaluation Procedures To Be Used | Criteria of Successful Performance |
| 1. Sue Ellen will identify the following relationships or concepts:<br><br>short - tall<br>front - back<br>inside - outside<br>all - some<br>push - pull<br>between - middle<br>some - more<br>top - bottom<br>push - pull | | 1. Given objects and people as required to represent the relationship, the child will<br>1) identify the item,<br>2) manipulate the objects or<br>3) follow a direction as requested by the trainer. | 1. For each relationship, the child must perform the task three consecutive times with 100% accuracy. |
| 2. Sue Ellen will identify categories. | | 2. Given 10 pictures of common objects and asked to "Show me something to eat, drink, wear, ride in, play with," Sue Ellen will point to an appropriate picture. | 2. Asked 10 such questions, she will respond with 80% accuracy on 3 consecutive trials. |

Instructional Area: Communication Skills: Expressive Language

*Present Educational Levels: Expressive Language*
Sue Ellen is able to imitate, in isolation, all consonant and vowel sounds except "th." She named 9 out of 10 common objects in the Emerging Language Program (ball, car, doll, dog, cat, truck, airplane, boy, girl, cow). Imitative responses to the question "What is this?" consisted of the pivot plus noun (i.e., a ball, big car). She uses 1-and 2-word phrases in spontaneous speech.
Annual Goal: Sue Ellen will use complex grammar.

| Short-Term Objective | Instructional Methods Media/Material Title (s) (Optional) | Evaluation of Instructional Objectives | |
| --- | --- | --- | --- |
| | | Test, Materials Evaluation Procedures To Be Used | Criteria of Successful Performance |
| 1. Sue Ellen will increase her production of 3 (4,5) word phrases in 1 to 1 setting with teacher. | 1. Emerging Language (Hatten, Go man, Lent) | 1. Assessment on objectives 34 - 44 in Emerging Language. | 1. Successful completion of each objective at 90% accuracy. |
| 2. Sue Ellen will increase her production of 3 (4,5) word phrases in spontaneous expressions of speech. | | 2. A systematic observation of spontaneous utterance during 5, 20 minute time samples. | 2. An average phrase length of 3 words in patterned arrangement. |

**FIGURE 2-1. SAMPLE I.E.P.***

---

*Identifying information about the child, Sue Ellen, would ordinarily be presented on a separate page of the I.E.P. Information about present educational levels would also be presented on separate pages of the I.E.P. form.

Sue Ellen was 8 years, 5 months at the time I.E.P. was prepared. She attends a self-contained class for the multiply handicapped. In addition to this placement, she receives consultative speech services, physical therapy, and adaptive physical education.

peers. This component of the law is referred to as educating the handicapped child in the "least restrictive environment," which is the more proper way of referring to mainstreaming. To educate the handicapped child in the least restrictive environment is *not* synonymous with dumping all the handicapped in the regular classroom and hoping the teacher will somehow cope.

Certain rights of parents are guaranteed by P.L. 94-142 and other recent legislation and litigation. Parents have a right to have their child evaluated and to be informed of the results of the evaluation. They must be consulted about the child's educational program prior to its implementation and have the right to have the program reviewed periodically to assess its success. If parents disagree with the school's approach, they have the right to an impartial due process hearing to decide the matter. Parents have the right to expect that due process will be followed throughout screening, assessment, and programming for their child.

It is easy to see that new roles for all teachers are associated with the provisions of Public Law 94-142. The law also provides for preservice and inservice training for teachers to enable them to implement the provisions of the law. Attitudes toward integration of nonhandicapped and handicapped children and teachers' expectations for the progress to be made by the handicapped are important considerations, too.

Teachers have a unique role to play in the integration of the handicapped into regular education. They also play a unique role in the education of gifted and talented children. Gifted children are those with superior intellectual ability, usually measured by tests of intellectual ability and demonstrated high achievement. Talented children are those who have especially advanced skills and abilities in a single area rather than generalized superior abilities. For example, talented children often have special abilities in music, languages, or dance.

Giftedness in young children often shows up early in the language arts areas. For example, children who are gifted often talk very early, and many are speaking in compound and complex sentences shortly after their first birthday. They tend to be early readers. Some gifted children crack the phonic code by the age of three. It is not at all unusual for a gifted first grader to be reading high school-level material.

Curriculum implications for gifted children primarily involve modifications in the content of the material used with the children, the teaching methods, and/or the setting in which the instruction takes place. Provisions for gifted children involving the content of material emphasize more complex ideas and higher levels of abstraction than would typically be recommended for children of the same chronological age. Attention to thinking skills such as comparing, summarizing, classifying, interpreting, criticizing, organizing, and judging is a must. Taxonomies of thinking skills, which encourage teachers to go beyond the simple level of knowledge acquisition, are often recommended as a means of encouraging teachers to use a more process-oriented style of presentation. Alternatives in setting for instruction involve acceleration to higher grade levels, use of special resource rooms, special classes, special summer or after-school programs, and early admission programs. For young children, early admission to school is a possibility; for those who are older, early admission to high school or college programs is an option (21). Sample pages from an I.E.P. for a young gifted child are shown in Figure 2-2.

At this point you might be thinking about the earlier section on developmental theories and wondering if any single theoretical perspective is recommended for either the handicapped or the gifted. The simple answer is "no." Many professionals think the behaviorist approach works well with handicapped children, and the cognitive-interactionist point of view is often suggested for use with the gifted. But there is no solid research evidence that absolutely supports such recommendations. As before, the critical aspect of designing programs for either the handicapped or the gifted seems to be the *consistent* application of some set of beliefs, whatever those beliefs might be.

## LINKS BETWEEN PHILOSOPHY, THEORY, AND PRACTICE

We propose that instructional practices and procedures logically follow from a set of theories about learning and development. We want to add the idea that the theories should have their roots firmly imbedded in a philosophy about the nature of people and the ways they grow, change, and are changed. Although it may sound dreadfully dull, we are suggesting that a person's philosophy of education is, in the final analysis, what undergirds educational decisions.

### Philosophy

Philosophies are abstract ideas. Even though we recognize that philosophy is difficult to describe, we know that each of us has a philosophy — a perspective on life. Each of us probably subtly modifies and shapes our personal philosophy unconsciously with each new experience and encounter. Nevertheless, it can be demonstrated that anyone's basic orientation to dealing with other human beings and to problem solving remains relatively stable and constant over time and situations.

If you look carefully at the various philosophical positions that underlie different theories of learning and development, you will probably find that you are in closer agreement with one philosophy more than the others. If your ideas, or philosophy, about human behavior are not yet uncovered or

# INDIVIDUALIZED EDUCATIONAL PROGRAM FOR GIFTED CHILD

*Present Educational Level:* Cathy was 7 years, 9 months at the time this I.E.P. was prepared. She had achieved an IQ score of 160 on an individual intelligence test and her reading achievement was assessed at 11th grade level in reading comprehension. She is placed in a regular classroom.

Instructional Area: Language Arts

Annual Goal: To *maintain* Cathy's reading ability and interest at the present level, with an enrichment of scope of material and mode of learning.

| Terminal Behavior | Instructional Methods Media/Material Title(s) (Optional) | Evaluation of Instructional Objectives | |
|---|---|---|---|
| | | Conditions | Criteria |
| Cathy will be introduced to a greater variety of children's literature written at or above her present reading level. | (a) Newberry award winners.<br><br>(b) Autobiographies, biographies, novels, short stories.<br><br>(c) Children's classics, myths, folktales, fables. | (a) Use of independent and group work on activities which require higher levels of thinking (synthesis, analysis, evaluation.<br><br>(b) Use of activities which do not rely too heavily on handwriting ability, i.e., handwriting should not be the limiting factor. | Cathy will be able to discuss with her teacher and/or other children the style, tone, figurative language, setting, and point of view of the material. |
| Cathy will have an understanding of basic grammatical structure commensurate with her ability. | (a) Using material and methods which minimize routine and drill. | (a) Use of oral and written exercises at the appropriate level as determined by teacher-made or teacher-supplied exercises. | Cathy will demonstrate an understanding of basic grammatical structure as determined by teacher-made tests or evaluation. |
| Cathy will be able to plan, organize, and present an oral speech to her peers with note cards, but without verbatim transcript. | (a) Materials and topics of interest to Cathy. | (a) Presentations will be made during class; the group size, length of presentation, and scope will be appropriate to Cathy's present level of public speaking skills, as determined by the teacher. | Level of performance will be determined by peer, teacher, and self-evaluation. |

Instructional Area: Critical Thinking

Annual Goal: To improve critical thinking skills

| Terminal Behavior | Instructional Methods Media/Material Title(s) (Optional) | Evaluation of Instructional Objectives | |
|---|---|---|---|
| | | Conditions | Criteria |
| Cathy will be able to *analyze* reading material for appropriate author style. | Use of library books, children's magazines. | Discussions will be held with peers and the teacher to exchange opinions on authors' style of writing. Foster the acceptance of different points of view. | Given a story or short passage, Cathy will discuss the appropriateness or inappropriateness of the author's writing style. |
| Cathy will be able to formulate, verify and defend her *own* position on an issue of interest. | Tape recorders, children's newspapers. | Opportunity will be provided for Cathy to present her point of view to her peers, both through oral and written presentations. | Cathy will select and defend her position on a topic of interest. |
| Cathy will formulate *alternate hypotheses* for the solution of problems. | Science experiments, social studies activities. | Activities that require divergent thinking will be provided. | Using brainstorming techniques, Cathy will develop logical alternatives to the solution of a problem. |
| Cathy will be able to collect and *synthesize* material from a variety of sources to solve a problem. | Use of encyclopedias, textbooks, films, interviews. | Activities that require the collection, synthesis, and analysis of information will be provided to enable exploration in depth. Questions should be open-ended. Ready access to library facilities. | Given an appropriate problem, Cathy will evaluate, synthesize and analyze materials from a variety of sources to discover a logical solution. |
| Cathy will demonstrate the ability to be *flexible in thinking* by listening to the opinions of others and adapting her own ideas when appropriate. | Group discussions, lectures, tape recordings, films, children's newspapers. | Cathy will have the opportunity to listen to opinions that are different from her own, both from class discussions and the media. | Given an opportunity for group exchange of ideas, Cathy will demonstrate a willingness to adapt her own ideas when a logical argument is presented. |

**FIGURE 2-2. SAMPLE I.E.P.**

out in the open, it is important to try and discover your position. Green put it very well:

> [The teacher's] intentions will inevitably be affected by the assumptions he makes regarding human nature and human possibility. Many of these assumptions are hidden; most have never been articulated. If he is to achieve clarity and full consciousness, the teacher must attempt to make such assumptions explicitly; for only then can they be examined, analyzed, and understood. (8:70)

A philosophy is commonly regarded as a perspective on the world and the nature of people. It forms part of our belief, or value, system. It is part of an often unarticulated foundation for our behavior. When we are required to make a response — decide whether to laugh at a bad joke, for example — we usually do not stop and think whether our philosophy dictates to laugh or not to laugh; we simply react at the time. Over time and the course of many, many reactions, however, outsiders would no doubt be able to see a pattern in our behavior. We might be characterized as a person who never laughs at bad jokes or conversely as someone who usually does for the sake of being polite. The fact that we typically react one way and not another is ultimately related to our basic views on life, human nature, and getting along with others. The point of all of this — even though you may be thinking that we are getting pretty far afield from language arts — is that our personal orientation to life *does* affect the way we behave as teachers, just as it affects other behavior.

As you will see as we continue to develop these ideas, theories of development and learning can be traced back to a more basic philosophy. This means that if you can discover your basic orientation to life, or your philosophy, you will narrow the possibilities of developmental theories that you might adopt. You might think of hierarchies of philosophy, theories, and educational practices. Philosophy forms the very broad base; the number of theories related to a particular philosophy is somewhat general but more specific than the philosophy. And, finally, the number of practices tied together with aspects of the theories is very large indeed. The diagram in Figure 2-3 is one way of visualizing the hierarchy between philosophy, theories, and practices.

The links between philosophy, theories, and practices become more obvious when we think of philosophy as a kind of large, all-encompassing umbrella. Several related theories are clustered under the "philosophy umbrella." Then, in turn, many educational practices are clustered under the smaller "theory umbrellas."

## Theories and Related Practices

We think of developmental theory as a set of related principles that explain or predict the course of man's development (20). Practices are the behaviors and experiences provided for children that are deliberately planned as a means of fostering development.

Many teachers are familiar with the use of theory to provide an explanation for certain practices. We might think of this situation as *theory-justified practices.* Perhaps the sequence of events should be the

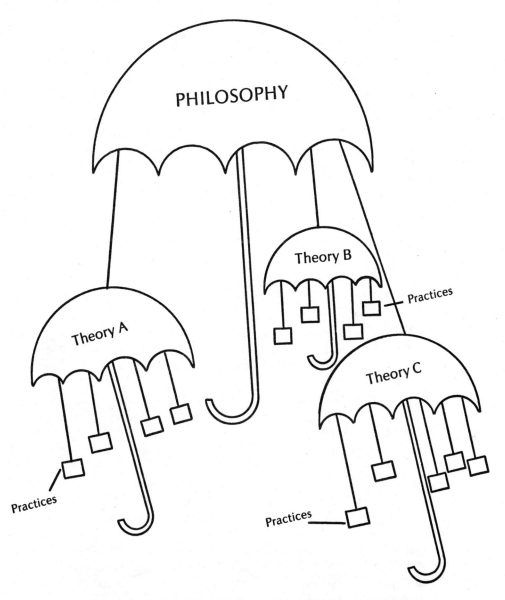

FIGURE 2-3.  HIERARCHY OF PHILOSOPHY, THEORY, AND PRACTICE

other way around with the theory coming first. Then the practices that are logically related to the theory should be developed. This situation would result in what we might call *theory-derived practices*. The teacher's consistency from day to day and content area to content area is likely to be better when theory-derived practices are used.

Deriving educational practices from a theory base maximizes the possibility of consistency but does not guarantee that identical programming practices will result for all who start with the same theory base because programming practices represent an individual's *interpretation* of theory. Thus, it is possible to have a variety of seemingly different practices all related to the same theory.

Regardless of the theory that is used as a basis for deriving program practices, there are common parts of theories that are useful. Some of the more esoteric components of theory and related research are not especially relevant to day-to-day program planning for young children, and these aspects will not be included here. Instead, we will look at those aspects of theory that are helpful in making decisions about educational practices.

## Useful Aspects of Theories

Theories of learning and development spell out certain assumptions about the organism and about how learning and development takes place. Certain developmental expectations can be associated with each theory. Descriptions of the process through which change (growth/learning) occurs can be found in the theories. These change processes differ from theory to theory. If we understand the basic assumptions of the theory, the developmental expectations, and the change processes, we can make logical inferences about the conditions that are expected to facilitate learning and development and about the implications for teachers' behaviors. Subsequently, we can logically select child activities, determine relevant content and establish an appropriate setting. A general process of inferring educational practices from theory is illustrated in Figure 2-4 (22:310).

Discussions about relationships between theory and practice are common in education. What is usually missing from the discussion is the link with philosophy. Philosophy is the initial entry point into the sequence of program planning events, but it is often hidden and unidentified.

We pointed out earlier that it is important to discover which philosophy lies at the heart of an individual's belief system because it establishes the subsequent choice of which theories (and related practices) are relevant. Philosophy establishes which particular hierarchy of philosophy, theories, and practices will be used. Basically, there are three such hierarchies: maturationist, cognitive-interactionist, and behaviorist.

The remainder of this chapter is devoted to a detailed look at each of

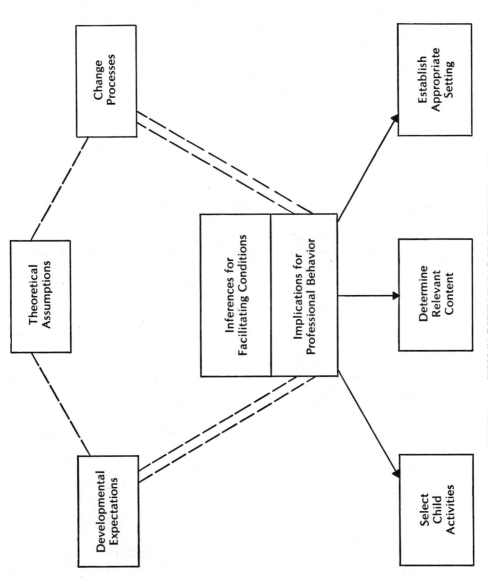

FIGURE 2-4. STEPS IN DETERMINING PRACTICE FROM THEORY

these three viewpoints on development. The common parts of theories (mentioned above) that are useful in deriving program practices are described for each of the three hierarchies. Special attention is given to examples of child activities, content, and setting from the language arts curriculum. Aspects of existing language arts programs related to the three hierarchies are described.

## The maturationist position

*Philosophy.* Examples of this value system date back to the time of Greek culture nearly three hundred years before Christ.* The human being is viewed as a unit, and it is thought that the same factors that influence biological development also operate to determine psychological and cognitive development. The phrase, "man is a product of his biology," is a key concept in the maturationist view.

The reasoning goes something like this: Essentially people come into the world equipped with innate, predetermined patterns of behavior, which are accompanied by internal, regulatory mechanisms. This view is sometimes labeled "genetic predeterminism." Those who embrace this view are often termed "romantics" or "idealists."

When people are viewed as a product of biology, development is thought to be predetermined, and maturation occurs primarily as a function of time. In other words, new behaviors are expected with increasing age. The impetus for development is considered to be internal. The environment is necessary, but given an adequate nurturing environment, the biological potential of the individual, whatever that is, will be realized.

The child is seen as a tiny seed, with everything necessary to become full grown imbedded in the seed at birth. The environment, then, provides the nutrients in which the seed unfolds. The process of development is like the process of plant growth with the gradual unfolding of the parts and characteristics of the organism over time.

A German, Friedrich Froebel, coined the word kindergarten, which means "child's garden." He derived his ideas about early childhood programs from his basic belief in genetic predeterminism. The term *kindergarten* was both a literal and figurative one, since it captured Froebel's idealism and, in actual practice, his program for children was conducted in an outdoor garden. The teacher was seen as the child's gardener, who provided proper conditions for growth and development.

In the maturationist perspective, development is thought to be time-related. Learning cannot be speeded up, but failure to learn at the

---

*A fascinating account of the stability of contrasting views across time can be found in "Conceptions of Development," in R.F. Biehler, *Child Development: An Introduction* (Boston: Houghton Mifflin, 1976), pp. 2-81.

"critical period" may influence the chance for complete and full development. It is felt that the organism is primed to learn during the critical periods and may not learn the skill as easily if the critical period is missed.

*Theories.* There are several theories related to the romantic world view. The maturationist theory of Arnold Gesell and his colleagues (7) emphasizes the whole child and views developmental change as occurring because of the natural unfolding and maturing of physiological structures. Ages are important benchmarks along the course of development, since each age is characterized by certain personality patterns, language accomplishments, patterns of cognition, and other skill achievements. Tables of normal development found in any basic psychology textbook were constructed by reseachers and psychologists to document developmental expectations for each age level.

Gesell began his work at the Yale Guidance Clinic in the 1920s. The phrase "ages and stages" has become synonymous with his and other theories associated with the maturationist perspective. Ideas such as the characterization of the toddler seeking independence and some autonomy and the "terrible two" have arisen as a result of interest in the work of Gesell and others who translated the maturationist position into developmental theories.

Children are thought to move from one stage to another at their own point of readiness. This belief gives rise to the notion that it is useless to attempt to teach children skills that are associated with older ages prior to their reaching that chronological age level. If, for example, the expected time for learning to read is age six or thereabouts, maturationists would consider the earlier teaching of reading to be inappropriate and inefficient because they maintain that children are not ready to benefit from the early instruction.

The psychoanalytic theory of Sigmund Freud includes a stage structure that is related to the child's age and ability to comprehend reality. The child is thought to move through predictable stages of psychosocial development. Freud presented certain theoretical constructs of personality development and emotions such as id, ego, superego, libido, and so forth as key concepts in understanding the development of the child. Each of these terms has a specific definition in Freud's writings, and more than a brief or superficial understanding of the concepts is required to understand a child's psychosocial development according to Freudian theory.

The central idea of the theory is that feelings and emotions, which he thought had a biological basis, have a primary role in development. He constructed a developmental sequence based almost entirely upon the resolution of internal conflicts at various stages of development. Certainly, many of the components of his theory are commonplace. We speak glibly of the id and ego. We talk informally about defense mechanisms. If people eat or smoke too much, we sometimes jokingly say they are "fixated at the oral stage." We talk about digging into our subconscious for clues to reactions and feelings. Freud did not receive professional recognition during his own lifetime, but even so, his ideas continue to have an important impact on approaches to education.

The maturationist position on language development became popular in the 1960s. Linguists were studying language acquisition by children, and some linguists theorized that the complexity and abstractness of language must be innate. They reached this conclusion in part because of the consistency of language acquisition by children, even those who did not have favorable environmental circumstances.

Chomsky (3) wrote about an innate concept of language. He and others pointed to the universal features of all languages and suggested that all children learn language by the same basic rules. Lenneberg (14) also presented a case for biological determinants of language. He stated that people's unique ability to produce and understand language is an inherited characteristic that is specific to the human species. He maintained that the development of language in children is based on highly specialized biological mechanisms including articulatory apparatus, specific brain centers for language, and a specialized auditory system.

More detailed information about theories of language development can be found in Chapter 4. They are briefly discussed here as a reminder that theories about different aspects of development can be grouped together under one general, overall, developmental perspective. It is as if Gesell, Freud, Lenneberg, and Chomsky are all walking under the umbrella of maturationism.

*Practices.* The term *developmental* is frequently used to refer to programming practices and methods derived from theories related to the maturationist view. Practices focus on the stage-patterned process of development and the healthy resolution of conflicts. An enriched language environment is the vehicle for activating the child's normal biological capacity for language. Language is used extensively to label the child's environment. A learning environment based on the play activities of children is usually employed by advocates of the maturationist perspective on development.

Many current educational practices are based on the notion that given a supportive teacher and a nurturant environment, the child will eventually perform expected, desired behaviors. Gesell's idea of readiness is crucial to practice under this perspective. The school of thought represented is the "don't-rush-them" school.

Teachers need to become familiar with age-related behaviors and related experiences for children to insure that appropriate materials and activities are available for children. They want to be sure to take advantage of critical or sensitive periods for development and need to have the tables of expected development firmly entrenched in their memories. These teachers stress social and emotional objectives and tend to deemphasize cognitive objectives.

Teachers are especially concerned with the warm, supportive classroom climate they can make ready for children. Much of the teaching goes on behind the scenes in setting up a rich, inviting place for children. Teachers tend to be somewhat unobtrusive and indirect in actual interactions with children, letting the children take the lead. Thus, the term *child-centered* has come to be associated with the maturationist perspective.

The child is generally in a situation that provides optimum opportunities for development to proceed according to the child's own particular predetermined pattern. Childern typically initiate their activities, choosing what they will do, when, and for how long. A fair amount of freedom is given to the children because it is assumed that they naturally gravitate toward activities that are most appropriate for their level of development.

Certain teaching practices are related to Freudian theory. These involve a style of teaching in which the promotion of self-esteem, the expression of feelings, and the healthy resolution of conflict situations are primary goals. Teachers provide interpersonal social and emotional support for children.

Some teachers may not say they are teaching according to the ideas of Freud, Gesell, or Chomsky. But on close inspection, much of what goes on in their classrooms is obviously related to encouraging social and emotional development and providing for readiness activities considered normal for a certain age group of children.

If you were to interview these teachers, they would very likely have some of the following ideas about development and teaching:

— Development is the unfolding of predictable patterns of behavior.
— Much of what we know is already present in the genes at birth.
— The aim of instruction is to provide optimum conditions for knowledge to show itself.
— Pushing children prematurely can be damaging in the long run.
— Children need to be free of emotional problems so they can develop intellectually.
— When language is used in instruction, it should be carefully matched to the child's level of readiness.
— Teachers can rely on the spontaneous choices of activities by children.
— Dimensions of development cannot be separated from one another; we deal with the whole child.
— Teachers are responsible for supervising free play.
— Teachers should provide children with experiences that are enriching and real, not symbolic and abstract (5).

Considering these statements and the description of the maturationist perspective on development, can you make a decision about whether you belong in this "camp"? Where do you stand?

*The theory-practice link for language teaching.* The general process for inferring educational practices from a theory was presented earlier (see Figure 2-4). We suggested that the following aspects of a theory could be identified and used in making educational programming decisions: (1) theoretical assumptions, (2) developmental expectations, and (3) change processes. Inferences for facilitating conditions and implications for teacher behavior are inferred from the three common aspects. Subsequently, child activities, relevant content, and appropriate setting are derived. An example of the link between theory and practice in the area of language learning for the maturationist perspective is given in Figure 2-5 (22:315). Inspection of this illustration of the process of deriving educational practice from common aspects of a theory will indicate an internal consistency. Certainly, different interpretations, different practical applications, and different program goals could have been specified. This is simply one way of documenting the internal consistency that is achieved when a theory-derivation rather than a "catch-as-catch-can" type of planning is used.

Let's take a closer look at the ideas presented in Figure 2-5. Notice that the idea of genetic predeterminism is the major theoretical assumption. The other aspects of the derivation process are ultimately related to this assumption. Notice that the idea of the nurturing role of environment is embodied in this theoretical assumption. We infer then that an enriched language environment is better than a limited one.

Those who embrace this position believe that language facility gradually increases with the increasing age of the child. In other words, their developmental expectations are tied to increasing age. Their views of the way in which change occurs are to see change as a combination of the readiness (critical or sensitive period) of the child and the availability of the right materials and activities in the environment. What inferences can be drawn from this general set of beliefs about development? We might ask, "What conditions can be expected to facilitate development?" The answers are as indicated in Figure 2-5. The position is that, given the right environment, children will learn because they are naturally motivated to do so. Children are seen as having a natural and spontaneous desire to express themselves, therefore, they are expected to use language. Children are seen as naturally curious and interested and as having a positive image of themselves as learners.

What do these ideas imply for the behavior of the teacher? The teacher is expected to be aware of the developmental levels of children. If she is working with three-year-olds, she would expect the children to have about 1,000 words in their speaking vocabularies. Based on information derived

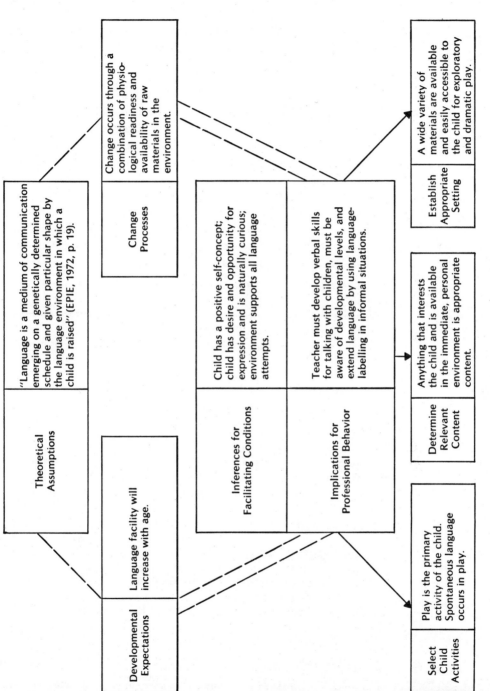

**FIGURE 2-5.  EXAMPLE OF THEORY-PRACTICE LINKS FOR THE MATURATIONIST POSITION**

| Theoretical Assumptions | "Language is a medium of communication emerging on a genetically determined schedule and given particular shape by the language environment in which a child is raised" (EPIE, 1972, p. 19). |
| --- | --- |

| Change Processes | Change occurs through a combination of physiological readiness and availability of raw materials in the environment. |
| --- | --- |

| Developmental Expectations | Language facility will increase with age. |
| --- | --- |

| Inferences for Facilitating Conditions | Child has a positive self-concept; child has desire and opportunity for expression and is naturally curious; environment supports all language attempts. |
| --- | --- |

| Implications for Professional Behavior | Teacher must develop verbal skills for talking with children, must be aware of developmental levels, and extend language by using language-labelling in informal situations. |
| --- | --- |

| Establish Appropriate Setting | A wide variety of materials are available and easily accessible to the child for exploratory and dramatic play. |
| --- | --- |

| Determine Relevant Content | Anything that interests the child and is available in the immediate, personal environment is appropriate content. |
| --- | --- |

| Select Child Activities | Play is the primary activity of the child. Spontaneous language occurs in play. |
| --- | --- |

from normative tables, she would expect about 80 percent of their utterances to be intelligible and that they would have grammatical structures about the same as adult colloquial speech, with some occasional mistakes. If four-year-olds comprised the group in the program, she would have slightly different expectations. She would expect a speaking vocabulary of some 1,500 words and, with normal children, would expect language to be fairly well established. Similar statements about developmental expectations could be made for other age groups as well.

A crucial behavior for teachers using this approach is talking with children. The teacher uses language labeling in informal situations and must be aware of these opportunities, so that they can be captured and used for informal, indirect extension of language. The teaching style is very subtle but not unplanned. This conversational approach to extending language must be deliberately exploited by the teacher. Delightful examples of verbal techniques for different ages are given by Pitcher and Ames (19:194-198) in the excerpts which follow.

*Verbal Techniques at Different Ages:*

*2 Years*

Verbal techniques are now beginning to be more important than physical, whereas at eighteen months the opposite was true. It is important to keep language simple, concrete, and repetitive. There is no need to fear boring the 2-year-old with repetition. The world is all so new to him that repetition helps him to feel comfortable. It is, however, best to keep language at a minimum. Adults who talk too much to the 2-year-old inevitably use words he does not understand. Such verbosity from adults may set up patterns of not paying attention in the child.

Often it is necessary to follow or to support verbalization with action. Thus, rather than simply saying, "Go wash your hands," a teacher leads a child to the washbasin as she utters this direction. Similarly it is better to say the more specific "Put the blocks on the shelf" than simply "Put the blocks away." Also it is useful to supplement the suggestion with demonstration.

*2 1/2 Years*

Questions such as "Where does your coat go?" can be good motivators. But it is important to avoid questions which can be answered by "No," such as "Do you want to ——?" or "Would you like to ——?" In general, it is good to avoid giving choices, for children find, as soon as they have made a choice in one direction, that the other is highly desirable.

Face-saving directions are useful, such as, "You could ——," or "How about ——?" It is wise not to meet the child head on with a too direct command, unless this is absolutely necessary. Verbalization about some neutral topic can be used as a distraction when children become especially negative or insist, "Me do it myself." The teacher can talk about something else, while actually doing something for them (such as putting on a snowsuit with which they have had great difficulty). Or a running commentary which does not cue them to a negative response, such as "I wonder if you could go down that big slide; I wonder if it's too high for you," may motivate them to a desired activity.

*3 Years*

Language now takes on a whole new texture and dimension. It is no longer necessary to repeat so much, or to say just the right thing. Spontaneous, two-way conversations are now coming in. A remark from a teacher often sets a child off on a series of associative responses.

*3 1/2 Years*

Going to extremes, such as speaking very loudly or very softly, works well with children of this age. They themselves, too, like either to shout or whisper. Indeed, since most behavior tends to be exaggerated at this age, the teacher must be careful not to let extreme behavior get out of hand. The *timing* of techniques is therefore important to prevent excessive exuberance or negativism.

The element of surprise can be a timely distractor or motivator: "Do you know what?" is usually a question that interrupts a child's actions or thoughts, and makes him receptive to the idea of some pleasant information. The idea of something new and exciting can be emphasized by the use of such words as "surprise," "new," and "different." Also a child can be distracted from undesirable behavior by some question such as, "Did you ever go to the zoo?" etc. Verbal praise and expressions of affection continue to be useful and important: "I like you," "You're my friend." One cannot, apparently, overuse this technique.

*4 Years*

Praise and compliment, for appearance or activity, continues to be one of the most effective techniques for making things go smoothly. The remark, "That's the handsomest shirt I ever saw," is certain to bring appreciative response in a child. In praising activities and abilities, however, it is important to use new and interesting adjectives and not to praise something which the child, now much more self-critical, knows to be poor. Instead of saying an artistic creation is good, for instance, it is better (when it is clearly *not* a talented production), to remark, "That's an *interesting* painting," or "That's pretty good, especially since it's the first time you've ever drawn a horse."

Specified excerpts from THE GUIDANCE NURSERY SCHOOL, Revised Edition by Evelyn Goodenough Pitcher & Louise Bates Ames. Copyright © 1964, 1975 by Gesell Institute of Child Development, Incorporated. Reprinted by permission of Harper & Row, Publishers, Inc.

The program as a whole is designed to invite the curious child to engage in many different kinds of experiences. There is considerable attention to manipulation and sensory experiences. Think of the language-labeling possibilities surrounding experiences in seeing, feeling, tasting, hearing, and smelling elements of the environment! Typical activities that bridge home and school are used to provide additional experiences for the natural unfolding of language in the young child. The teacher values play as a method of instruction. The most important method (if you can even call it by that formal label) for achieving the developmental goals in such a program is to advance the functional use of language in the context of the child's own activities and play.

As you can see from Figure 2-5, this discussion has naturally led to descriptions of child activities, content, and setting from a description of expected teacher actions. Since play is the primary activity of young children, many play activities are available for children with the expectation that spontaneous language will occur during the play.

What content is appropriate? Anything and everything — so long as it is something that interests the children and is a part of the real, immediate environment. If a child brings a seashell to school following a trip to the shore, then seashells constitute appropriate content. If a child has new shoes, shoes become content. If a new pet has been placed in the classroom, characteristics of the pet and ways of caring for it become appropriate content. The list is limitless.

What does a classroom for young children look like when the teacher takes a maturationist view? We might characterize the setting as stimulating, open, enriched, and natural. There would probably be areas of the room set aside for block building, painting, and clay modeling; looking at books in a quiet corner would be encouraged; a housekeeping center would be available to provide the transition between home and school and to provide an outlet for social and emotional learning. Other forms of dramatic play would be visible in the costumes and props set about the room. Toys to stimulate the development of large muscles and coordination would be found in such a classroom. Sand and water facilitate sensory experiences and the language learning that comes with them, and they would be standard equipment in many early education classrooms. Pictures of family and pets might be available, because they are real and natural parts of the children's lives. Special displays might be arranged from time to time to spark curiosity in the children. Typical daily activities such as snack time would be used to label and discuss the environment and experiences of the children.

*A sample program.* The Bank Street early childhood program (2) is often used as an example of the maturationist view in action. In fact, some aspects of the Bank Street program go beyond the maturationist view, but because of its long-standing reputation as a program that espouses a maturationist view, we will use it as an example here. As might be expected, goals for the program involve developing the ability to function in a social group, to expand the child's world, gradually to develop facility with abstract symbols, and to develop cognitive processes. No single, specific goal exists for the language arts area because language is viewed as a process and not as an end product. The teacher's role is one of waiting and carefully looking for evidence that children are mastering the developmental tasks expected for their age level. A warm, loving, caring style of working with the children is expected of the teacher; the provision of a natural and comfortable setting constitutes part of the teacher's role.

The teacher's verbal behavior is characterized as gentle and firm. There is an emphasis on clear articulation, and care is exercised in choosing words to extend language informally. The questions put to the children are carefully phrased, so that the children's responses are positive and natural. In general, the teacher is someone who has a good stock of child-oriented small talk.

Special materials are not required in the Bank Street program. Those things that are considered typical or traditional nursery school materials — blocks, toys, paint, clay, sand, water, puzzles, games, books, wheeled toys, costumes, and dolls — are used extensively. The content incorporates home and school into the children's activities. The playground, neighborhood, home, and school are important themes in the curriculum.

*How about you?* There is really no need to launch into an extensive listing of activities and materials for those of you who feel this developmental perspective is for you. Now that you have a basic understanding of what is involved, you can choose from among the wealth of ideas provided in the chapters in this book. You will know which activities to choose and which to reject on the basis of your beliefs about development.

## The behaviorist position

*Philosophy.* In contrast to the biologically predetermined view of man, there is a view of man which ascribes to environment the major role of shaping man's destiny. "At the core of this perspective is the thesis that *man grows to be what he is made to be by his environment.*" (12:4). Biological endowment is minimized, and the role of the environment as the determining factor in development is emphasized.

The child is seen as being born as a blank slate, or, as Locke said, "tabula rasa." Initially, the behavior of the child is thought to be random and somewhat purposeless. Environment is thought to provide the structure for human behavior. Ultimately people will become a product of the special individual stimulus situations and reinforcing elements of their particular, unique environment.

Those who hold this position on human development are often called "empiricists" because they talk about development in terms of how it has been demonstrated or observed. In other words, they have empirical evidence about inputs and outputs. They do not have such evidence about what goes on inside the organism, so they choose not to talk about it. This does not necessarily mean they reject the concept of internal processes. They simply maintain that because the internal processes are not observable, they cannot include them in an empirical explanation of development.

The phrase "cultural transmission" is another important way to characterize this world view. There is an assumption that what is important in the development of the human being is the learning of academic and social skills and the roles of the culture. The role of early education is viewed primarily as preparation for later education. Again, we can go back to the times of Plato and Aristotle to find examples of this world view. (By the way, have you decided which is the behaviorist and which is the romantic? Is it Plato? Is it Aristotle?)

*Theories.* Theories of learning and development derived from this view of human beings do not focus on emotions, feelings, or inner states. Instead they consider overt, visible acts and behaviors. There is an emphasis on documenting the inputs (stimuli) and outputs (products) of development. The basic building block of behaviorist theories is the stimulus-response unit. Some people refer to this group of theories as the "black box" approach. Baldwin put it this way:

> If we came upon a mysterious black box with various appendages that acted and behaved and responded to stimuli, we might watch it carefully, put it into different sorts of experimental situations, and finally develop a theory about the mechanism inside the box that would explain its reactions. Or, we might be content with writing down a set of empirical laws that related properties of the situation to the characteristics of the response. The advantage of the black box strategy is that we are not tempted to attribute to the box any of the subjective feelings and thoughts that we ourselves experience. (1:392)

This point of view is commonly referred to as *behaviorism;* in it, development is portrayed as an accumulation of new skills. The child is seen as a mirror, reflecting environmental experiences. Learning is thought to be observable, countable, and measurable. Complex learnings are explained as chained sequences of simpler-level learnings. A response is said to be established when reinforcement is keyed to performance and, therefore, it is said that learning is *operant.*

Theorists such as Watson, Thorndike, Skinner, and Bandura take this approach to development. For these theorists, respondent and operant conditioning serve as fundamental explanations of the acquisition and modification of behavior. Behaviorists attempt to describe the mechanisms of learning independent of content. They are not concerned that the content of the learning experience is realistic and within the child's immediate realm of experience nor are they concerned about the ages and stages of development as are the maturationists. Behaviorists maintain that it is possible to teach anyone anything, as long as the environmental circumstances are properly arranged and appropriate reinforcing events are provided.

For the behaviorists, language learning is viewed as being the same as any other learned behavior; that is, it is governed by basic learning principles. Systematically reinforcing children as they respond or imitate adult models is at the heart of the behaviorists' explanation of language learning. Skinner explained language development as beginning when the parent first reinforces the babblings of the child that most closely resemble adult speech (23). Other behavioral theorists see imitation as a major vehicle in language learning.

Language development is seen as essential for learning, as the academic skill necessary for learning other academic skills. This viewpoint is similar to the view of early education as preparation for later education. Before children can learn academic skills, behaviorists think they must be able to speak correctly. The quality and quantity of the child's language is viewed as dependent on available language models in the environment and the reinforcement received. In school situations, the teacher is an important model. At home, parents are key models.

*Practices.* Programming practices and methods based on behaviorist theories are built on the idea that the curriculum planners and teachers should decide what the child is to learn. Development can be specifically enhanced through carefully preplanned sequences of lessons. It is incumbent upon the teacher to arrange the environment carefully and to provide appropriate reinforcing situations, so that learning will occur. B. F. Skinner said that if the child does not learn, it is not the child who should get the F; it is the teacher who has failed.

A variety of terms are used to describe teachers who have adopted this viewpoint of development and translated it into educational practices. Some of the terms are flattering, others are not. Teachers have sometimes been referred to as "environmental engineers" or "manipulators." For those who take the behaviorist position, the primary means of effecting change or learning in the child is through manipulating the environment. Teachers are directive; they initiate activities. The teacher specifies the desired changes the child is to undergo, arranges activities that will result in those changes, and is careful to reinforce changes when they do occur. The child is seen as a responder to the environment. For these teachers, the approach is seen as efficient, systematic, commonsense.

If you were to interview educators who take a behaviorist view of learning and development, they might make statements such as these:

— Knowledge is acquired piece by piece and is cumulative.
— The major goal of instruction should be to help the child get the "right" answer.
— Our behavior is largely shaped by the environment.
— Different areas of development (e.g., intellectual, motor) can be separated from each other for purposes of instruction.
— If the instructor takes the time to carefully build up response patterns, learners can be taught practically anything.

— Teachers need to have a highly structured schedule of daily activities.

— Teachers are expected to present lessons to children so they can achieve specific objectives.

— The general goal of schooling is to teach children academic skills.

— Teachers need to provide reinforcement for correct responses to children through the use of verbal praise and concrete rewards (5).

Do you find yourself in agreement with many of these statements? Are you beginning to identify yourself with the behaviorist position? Where do you stand?

*The theory-practice link for language teaching.* Similar to the approach used in illustrating the translation of the maturationist theories into language teaching practices, we again present an example (22:319) of the theory-practice link. This time the example (see Figure 2-6) illustrates the application of the behaviorist perspective on development. Again, it is possible to find an internal consistency among the components of the derivation process. Each part of the example is logically related to the others.

The assumption drawn from behaviorist theories that has special relevance for language learning is a response to the chicken-egg controversy about the relationship between language and thinking. For the behaviorists, language clearly comes first; it is considered essential to the development of cognitive skills. Remember that this is an assumption — it is not proven fact. We shall see later that another group of theorists takes quite a different position in the debate.

In terms of developmental expectations, recall that behaviorists believe children will learn whatever we teach them. Therefore, it is logical to believe that language skill increases with appropriate practice. As expected, change processes are mainly concerned with the provision of direct instruction and the control of reinforcing conditions.

In answer to questions about the conditions that are most likely to facilitate language development, it can be seen that behaviorists believe that if the child is exposed to sequenced instruction in language content at the appropriate skill level, the development of language is enhanced. Task analysis and diagnosis of current levels of functioning become important when conditions to facilitate development are considered. Thus, one of the implications for teachers' behavior is that they must be able to diagnose the children's present levels of language functioning. Teachers should also be skilled at formulating a sequence of specific language learning objectives based on a careful task analysis of what must follow the child's present functioning. Further, the teacher is expected to use a structured pedagogy (when one knows where one is going, there is no need to dillydally along the way), and, of course, since reinforcement is a key element in the

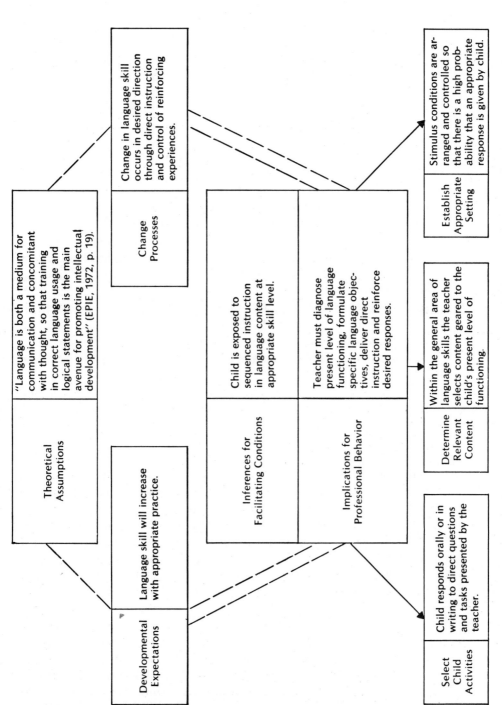

**Theoretical Assumptions**

"Language is both a medium for communication and concomitant with thought, so that training in correct language usage and logical statements is the main avenue for promoting intellectual development" (EPIE, 1972, p. 19).

**Change Processes**

Change in language skill occurs in desired direction through direct instruction and control of reinforcing experiences.

**Developmental Expectations**

Language skill will increase with appropriate practice.

**Inferences for Facilitating Conditions**

Child is exposed to sequenced instruction in language content at appropriate skill level.

**Implications for Professional Behavior**

Teacher must diagnose present level of language functioning, formulate specific language objectives, deliver direct instruction and reinforce desired responses.

**Establish Appropriate Setting**

Stimulus conditions are arranged and controlled so that there is a high probability that an appropriate response is given by child.

**Determine Relevant Content**

Within the general area of language skills the teacher selects content geared to the child's present level of functioning.

**Select Child Activities**

Child responds orally or in writing to direct questions and tasks presented by the teacher.

**FIGURE 2-6. EXAMPLE OF THEORY-PRACTICE LINKS FOR THE BEHAVIORIST POSITION**

perspective, the teacher must be able to supply appropriate reinforcers for children's correct responses.

Teaching strategies that are based on empirically validated learning principles form the core of the structured pedagogy. Let's consider some of these strategies in greater detail. Many behaviors can be taught using a modeling strategy. Someone performs (models) the desired behavior, and the child imitates it. Modeling is frequently used in teaching children to speak in complete sentences. The teacher might say, "I have a red ball. Now you say it." She would pause and expect the child to respond with "I have a red ball."

Chaining is another strategy often used in sentence work with young children. Behaviors can be chained either forward or backward. In either case, the entire sequence for the task must be determined in advance. In backward chaining, the teacher provides everything but the last step and the child is expected to produce the last behavior in the chain. In the example used above, the teacher would say, "I have a red . . . .," and the child would fill in "ball" to complete the chain. This procedure continues with the teacher working backwards until the entire chain has been learned and produced by the child. Forward chaining operates on the same principle, but the chain is worked from front to back rather than the reverse.

Prompting is another important teaching strategy. A prompt is something — a stimulus — that a teacher uses to get a desired response. It is a way of arranging the environment so that the child is likely to produce the desired response. A prompt is that little bit of extra push needed to help the child perform a behavior. Eventually we want the children to perform the behaviors without the prompts, so that it is important to choose prompts that can be easily faded. *Fading* refers to the process of gradual elimination. Prompts should be carefully chosen to help the child focus on the significant aspects of the task. An example of the use of prompting can be demonstrated through the use of special paper to teach the placement of letters on the paper in manuscript writing. Young children often have difficulty remembering where letters begin and end on the lines of the paper. A paper that is lined with the top line in red, the middle line in yellow, and the bottom line in green provides the necessary visual cues. The child learns that capital letters are started at the red line and come all the way down to the green line. They learn that lower case letters that occupy only a single space, a, c, e, and i for example, are started on the yellow line and brought down to the green. These cues make the tasks more manageable. The child doesn't have to fight through a confusing array of blue lines, all looking alike. Gradually the intensity of the colors could be faded, or lightened, so that the child comes to have a sense of where the letters belong on the lines and is subtly discouraged from relying completely on the colored lines.

Behavioral rehearsal is a technique that consists of having the children practice a task over and over again. Counting to ten is a classic example of a task that is practiced repeatedly. Tasks can also be rehearsed in a dramatic play situation, especially if the tasks are not a part of the school program. Teachers are encouraged to use task-imbedded reinforcers to keep the repeated practice interesting. In other words, aspects of the task that will keep it novel can function as reinforcers and should be used as such. In counting to ten, for example, children could squeak to ten like mice, they could roar to ten like lions, they could sing to ten, and so on.

Another important teaching strategy for behaviorist teachers is discrimination training. This is a strategy that helps the teacher bring certain behaviors under the control of specific stimuli. Often we want children to discriminate between two stimuli. Other times we are interested in having children choose a given behavior in a given situation; for example, we might want them to sit in a circle during story-telling time. General principles of discrimination training involve: (1) providing distinctive prompts, (2) giving many instances for children to practice and be reinforced in the presence of the discriminative stimuli, (3) reducing the opportunities to practice the incorrect behavior in the presence of the discriminative stimuli, and (4) fading the prompts. The following example (6) is a step-by-step approach to discrimination training in response to the problem that Susan doesn't correctly identify her name tag on her chair or her toothbrush. The objective is to have Susan identify *Susan* when she sees it. She will need to be taught to discriminate between *Susan* and other names in the group of children in her class. Here's what the teacher might do:

1. List the other stimuli in order of maximum to minimum difference from the stimulus being taught — Susan. 1. Joe   2. Henry   3. Marcia   4. Sally
2. List some other stimuli that would even be more different from the stimulus *Susan,* for example, colored shapes, animal pictures, lines.
3. Order these in terms of maximum to minimum difference from the stimulus *Susan.*
   1.  animal pictures.   2. colored shapes.   3. lines
4. Think of stimuli that are not names of children in the group but are very close to the name.
   For example, individual letters, non-name words, words of similar length, words of similar configuration, other words that begin with capital letters.
5. Order these from maximal to minimal difference from the stimulus *Susan.*

      1. individual letters
      2. non-name words
      3. words of similar length
      4. words of similar configuration
      5. other words that begin with capital letters
  **6.** Write a series of paired stimuli in which the child is to identify *Susan* by beginning with the order generated in step 3 above, then going to the order in step 5, and finally going to the order in step 1.

Some examples of the actual discrimination materials are given on page 57. More than one example for each pairing should be used (6).

Perhaps you have noticed throughout the discussion of teaching strategies that the children's activities are usually to respond orally or in writing to direct questions and tasks presented by the teacher. Selection of the content for the lesson is frequently based on the task analysis. In other words, it is whatever comes next in the sequence the child is working on. In the example about Susan, the child's name was the content. Other content evolved naturally from a determination of the maximally and minimally different stimuli to be used in the discrimination training. Establishing the appropriate setting is often imbedded in the teaching strategy employed. Prompts are really a part of the setting. They set up conditions that make it likely that the desired response will be given by the child. A response that is not given cannot be reinforced, so that it is essential to get the child to produce the behavior somehow so that it can be reinforced.

In many behaviorist-type classrooms, there are special areas of the room set up for teaching new skills and others set aside for maintaining the behaviors under more natural circumstances. There might, for example, be teaching booths or cubicles for the new skill teaching part of the schedule and more traditional nursery school activities set up in other parts of the room. This encourages teachers to watch for behaviors recently acquired and reinforce them in the more natural setting. This is an important aspect of the setting because children are not expected to perform the behaviors in the artificial settings of the booths or cubicles forever. Rather, they are encouraged to use them in their day-to-day interactions.

*A sample program.* The DISTAR program stands as one very obvious example of the behaviorist theories in action in language learning (4). This program was derived from a preschool program initiated by Engelmann and Bereiter in the 1960s. Major goals for the program are to develop skills in language, reading, and arithmetic. The approach to reading is phonic. Language teaching pervades the program. Teachers are expected to follow the teacher's manual in providing direct instruction. Patterned drills are often used. Unison responses are typically expected from the children. Cues such as hand clapping and signals are used extensively. Questions are used liberally as are examples and brief explanations.

| What stimuli are being paired (easiest to hardest discriminations)? | What do the teaching materials look like? |
|---|---|
| 1.  animal pictures, Susan | Susan        🐱<br>"Show me your name." |
| 2.  colored shapes, Susan | ●        Susan<br>"Show me your name." |
| 3.  lines, Susan | <        Susan<br>"Show me your name." |
| 4.  individual letters, Susan | Susan        B<br>"Show me your name." |
| 5.  non-name words, Susan | dog        Susan<br>"Show me your name." |
| 6.  words of similar length, Susan | jumps        Susan<br>"Show me your name." |
| 7.  words of similar configuration, Susan (note shape of the words) | Beams        Susan<br>"Show me your name." |
| 8.  other words that start with capital S, Susan | Short        Susan<br>"Show    me    your    name." |
| 9.  names of children in group, Susan | Susan        Joe<br>"Show me your name." |

Teachers are looking for "correct" answers, and they provide the reinforcement, usually verbal praise. As would be expected the material is very carefully sequenced according to task analyses and the learning principles used in the lesson. Materials are generally pencil-and-paper type, and there is a great reliance on having the children's attention focused on the teacher's master book. The emphasis is on labeling, naming, describing, following directions, and categorizing. Teachers use a rapid drill technique with small groups of three to eight children. Teachers must be familiar with the materials to use them effectively with the children. Note the explicitness of the directions in the sample pages from the DISTAR Teacher Presentation Book (4) which follow. It is not at all unusual to find DISTAR teachers engaging in a bit of behavioral rehearsal of their own in order to conduct the lessons smoothly!

*How about you?* As we suggested earlier, many of the other activities presented in this book may be appropriate to the behaviorist approach to language arts teaching. You have been given some very basic information about the approach. If it fits with your view of learning and development, you will know which activities to choose, which to adapt, and which to reject on the basis of your beliefs and understanding of the behavioral approach.

### The cognitive-interactionist position

*Philosophy.* The organismic world view sees people themselves as the organizing, formative power in merging environment and genetic endowment in an interactive process. Langer said that *"man develops to be what he makes himself by his own actions"* (12:7). Before, we thought of people as products of heredity or environment. Now we might think of people as a product of their own design. According to this view, people develop themselves from within, not according to a genetic blueprint or completely at the mercy of environmental dictates. Instead development is thought to be caused by a kind of self-organization.

Those who take the cognitive-interactionist position see the human being as more than a simple sum of the contributions of heredity and environment. The organismic, or dialectical, view recognizes both the advantages and the limits of both environment and heredity. There is a role for people that maximizes self-determinism. When people are viewed as a product of their own design and free will, development is thought to occur through active, self-structuring by people themselves. In this perspective, development occurs when people's self-organization is matched or challenged by experiential events.

*Theories.* Who are the theorists who walk under the umbrella of the organismic perspective? Those who have made important contributions to theory development related to this philosophy are Piaget, Dewey, and

# LESSON 50

### TASK 1 Actions

It's time for some actions.

a. Everybody, hold your hand in front of your eye. Signal. Wait. What are you doing? Signal. *Holding my hand in front of my eye.*

b. Everybody, hold your hand in front of your nose. Signal. Wait. What are you doing? Signal. *Holding my hand in front of my nose.*

c. Everybody, hold your hand over your shoulder. Signal. Wait. What are you doing? Signal. *Holding my hand over my shoulder.*

d. Everybody, hold your hand on your wrist. Signal. Wait. What are you doing? Signal. *Holding my hand on my wrist.*

e. Everybody, hold your hand on your chest. Signal. Wait. What are you doing? Signal. *Holding my hand on my chest.*

f. Repeat *a* through *e* until all children's responses are firm.

g. Everybody, hold your hand on your chest. Signal. Wait. What are you doing? -- Signal. *Holding my hand on my chest.* Say the whole thing. Signal. *I am holding my hand on my chest.*

h. Everybody, hold your hand over your shoulder. Signal. Wait. What are you doing? Signal. *Holding my hand over my shoulder.* Say the whole thing. Signal. *I am holding my hand over my shoulder.*

i. Everybody, hold your hand on your wrist. Signal. Wait. What are you doing? Signal. *Holding my hand on my wrist.* Say the whole thing. Signal. *I am holding my hand on my wrist.*

j. Everybody, hold your hand in front of your nose. Signal. Wait. What are you doing? Signal. *Holding my hand in front of my nose.* Say the whole thing. Signal. *I am holding my hand in front of my nose.*

k. Everybody, hold your hand in front of your eye. Signal. Wait. What are you doing? Signal. *Holding my hand in front of my eye.* Say the whole thing. Signal. *I am holding my hand in front of my eye.*

l. Repeat *g* through *k* until all children's responses are firm.

m. Everybody, hold your hand in front of your nose. Signal. Wait. What are you doing? Signal. *Holding my hand in front of my nose.* Are you holding your hand in front of you eye? Signal. *No.* Say the whole thing. Signal. *I am not holding my hand in front of my eye.*

n. What are you doing? Signal. *Holding my hand in front of my nose.* Say the whole thing. Signal. *I am holding my hand in front of my nose.*

### Individual Test

Repeat *a* through *n,* calling on different children for each step.

### TASK 2  Days of the Week

Let's do the days of the week.

a. Everybody, how many days are there in a week? Signal. *Seven.*

b. Everybody, say the days of the week. Signal. *Sunday, Monday, Tuesday, Wednesday, Thursday, Friday, Saturday.*

c. Again. Signal. *Sunday, Monday, Tuesday, Wednesday, Thursday, Friday, Saturday.* Repeat *c* until all children's responses are firm.

d. Everybody, I'll say some days of the week. When I stop, tell me the day that comes next. Listen. Wednesday, Thursday, Friday. Pause. Signal. *Saturday.*

### Error

The children don't say **Saturday.**

From *Distar® Language I: An Instructional System,* Teacher Presentation Book B by Siegfried Engelmann and Jean Osborn. © 1976, 1972, 1969, Science Research Associates, Inc. Reprinted by permission of the publisher.

**FIGURE 2-7.  EXCERPTS FROM DISTAR TEACHER PRESENTATION BOOK**

**Correction**

1. My turn.  Wednesday, Thursday, Friday.
   Pause.  Saturday.  I said the day that
   comes next.
2. Your turn.  Wednesday, Thursday, Friday.
   Pause.  Signal.  *Saturday.  You said*
   *the day that comes next.*
3. *Repeat d.*
e. *Listen.  Monday, Tuesday, Wednesday,*
   *Thursday.  Pause.  Signal.  Friday.  Listen.*
   Sunday, Monday.  Pause.  Signal.  *Tuesday*
   Repeat e until all children's responses
   are firm.

**Individual Test**

**Repeat** *d* and *e,* calling on different
children.

**TASK 4  Pronouns—Actions**

Here's the first action.
a. Everybody, let's all touch our hips.
   Signal.  You touch your hips.
   Keep touching them.
b. What are you doing?  Signal.  *Touching my*
   *hips.*  Say the whole thing.  Signal.
   *I am touching my hips.*
c. Point to everybody.  What are we doing?
   Signal.  *Touching our hips.*  Say the whole
   thing.  Signal.  *We are touching our hips.*
d. Look at me.  What am I doing?  Signal.
   *Touching your hips.*  Say the whole thing.
   Signal.  *You are touching your hips.*
e. Point to a boy.  Look at him.
   What is he doing?  Signal.  *Touching his*
   *hips.*  Say the whole thing.  Signal.
   *He is touching his hips.*
Here's the next action.
f. Everybody, let's all wave.  Signal.
   You wave also.  Keep waving.
g. What are we doing?  Signal.  *Waving.*
   Say the whole thing.  Signal.
   *We are waving.*
h. Point to two children.  Look at them.
   What are they doing?  Signal.  *Waving.*
   Say the whole thing.  Signal.
   *They are waving.*

i. Point to a girl.  Look at her.
   What is she doing?  Signal.  *Waving.*
   Say the whole thing.  Signal.
   *She is waving.*
j. Point to a boy.  Look at him.
   What is he doing?  Signal.  *Waving.*
   Say the whole thing.  Signal.
   *He is waving.*

k. Look at me.  What am I doing?  Signal.
   *Waving.*  Say the whole thing.  Signal.
   *You are waving.*
Let's do this again and see how fast we can
go.
l. Repeat a through k until all children's
   responses are firm.  Then say:
   That was very good.

**Individual Test**

Repeat a through k, calling on different
children for each step.

**TASK 5  Concept Application**

You're going to figure out a hard problem
about a dog.
a. Listen to the rule.
   The dog that is sitting will bite.
   Everybody, say the rule with me.  Signal.
   Respond with the children.
   *The dog that is sitting will bite.*
b. Again.  Signal.  Respond with the children.
   *The dog that is sitting will bite.*
c. All by yourselves.  Say the rule.  Signal.
   Do not respond with the children.
   *The dog that is sitting will bite.*
d. Again.  Signal.
   *The dog that is sitting will bite.*
e. Repeat a through d until all children can
   say the rule.

Let's look at the dogs on the next page.
Turn the page quickly.

**FIGURE 2-7.   EXCERPTS FROM DISTAR TEACHER PRESENTATION BOOK —**
**CONTINUED**

Vygotsky. A characteristic of the theories related to this view is the use of stages to indicate the levels of organization people reach at given points in development. Typically a stage refers to a level of internal organization that is qualitatively different from other stages.

The stage component is a well-known part of Jean Piaget's theory of cognitive development. Terms such as preoperational and sensorimotor stages are commonplace in the educational vocabulary as a result of Piaget's thinking and writing. In Piagetian theory, the stages are characterized by specific types of mental operations. Piaget believes that maturation, environment, and social experience, along with what he calls equilibration, all contribute to the child's attempts to organize and structure his world (18).

In the area of language development, cognitive theorists are concerned with which develops first, language or thought. In general, this group of theorists believes that language does not determine thought processes, but that thought processes and language processes interact and accommodate to one another. For Vygotsky thought and speech are separate entities until about the age of two years when they join and initiate a new form of interactive behavior (24). An example may make this idea clearer. Vygotsky makes a distinction between spontaneous and scientific concepts. A spontaneous concept is the child's learning of the word "brother" from concrete, immediate experiences. The scientific concept develops later when the child comes to understand ideas such as "brotherhood" and "all men are brothers." For Vygotsky, the word originally serves as a signal to a concept, but later the word becomes the concept itself as a result of the child's cumulative experiences.

In contrast, Piaget believes that the child's thought derives from internalized actions. He feels that language develops along with nonverbal cognitive structures. The following statement by Pflaum is an excellent summary of Piaget's position on language development:

> During his forty-five years of study of cognitive growth, Piaget has not changed his position on the role of language in thinking drastically. He continues to believe that language ability is generally determined by the level achieved in cognitive development; however, there are points where language does stimulate cognitive growth to a certain extent. For example, language enables children to detach thought from action at the start of the preoperational stage. Thus, thought becomes symbolic and, because language too is inherently symbolic, it becomes the natural medium for representing absent objects and past events. This ability to represent is a hallmark of the beginning of the preoperational stage, and language is one important source used by children as they move into this stage (17:6).

Further developing Piaget's position on language and thought, Pflaum states that, "Piaget would contend that the strategies used in learning language are not used to create new thinking abilities. Instead, language services thought" (17:7). The cognitive-interactionist position on the interrelationships between language and thought is quite different from that of the behaviorists. We shall see how this organismic position translates into language teaching practices which are considerably different from those espoused by the behaviorists.

*Practices.* Program practices and instructional strategies derived from the cognitive-interactionist theories generally are built on two basic assumptions: (1) The child progresses through a sequential series of stages of development, which must be taken into account in program planning; and (2) Active participation by the child in manipulating and organizing experiences is essential for development. The teacher follows a "wait-challenge-wait" procedure. Children are allowed to accumulate their own experience at their own rate at a certain level until that level is well established. The teacher's responsibility is to arrange activities that challenge current levels and stretch the child to higher levels. Under this approach, the child and the teacher have complementary roles; each alternates between passive and active roles.

If you were to interview teachers at work in programs representing the cognitive-interactionist view of human development, you would get some clues from their conversation to indicate how they apply theoretical ideas to real teaching situations. They would make comments such as these:

— Development can be seen as qualitative change in internal structures.
— The aim of instruction should be to guide children to inquiry.
— We need to stress finding order and relationships and should concern ourselves with classification, seriation, etc.
— Humans are active organisms, using adaptive behavior to meet environmental forces halfway.
— Different domains of development can be studied in isolation, but are so interrelated in children that they must not be taught in isolation.
— One stage of development is a prerequisite to the next and successful completion of one stage is needed before moving on.
— Teachers should use the guided discovery approach to teaching.
— Projects which cut across several subject areas should be used.
— Both teachers and children need to be engaged in manipulation and experimentation.
— The overall goal of education is to stimulate children toward involvement and self-direction in learning (5).

Once again we challenge you to examine your own beliefs. Where do you stand? Are you basically a behaviorist? A maturationist? A cognitive-interactionist? Undecided? Need more time to think about it?

Even if you are not quite ready to commit yourself, perhaps your awareness of the different positions on human development has been raised sufficiently so that you are more sensitive to the links between philosophy, theory, and practice.

*The theory-practice link for language teaching.* As before, we will present an example of the application of the cognitive-interactionist position on development to language. The example is given in Figure 2-8 (22:321).

Notice that the theoretical assumptions about language primarily involve the interaction between language and thought. Knowledge, thought, and language are inextricably tied. One important implication of this position is that any teaching aimed at development of the intellect will simultaneously develop language, and vice versa. In terms of developmental expectation, limits set by the stage of development are important considerations. It is also assumed that intellectual functioning will increase as language competence improves.

With regard to change processes, change is thought to occur in the area of language in the same way as it does in other areas of development: the building of experiences on each other, forming more complex structures, or schemata. The building is done through a series of adaptations made up of assimilation and accommodation experiences. As the child has an abundance of assimilation experiences in which new situations are fitted into old schema, the use of accommodation elevates the child to a higher level of functioning. Accommodation is the changing of ideas to fit new situations.

The developmental expectation as well as the theoretically determined change processes must be used in drawing inferences about the conditions that will facilitate development. Because change occurs when new language schemata are built through the processes of assimilation and accommodation, it follows that the child must be actively involved in situations which are expected to promote assimilation and accommodation. Teachers' behaviors related to providing experiences for children are especially important. Teachers must understand which stage or level of mental operation is current for the child and provide experiences appropriate to that level. They must also be sure that the experiences they provide are ones that will involve the child in the activity. Recall that the child must be actively involved in solving problems in order to build new schemata. Different types of experiences and different lines of inquiry are related to different stages or levels of mental development on the part of the children.

As is seen in the suggestions in Figure 2-8, child activities should be such that the child can mentally manipulate and act on information and materials. The content for language experiences should not be beyond the level of the symbolic schemata already present in the child. Teachers are

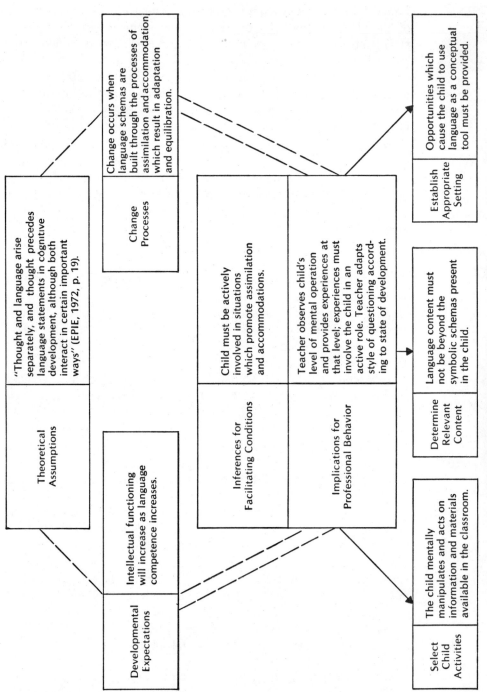

**Theoretical Assumptions**

"Thought and language arise separately, and thought precedes language statements in cognitive development, although both interact in certain important ways" (EPIE, 1972, p. 19).

**Developmental Expectations**

Intellectual functioning will increase as language competence increases.

**Change Processes**

Change occurs when language schemas are built through the processes of assimilation and accommodation which result in adaptation and equilibration.

**Inferences for Facilitating Conditions**

Child must be actively involved in situations which promote assimilation and accommodations.

**Implications for Professional Behavior**

Teacher observes child's level of mental operation and provides experiences at that level; experiences must involve the child in an active role. Teacher adapts style of questioning according to state of development.

**Establish Appropriate Setting**

Opportunities which cause the child to use language as a conceptual tool must be provided.

**Determine Relevant Content**

Language content must not be beyond the symbolic schemas present in the child.

**Select Child Activities**

The child mentally manipulates and acts on information and materials available in the classroom.

FIGURE 2-8. EXAMPLE OF THEORY-PRACTICE LINKS FOR COGNITIVE-INTERACTIONIST POSITION

expected to set the stage for concept acquisition rather than attempting to teach specific responses. They are expected to call children's attention to dissonant information and to ask children to justify their responses. The assumption is that if children are given interesting activities at the appropriate level (in terms of their mental operations), they will not perform the activities in routine, thoughtless fashion, but will think about what they are doing and about the consequences of their transactions.

Since thought and language are so tightly related, it is felt that an early education program should be designed so that language permeates the entire day. Special lessons devoted to the development of cognitive skills are often recommended. In these lessons, teachers are expected to verbalize each child's transaction and to encourage the child to verbalize what he or she is thinking. As children explore and manipulate they make certain discoveries. Some of these discoveries are wrong, but over a period of time they assimilate enough data from experiences to make corrections. Whenever possible, feedback is provided, so that the children can figure out whether or not they are on the right track. The teacher's role is to stimulate and guide, not to teach specific responses, not to tell the children the right answer, nor even to tell them that they are wrong. The teacher must have confidence in the children's ability to learn on their own. When they are wrong, the teacher may ask questions or call attention to cues that were missed, so that the children have more data to assimilate, but giving them the right answer will not convince them. They must be convinced by their own actions.

Many of the foregoing suggestions for planning children's activities and determining teacher behavior are drawn from an early education curriculum developed by Lavatelli (13). There are other Piagetian curriculum derivations, and some differ from the Lavatelli curriculum. It is important to recall the point made earlier that each program is an interpretation of theory. We need not quarrel with one interpretation of the theory versus another but ought to be convinced that there are logical relationships between the important aspects of the theory and the curriculum derivations as they are interpreted by any program planner.

*A sample program.* In addition to the Piagetian curriculum developed by Lavatelli, programs for young children based on Piagetian thinking have also been published by Weikart (25) and, more recently, by Kamii and DeVries (11). Pflaum provides detailed recommendations for an early childhood level language development program in her book, *The Development of Language and Reading in the Young Child* (17). Pflaum's suggestions are derived from a Piagetian framework; they will be used as examples in this chapter.

Pflaum's position is that language provides children with learning strategies that can be applied in general cognitive development, and so the program is designed to maximize language abilities. In general, informal contacts with children rather than formal lessons are preferred. Teacher assessment of children's development is an important part of the plan, because it is important to know which type of language information children are ready for next.

The second major component of the program involves vocabulary development. As Pflaum put it:

> ... adults must help children to acquire attributes of concepts so that their in-depth understanding of words expands. The adult function is to help children focus on the relevant features of words they use. There are, then, two parts to instruction in language meaning. One is to encourage vocabulary growth in terms of quantity, while the other provides .opportunities for children to further their understanding of word meaning. All components of the language program are based on teacher assessment and take place in child-structured situations as well as in informal, planned lessons determined by teacher judgment and student need. (17:68)

Teachers are provided with suggestions, in checklist format, for evaluating children's present levels of attainment in syntactic development and phonological growth. Other procedures are recommended for assessing language meaning. The teacher is advised to be informal in teaching style and to focus efforts on providing data that will be helpful to children as they form their own rules. Content arises out of natural activities of the classroom. Both adult naming of words and adult questioning about word features are considered important.

Some examples of instructional activities from Pflaum's book (17:89, 91-92, 94-95) are as follows:

Illustrative Instructional Activities to
Enhance Syntactic Development
1. Period of Acquisition of Basic Structures (Generally Three and Four Year Olds)

*Topic*

Subject-Verb-Object Sentences

*Sample Dialogues*

Interaction at this point will be spontaneous. The following examples are intended to illustrate types of adult responses which are helpful to the child's growing syntactic knowledge.

A. *Expansion.* In these responses, adults repeat the child's structure in mature form.
      *Child:*    "Look, Teacher. *Smash snake.*" (Another child has just

smashed the speaker's plasticene snake.)

*Teacher:* "Oh, too bad. *Johnny smashed the snake.*" (Teacher emphasizes the expansion of the child's structure.) "Billy, make a new one, and maybe Johnny will help."

*Child:* "Hurt finger."

*Teacher:* "Oh, I'm sorry. You hurt your finger. Let's fix it."

B. *Prompts.* Adults prompt for words and then repeat the words in mature sentence structure.

*Child:* "Look, snake." (He points to a plasticene snake before him.)

*Teacher:* "Oh, you made a . . .?"

*Child:* "Snake."

*Teacher:* "You made a nice snake."

*Child:* "Want drink."

*Teacher:* (Looking around): "Who wants a drink?"

*Child:* "Me."

*Teacher:* "Oh, Billy wants a drink."

*Child:* "Gimme." (Points to toy.)

*Teacher:* "What toy do you want, Billy?"

*Child:* "Truck."

*Teacher:* "OK, Billy, you want a truck."

## Topic

Negative Word in the Middle of a Sentence

### Activities

A. Beginning development of the concepts *same* and *different* emerge when two identical groupings of objects or pictures are placed on the table and the following dialogue results:

*Teacher:* "This pile of blocks is the same as this one."
*Teacher* (adding blocks to one pile): "Are they the same now?"
*Children:* "No."
*Teacher:* "Right. They are not the same. Say that."
*Children:* "They are not the same."

B. "In the foolishness game," the teacher names a well-known object incorrectly. The child responds, "You're silly. That's not a _____. It's a _____." The teacher then encourages the child to be the "silly one."

## Topic

Wh-word Questions

### Activities

A. Songs, nursery rhymes
   1. Songs, nursery rhymes.
   2. In the "question-answer game," each child asks where an object is.

The game continues from child to child.

*Topic*

Use of Adjectives

*Activities*

A. The children expand simple sentences by using pictures and objects.

| | |
|---|---|
| *Teacher:* | "What do you see here?" |
| *Child:* | "A dog." |
| *Teacher:* | "Yes. What does he look like?" |
| *Child:* | "He's a big dog." |
| *Teacher:* | "What else?" |

*Topic*

Future Tense

*Activities*

A. Children can play a game of "wishing" by saying, "When I grow up, I will be a _____" or "On Saturday, I will _____."

B. In projecting from picture stories, the teacher selects pictures which portray events and asks the children to say what will happen. He then expands their comments to include the future tense.

One can see that dialogue between the teacher and child is an important instructional technique in this program. The ability to ask questions in the right way is also essential for the teacher in this program. Adults must be aware that they function as models for children, especially in the area of phonological development.

A major goal of the program is the expansion of both the listening and speaking vocabularies of young children. Pflaum recommends planned instruction to accomplish this goal but insists that this instruction should be as natural and informal as possible. The content is to be drawn mainly from the activities of the classroom. The teacher is advised to be sensitive to the interactive relationship between language and thought. Instructional procedures place the teacher in the role of namer so that children have the necessary labels, planner of events that will require additional labels, and planner of activities that will help children improve their classification abilities. Pflaum suggests:

Interactive involvement with objects and materials of many sorts, with people, with actions, and even with pictures, contributes to cognitive development. The language aspect of the process involves the naming of objects, actions, events, etc., but it also involves the critical elements of description, classification of events, explanation, and communication . . . . the teacher provides opportunities to make understanding explicit by interaction with children as they spontaneously involve themselves in the objects and with the people around them. (17:101)

*How about you?* In our discussions of the teaching practices and published programs derived from maturationist and behaviorist theories, we indicated that a basic understanding of the theory would allow you to review, choose, adapt, and use many of the activities described throughout this book. The same recommendation applies to the cognitive-interactionist position. If this is the style of teaching for you, use your basic understanding of the assumptions, developmental expectations, and change processes from the theory as guides in the review and selection of teaching activities in the language arts.

## WHERE DO YOU GO FROM HERE?

This chapter could have been written by concentrating on teaching "recipes." If that had been done, you would have been exposed to many ideas for use in language arts programs with young children. So what? What happens after you have tried all those ideas and are looking for something new? What happens when you encounter a child that you haven't found described in one of the recipe books? Then what?

The chapter was oriented in a very different way. We tried to persuade you to take the time to think through your system of beliefs about how people learn and develop, so that you can gain for yourself an understanding of the instructional approach you espouse. With your own conception of development firmly in place, those teacher recipe books will be more valuable because you can use them selectively, adopting ideas that fit your perspective, rejecting those that do not, and modifying others. The procedure is likely to result in a teacher who makes decisions that are related and consistent, one with the other; that consistency is bound to have positive results with children in language arts teaching and learning.

## REFERENCES

1. Baldwin, A.L. *Theories of Child Development.* New York: Wiley, 1967.

2. Biber, Barbara. "A Developmental-Interaction Approach: Bank Street College of Education," in Mary C. Day and Ronald K. Parker (Eds.), *The Preschool in Action* (Rev. Ed.) Boston: Allyn and Bacon, 1977, pp. 423-460.

3. Chomsky, N. *Language and Mind.* New York: Harcourt, Brace and World, 1968.

4. Engelmann, Siegfried and Osborn, Jean. *Distar Language 1: An Instructional System. Teacher Presentation Book B* (2d Ed.) Chicago: Science Research Associates, 1976.

5. Educational Product Report. *Early Childhood Education: How To Select and Evaluate Materials.* New York: Educational Products Information Exchange Institute, 1972.

6. Forsberg, Sara; Neisworth, John T.; Laub, Karen. *COMP Curriculum Guide.* University Park, Pa.: The Pennsylvania State University, HICOMP Outreach Project, 1977.

7. Gesell, Arnold, et al. *The First Five Years of Life: A Guide to the Study of the Preschool Child.* New York: Harper and Row, 1940.

8. Green, Maxine. *Teacher As Stranger.* Belmont, Calif.: Wadsworth Publishing Co., 1973.

9. Honstead, Carole. "The Developmental Theory of Jean Piaget," in Joe Frost (Ed.), *Early Childhood Education Rediscovered.* New York: Holt, Rinehart and Winston, 1968, pp. 132-145.

10. *Introduction to Individualized Education Program Plans in Pennsylvania.* Harrisburg, Pennsylvania Department of Education and King of Prussia, Pa.: National Learning Resource Center of Pennsylvania, 1977.

11. Kamii, Constance and DeVries, Rheta. "Piaget for Early Education," in Mary C. Day and Ronald K. Parker (Eds.), *The Preschool in Action* (Rev. Ed.). Boston: Allyn and Bacon, 1977, pp. 363-420.

12. Langer, J. *Theories of Development.* New York: Holt, Rinehart and Winston, 1969.

13. Lavatelli, Cecelia S. *Piaget's Theory Applied to an Early Childhood Curriculum.* Boston: Center for Media Development, 1970.

14. Lenneberg, Eric. *Biological Foundations of Language.* New York: Wiley, 1967.

15. Moffett, James and Wagner, Betty J. *Student-Centered Language Arts and Reading.* (2d Ed.) Boston: Houghton Mifflin, 1976.

16. Peters, Donald L. "Early Childhood Education: An Overview and Evaluation," in P. Robinson and L. Hom (Eds.), *Psychological Processes in Early Childhood.* New York: Academic Press, 1977.

17. Pflaum, Susanna Whitney. *The Development of Language and Reading in the Young Child.* Columbus, Ohio: Charles E. Merrill Publishing Co., 1974.

18. Piaget, Jean. *The Origins of Intelligence in Children.* New York: International Universities Press, 1952. (Originally published, 1936.)

19. Pitcher, Evelyn G. and Ames, Louise B. *The Guidance Nursery School.* (Rev. Ed.) New York: Harper and Row, 1975.

20. Reese, H. W. and Overton, W. F. "Models of Development and Theories of Development," in L. R. Goulet and P. B. Baltes (Eds.), *Life-span Developmental Psychology: Research and Theory,* New York: Academic Press, 1970.

21. Reynolds, Maynard and Birch, Jack. *Teaching Exceptional Children in All America's Schools.* Reston, Va.: The Council for Exceptional Children, 1977.

22. Seaver, Judith and Cartwright, Carol. "A Pluralistic Foundation for Training Early Childhood Professionals," *Curriculum Inquiry,* 1977, 7, 305-329.

23. Skinner, B. F. *Verbal Behavior.* New York: Appleton-Century-Crofts, 1957.

24. Vygotsky, L. S. *Thought and Language.* Cambridge, Mass.: M.I.T. Press, 1962.

25. Weikart, David P. "Relationship of Curriculum, Teaching, and Learning," in Julian C. Stanley (Ed.), *Preschool Programs for the Disadvantaged: Five Experimental Approaches to Early Childhood Education.* Baltimore, Md.: Johns Hopkins University Press, 1972, pp. 22-66.

# CHAPTER 3
# LISTENING

*We believe the attention given to listening instruction must be significantly increased if the best interests of pupils are to be served, especially those of pupils who have deficiencies in other curriculum areas and who may need to rely upon listening for most of their information and much of their recreation. (6:306).*

Although children may spend up to 58 percent of their time in school listening, according to one of the first studies of listening by Wilt (8) in 1950, relatively little research on listening skills has been conducted, especially as compared to the amount of research concerning reading. Interest in listening has increased, however, and since Wilt's study, more research has been conducted about listening itself as well as its relationship to reading.

Researchers who have studied the teachability of various listening skills have discovered that listening skills usually can be taught successfully. Children who have systematically been taught particular listening skills, such as critical listening skills (5), do show improvement in the application of those skills.

The relationship of listening skills to reading skills is not entirely clear in the research literature. The impact of auditory perception skills, including the ability to hear differences in sounds in words, upon reading ability may vary depending on the type of early reading instructional program. Spache (7), summarizing the results of research that studied the relationship of auditory perception and reading, concludes that highly phonic-oriented reading programs in the primary grades require almost a mastery of auditory perception skills in order for children to be successful in reading. Spache also urges that in this type of reading program, auditory perception and phonic skills be taught together to reinforce each other, rather than being considered as unrelated sets of skills.

In reviewing research studies concerning the relationship of auditory comprehension — the ability to understand what is heard — and reading ability, Spache concludes that there is "ample evidence that training programs in auditory comprehension tend to increase reading ability ... [because] they are simply stimulation of the same type of thinking that compose silent reading with the practice being in a parallel medium" (7:64).

Many textbooks (3:182, for example) on teaching young children to read recommend that the teacher begin with listening activities as a preparation for formal reading instruction. For example, when reading a story to children, the teacher should pose questions before reading to guide children's listening. Afterwards the teacher should encourage spontaneous reactions followed by questions for clarification.

Auditory comprehension, or the ability to understand what the child hears, has traditionally been used by teachers as a measure of a child's capacity to learn. Often specialists calculate the difference in levels between what the child can comprehend through listening and what he or she can comprehend through reading. Presumably if the auditory comprehension level is higher than the reading level, the auditory comprehension level represents the child's capacity; the child would therefore profit from instruction in word recognition skills which would enable the student to read at the level which he or she can comprehend through listening. On the other hand, if a child reads at a higher level than he or she can comprehend auditorally, training in auditory comprehension seems warranted. While research studies have reported varying relation-ships between capacity and auditory comprehension, depending on the measures of intelligence and listening ability, Spache (7) concludes that the median correlation found in a number of studies is 0.61, not as close a relationship as educators have assumed in the past. Nevertheless, listening comprehension may be used as one index of a child's capacity, especially as related to language processes.

In conclusion, for purposes of discussion in this chapter the listening skills are presented as clearly identifiable skills arranged, to some extent, in hierarchical order. This presentation is for the convenience of the reader so that the skills may be examined in depth. In reality, research (7) reveals that listening skills probably overlap to some extent and are not as clearly defined as might appear from this discussion.

## DIAGNOSIS AND ASSESSMENT

The game of "telephone" illustrates the importance of accurate listening for children and adults alike. As a simple message is passed around a circle of children, details change so that the message that the last person receives is usually rather different from the message originally sent. Most of us have also experienced lapses of memory after having been given directions for getting to a destination. Good listening is a practical necessity as well as the medium through which other learning occurs.

Before considering diagnosis and assessment of children's listening skills, we, as teachers, should first assess our own listening habits. Do we listen when someone is talking to us, are we planning what we will say next, or are we thinking of something else? Can we retell the events of a story accurately? Can we follow directions when they are given verbally? Since the teacher is the model in the classroom, we should first become aware of our own habits and become good listeners in all situations.

Try this activity to test your listening habits. First, evaluate yourself on the following checklist, using "1" for rarely, "2" for sometimes, and "3" for almost always:

_____**1.** Do you look at a person who is speaking?

_____**2.** When you speak, does what you say follow directly from the context of what the other person has said?

_____**3.** Do you interrupt when another person is speaking?

_____**4.** Are you able to follow directions given orally?

_____**5.** Are you able to sum up the "gist" or main ideas of something told to you?

Now, after evaluating yourself, ask a friend (preferably a good one) to observe you for a day or two and evaluate you on the checklist. Note whether there are any discrepancies between your evaluations and those of your friend.

We have said that good listening habits of the teacher are important in establishing good listening conditions in the classroom. Listening skills also can and should be systematically taught throughout the early childhood years. Many teachers unfortunately assume that because children can hear, they are listening. We are used to "tuning out" in our age of noise pollution. In many homes the television is never turned off until late at night. Frequently, one or more radios blare — perhaps also a tape recorder or record player. We learn at an early age to "tune out" in self-defense. However, we also need to learn to "tune in" when listening is important.

What listening skills may be taught to help a child "tune in"? All the following skills should be taught in preschool or kindergarten and developed throughout the elementary school.

    **I.** Auditory perception skills
      **A.** Auditory awareness
      **B.** Auditory discrimination
      **C.** Auditory memory
    **II.** Following directions
    **III.** Deriving word meanings from context
    **IV.** Auditory comprehension

All these skills are also included in most language arts and reading programs. Since listening and reading are really two sides of the same coin, listening skills should be taught not only for their own value but also as preparation for more formal training in reading skills. First, we will consider how diagnosis and assessment of these listening skills can take place with preschool and kindergarten children.

## Preschool and Kindergarten

**Auditory awareness.** Auditory awareness refers to the ability of the child to listen to sounds in the environment. Auditory acuity (the physical ability to hear) is obviously a prerequisite to auditory awareness, but it does not guarantee it. Training in auditory awareness helps children focus their attention on *listening for* sounds as opposed to just hearing them in the background. One type of activity that may be used to assess children's auditory awareness is to have the children close their eyes and identify sounds outside their classroom. Or the teacher can make various sounds (crumbling paper, slamming doors, opening windows, and so on), which the children identify. The same activities recommended for instruction may be used for diagnostic purposes to assess whether young children can identify familiar sounds. This skill is fundamental to the development of more sophisticated listening skills, which are necessary for functioning in a classroom.

**Auditory discrimination.** After preliminary work in auditory awareness, the teacher can begin training in auditory discrimination, having the children note whether sounds are the same or different. As the teacher presents instructional activities to preschool and kindergarten children, it can be noted who is able to hear differences in sounds and who is having difficulty. First, sounds in the environment (for example, the roar of a motorcycle and of a car) can be compared, having children decide whether the sounds are the same or different. Then the teacher can work with beginning letter sounds. For example, children can decide whether the words (presented auditorally only) *big, boy,* and *bat* all begin with the same sound. Then the children can be asked to pick out a word that begins with a different sound from others heard (for example, *big, cab, ball*). Finally, have the children supply words that begin with a particular sound (for example, have them think of words that begin with the same sound as in the beginning of *dog*).

After beginning sounds can be discriminated, ending sounds can be presented, probably most easily in rhymes. Simple nursery rhymes can be used to teach the concept of rhyming. If given incomplete nursery rhymes, children can supply the rhyming word ("Jack and Jill went up the _____"). Rhyming verses can be made up by the teacher to test whether children really have the concept of rhyming words or whether they have only a familiarity with a given nursery rhyme. For example, children should supply *light* in the following: "When it's dark at night, on goes the street _____." Children also delight in adding to a list of rhyming words (*man, pan, fan* . . .). Children who are unable to supply rhyming words need further instruction in the concept of likeness of the vowel and ending sounds.

After the concept of rhyming has been grasped, children then need to be taught the distinction between rhyming and ending sounds. They can be asked to identify whether all the words end the same (*hop, map, tip*) and then which word has a different ending among others (*bit, bag, hat*).

A note of caution should be added about using the terms *same* and *different* with young children. The listening exercises described above have no meaning if children lack the concept of same and different. It is probably easiest to teach the meaning of these terms first with objects in the environment. For example, the teacher, holding up two like balls, can ask whether these objects are the same or different. Then the concepts can be reinforced with worksheet exercises. (Mark the object that is different: ▢ ▢ ▢ ○ .)

**Auditory memory.** Auditory memory refers to the ability to repeat sounds heard. For example, if the children hear the teacher knocking on the table three times, they should be able to reproduce three knocking sounds. More difficult aspects of this skill involve asking children to repeat a series of numbers (3, 7, 2) or words (*tall, hug, bat*). Still more difficult is asking children to repeat whole sentences exactly and finally to retell stories. Training in auditory memory helps create a "set" toward listening and foster good listening habits. It probably also assumes importance in phonics-oriented reading programs, because children must retain the sounds in their auditory memories as they sound out words, blending the sounds together. Assessment of this skill may reveal that children with poor auditory memories may be the same ones who have difficulty following directions.

**Following directions.** The teacher should carefully observe the ability of individual children to follow directions. Children may be able to understand simple one-step directions (such as, "Close the door"), but they may be unable to remember directions involving several steps ("Close the door, open the window, and sit down, please").

Attention should be given to word choice in giving directions. Too often we overestimate children's knowledge of word meanings. Even if children do know the meanings of the individual words, sometimes we use complex linguistic structures that cause comprehension problems. For example, the directions "Give the ball, which is in the basket, to the boy who is standing at the head of the line" may cause problems even for children who know the meanings of the individual words. The use of the relative clauses may make the directions difficult for some children to comprehend. With young children teachers should probably use simple, direct sentences. It would be preferable to say, "Get the ball out of the basket. Then give it to Tom" (avoiding the construction "the boy at the head of the line" which is a vague and confusing referent).

Once the teacher determines whether a child's difficulty in following directions is due to poor auditory memory or to poor listening habits, then appropriate instruction can take place. If certain children habitually do not attend to directions, some of the techniques mentioned later in this chapter may help get their attention. If, however, the problem in following directions is due to poor auditory memory, only very simple one-step directions should be given at first. As the child is able to respond, the complexity may gradually be increased to two- and three-step directions.

A note of caution should be inserted, however, about a child who doesn't seem to be able to follow directions. Does a child have an undetected hearing loss? Or is another language spoken in the home? Observations should be made in other situations; cumulative records and/or information from parents may reveal physical or language problems.

While most schools routinely do screening for hearing losses through audiometric testing, the teacher should be alert to children who manifest symptoms of a hearing loss. The following have been suggested (6:16) as symptoms of hearing difficulties: earache, faulty pronunciations, tendency to favor one ear, breathing through the mouth, complaints of head noises or dizziness, unnatural pitch of voice, inattention or poor scholastic achievement, frequent rubbing of the ear, and blank expression when directions are given.

**Deriving word meanings from context.** This skill is a key one, which will help children immensely not only in listening but also in reading. Mature readers do not sound out every word; their eyes take in the general shape or configuration of a word and perhaps the first letter. Using the flow of the context or surrounding meaning, the word is recognized instantly with virtually no thought given to it. However, this system works smoothly only as long as the printed words are in the reader's reading vocabulary. In other words, the word is known, and the reader does not have to ponder the meaning. Similarly, in listening we do not attend to individual words unless an unfamiliar or unusual word is used. We are then usually able to understand its meaning through context.

When children learn to read, they typically have oral vocabularies of about 2,500 words. The vocabulary in beginning reading instructional books is usually controlled, so that average children meet in print only those words that they are familiar with orally. But what difficulties will be encountered by children who come to school with a limited oral language background? They may not have meaningful associations for the words they are supposed to recognize in print. In other words, the vocabulary used in the reading book may not be in their listening vocabularies — the words they understand when listening — or in their speaking vocabularies — the words they use in their own oral language. Since the words in the reading book have little meaning, these children typically have difficulty even in decoding or saying them.

The first step, then, is to assess the point where each child is in language development. It is important to expand children's listening and speaking vocabularies, because they form the bases for the later development of a reading vocabulary. Since oral language development is described in another chapter, we will concentrate on the assessment of a listening vocabulary in any child regardless of verbal abilities.

The teacher must, first of all, be aware of his or her own word choice. Constantly quiz children on the meanings of words that are used in conversation, in the conversation of other children, in books, films, television, and so on. The teacher, for example, might say, "Today we are going to *view* a filmstrip on animals. What are we going to do today?" Not only will this strategy keep children alert and in the habit of listening, but it will also build an awareness of word meanings. The teacher can see which children are able to use the context to derive the meanings of new words.

**Auditory comprehension.** Auditory comprehension corresponds to reading comprehension although the material is presented orally rather than in printed form. Auditory comprehension ranges from the very simple ability to retell an event in a story to much more complex story interpretation.

Even preschool children should be taught to respond at various levels of thinking to material presented orally. Research has documented that most thinking demanded by teachers' questions is at the literal level. Although questioning should begin at the literal level, it should also go beyond to higher levels of thinking. If children are never challenged by the teacher to go beyond the literal level in their thinking, they probably won't. Barrett's *Taxonomy of Reading Comprehension\** (1), which is an adaptation of Bloom's *Taxonomy of Educational Objectives* (2), is a vehicle for helping teachers formulate questions at all levels of thinking.

> 1.0 *Literal Recognition or Recall.* Literal comprehension requires the recognition or recall of ideas, information, and happenings that are explicitly stated in the materials read. *Recognition Tasks,* which frequently take the form of purposes for reading, require the student to locate or identify explicit statements in the reading selection itself or in exercises that use the explicit content of the reading selection. *Recall tasks* demand the student to produce from memory explicit statements from a selection; such tasks are often in the form of questions teachers pose to students after a reading is completed. Two additional comments seem warranted with regard to literal comprehension tasks. First, although literal comprehension tasks can be overused, their importance

---

\*Although the examples in each of the categories are logically ordered from easy to difficult, it is recognized that such a finite hierarchy has not been validated. Therefore, the user of the Taxonomy should view the examples as some of the tasks that might be used to help students produce comprehension products that relate to the type of comprehension described in each of the four major categories of the Taxonomy.

cannot be denied, since a student's ability to deal with such tasks is fundamental to his ability to deal with other types of comprehension tasks. Second, all literal comprehension tasks are not necessarily of equal difficulty. For example, the recognition or recall of a single fact or incident may be somewhat easier than the recognition or recall of a number of facts or incidents, while a more difficult task than either of these two may be the recognition or recall of a number of events or incidents and the sequence of their occurrence. Also related to this concern is the hypothesis that a recall task is usually more difficult than a recognition task, when the two tasks deal with the same content and are of the same nature. Some examples of literal comprehension tasks are:

   1.1 *Recognition or Recall of Details.* The student is required to locate or identify or to call up from memory such facts as the names of characters, the time a story took place, the setting of a story, or an incident described in a story, when such facts are explicitly stated in the selection.

   1.2 *Recognition or Recall of Main Ideas.* The student is asked to locate or identify or to produce from memory an explicit statement in or from a selection which is the main idea of a paragraph or a larger portion of the selection.

   1.3 *Recognition or Recall of Sequence.* The student is required to locate or identify or to call up from memory the order of incidents or actions explicitly stated in the selection.

   1.4 *Recognition or Recall of Comparisons.* The student is requested to locate or identify or to produce from memory likenesses and differences among characters, times in history or places that are explicitly compared by an author.

   1.5 *Recognition or Recall of Cause and Effect Relationships.* The student in this instance may be required to locate or identify or to produce from memory reasons for certain incidents, events, or characters' actions explicitly stated in the selection.

   1.6 *Recognition or Recall of Character Traits.* The student is requested to identify or locate or to call up from memory statements about a character which help to point up the type of person he was when such statements were made by the author of the selection.

2.0 *Inference.* Inferential comprehension is demonstrated by the student when he uses a synthesis of the literal content of a selection, his personal knowledge, his intuition and his imagination as a basis for conjectures or hypotheses. Conjectures or hypotheses derived in this manner may be along convergent or divergent lines, depending on the nature of the task and the reading materials involved. For example, inferential tasks related to narrative selections may permit more divergent or creative conjectures because of the open-ended possibilities provided by such writing. On the other hand, expository selections, because of their content, may call for convergent hypotheses more often than not. In either instance, students may or may not be called upon to indicate the rationale underlying their hypotheses or conjectures, although such a requirement would seem to be more appropriate for convergent rather than divergent hypotheses. Generally, then, inferential comprehension is elicited by purposes for reading, and by teachers' questions which demand thinking and imagination which are stimulated by, but go beyond, the printed page. Examples of inferential tasks related to reading are:

2.1 *Inferring Supporting Details.* In this instance, the student is asked to conjecture about additional facts the author might have included in the selection which would have made it more informative, interesting or appealing.

2.2 *Inferring the Main Idea.* The student is required to provide the main idea, general significance, theme, or moral which is not explicitly stated in the selection.

2.3 *Inferring Sequence.* The student, in this case, may be requested to conjecture as to what action or incident might have taken place between two explicitly stated actions or incidents; he may be asked to hypothesize about what would happen next; or he may be asked to hypothesize about the beginning of a story if the author had not started where he did.

2.4 *Inferring Comparisons.* The student is required to infer likenesses and differences in characters, times, or places. Such inferential comparisons revolve around ideas such as: "here and there," "then and now," "he and he," "he and she," and "she and she."

2.5 *Inferring Cause-and-Effect Relationships.* The student is required to hypothesize about the motives of characters and their interactions with others and with time and place. He may also be required to conjecture as to what caused the author to include certain ideas, words, characterizations, and actions in this writing.

2.6 *Inferring Character Traits.* In this case, the student may be asked to hypothesize about the nature of characters on the basis of explicit clues presented in the selection.

2.7 *Predicting Outcomes.* The student is requested to read an initial portion of selection, and on the basis of this reading to conjecture about the outcome of the selection.

2.8 *Inferring about Figurative Language.* The student, in this instance, is asked to infer literal meanings from the author's figurative use of language.

3.0 *Evaluation.* Evaluation is demonstrated by a student when he makes judgments about the content of a reading selection by comparing it with external criteria, e.g., information provided by the teacher on the subject, authorities on the subject, or by accredited written sources on the subject; or with internal criteria, e.g., the reader's experiences, knowledge, or values related to the subject under consideration. In essence, evaluation requires students to make judgments about the content of their reading, judgments that have to do with its accuracy, acceptability, worth, desirability, completeness, suitability, timeliness, quality, truthfulness, or probability of occurrence. Examples of evaluation tasks related to reading are:

3.1 *Judgments of Reality or Fantasy.* The student is requested to determine whether incidents, events, or characters in a selection could have existed or occurred in real life on the basis of his experience.

3.2 *Judgments of Fact or Opinion.* In this case the student is asked to decide whether the author is presenting information which can be supported with objective data or whether the author is attempting to sway the reader's thinking through the use of subjective content that has overtones of propaganda.

3.3 *Judgments of Adequacy or Validity.* Tasks of this type call for the reader to judge whether the author's treatment of the subject is accurate and complete when compared to other sources on the subject. In this instance, then, the reader is called upon to compare written sources of information with an eye toward their agreements or disagreements, their completeness or incompleteness, and their thoroughness or superficiality in dealing with a subject.

3.4 *Judgments of Appropriateness.* Evaluation tasks of this type require the student to determine whether certain selections or parts of selections are relevant and can contribute to resolving an issue or a problem. For example, a student may be requested to judge the part of a selection which most appropriately describes a character. Or he may be called upon to determine which inferences will make significant contributions to a report he is preparing.

3.5 *Judgments of Worth, Desirability, or Acceptability.* In this instance, the student may be requested to pass judgments on the suitability of a character's action in a particular incident or episode. Was the character right or wrong, good or bad, or somewhere in between? Tasks of this nature call for opinions based on the values the reader has acquired through his personal experiences.

4.0 *Appreciation.* Appreciation involves all the previously cited cognitive dimensions of reading, for it deals with the psychological and aesthetic impact of the selection on the reader. Appreciation calls for the student to be emotionally and aesthetically sensitive to the work and to have a reaction to the worth of its psychological and artistic elements. Appreciation includes both knowledge of and emotional response to literary techniques, forms, styles, and structures. Examples of tasks that involve appreciation are:

4.1 *Emotional Response to the Content.* The student is requested to demonstrate his reaction to a selection in terms of the visceral effect it had upon him. The emotional impact of a work may have to do with such things as its ability to stimulate and sustain interest, excitement, boredom, fear, hate, or amusement on the part of the reader.

4.2 *Identification with Characters and Incidents.* Tasks of this nature will elicit responses from the reader that demonstrate his sensitivity to, sympathy for, or empathy with characters and events portrayed by the author.

4.3 *Reactions to the Author's Use of Language.* In this instance, the student is required to recognize and respond to the author's craftsmanship in his use of words. Such tasks deal with the semantic dimensions of a selection, e.g., the connotations and denotations of words.

4.4 *Imagery.* In this instance, the reader is called upon to recognize and respond to the author's artistic ability to "paint word pictures" that cause him to visualize, smell, taste, hear, or feel the things the author is describing.

Barrett, Thomas C. "Taxonomy of Reading Comprehension," *Reading 360 Monograph* (1972). Lexington, Massachusetts, Ginn and Company — A Xerox Company. Reprinted by permission.

The teacher could ask selected questions from the taxonomy about even a picture book that is shared with young children. Certainly the categories are appropriate for questions about stories read to the children as well as those presented on tapes and records. Comprehension of factual information presented in a class presentation or on television can also be evaluated using the taxonomy. The categories can guide the teacher in formulating questions about children's presentations, even during "show and tell." The important point is that children should not listen passively, but be given *active* purposes for listening through guide questions based on the taxonomy categories. After listening, the questions aid in developing better comprehension and thinking as well as provide diagnostic information about children's auditory comprehension. If the child cannot respond to all levels of comprehension after a listening lesson, the teacher needs to emphasize those levels in instruction.

In using the taxonomy as an assessment tool, the teacher must be careful to distinguish between questions that require convergent thinking — those for which there is one correct answer — and those that require divergent thinking, or those for which several answers may be appropriate. Literal-level questions (for which the answers are stated in the material) and some inferential level questioning (for which answers are not stated directly) require convergent thinking; there is only one correct answer. Some of the inferential-level questions and evaluation and appreciation levels require divergent thinking, meaning that creative responses may be possible. Test questions in multiple-choice format should be of a convergent-thinking nature. Open-ended questions are appropriate to assess divergent thinking if the teacher is willing to accept almost any answer as correct, provided that the child can state a rationale for the answer.

To make sure you understand the categories of Barrett's taxonomy, try creating questions for some of the categories at each level of thinking using the story of "Goldilocks and the Three Bears."

Possible answers:

**1.1** *Recognition or Recall of Details.*
What did Goldilocks eat at the three bears' house?

**1.3** *Recognition or Recall of Sequence.*
What did Goldilocks do after she sat in the three bears' chairs?

**2.5** *Inferring Cause-and-Effect Relationship.*
Why did Goldilocks enter the three bears' house?

**2.7** *Predicting Outcomes.*
Before the children are told the ending of the story, ask the following: What do you think will happen to Goldilocks when the three bears come home?

**3.1** *Judgments of Reality or Fantasy.*
Could this story really have taken place? Why or why not?

**3.5** *Judgments of Worth, Desirability, or Acceptability.*
Was Goldilocks right to have entered the three bears' house? Why or why not?

**4.2** *Identification with Characters and Incidents.*
How did you feel when the three bears found Goldilocks asleep in the little bear's bed?

## Primary Grades

As has been stressed so far in this chapter, the teacher must know which students need more instruction in each of the listening skills. How does the teacher know the level at which each child can comprehend? How can each pupil's skill development be diagnosed? How does diagnostic information about listening abilities help the teacher plan appropriate reading instruction?

In answer to the last question, we know that some relationship exists between reading and auditory skills. The auditory perception skills, discussed earlier in this chapter, are commonly taught to young children as preparation for phonics instruction in the primary grades. Assessment of the development of these skills is important in order to know at what point a more formal program of phonics can be used. For example, working with rhyming words, an auditory discrimination skill, prepares children to hear the likenesses and differences among the vowel sounds, one of the phonics skills. It would be inappropriate to teach children the various long and short vowel sounds if they cannot pick out rhyming words.

As stated at the beginning of this chapter, the relationship between auditory comprehension and reading comprehension has been the subject of much research. It would seem reasonable, moreover, to assume some relationship. If a child is having difficulty with reading comprehension skills, such as stating the main idea of a paragraph, instruction in the same comprehension skill through listening to a paragraph read orally would be a logical prerequisite to working with the skill in written material. The child is relieved of reading the written words and can concentrate on the comprehension skill. After the child has grasped the skill through listening, instruction may continue using reading materials. Sometimes teachers prefer to teach a comprehension skill simultaneously through listening and reading so that learning in the two modalities reinforces skill acquisition. In order for this instruction to be effective, the teacher must assess both the listening and reading levels and skill development of each child.

Formal standardized listening tests do not provide much help in diagnosis of skill strengths and weaknesses. They do yield a score which indicates the grade level at which the child can successfully listen to the test material. The child's score is compared to scores of a norming group, a supposedly representative group of children of the same age. The score, then, indicates how the child did on the test in relation to other comparable children who have taken it. It does not, however, indicate the child's strengths and weaknesses in skill development. Two children may attain the same score on a norm-referenced achievement test but have very different skill needs.

Although several standardized tests of auditory comprehension[1] exist, most schools do not give standardized listening tests as routinely as they give standardized reading tests. Most reading readiness batteries include assessment of auditory perception skills. In addition some individual tests of auditory perception skills[2] are available. Often the classroom teacher, however, must rely on a specialist to give an individual assessment. The teacher, therefore, must judge the listening levels of individual children as well as diagnose their strengths and weaknesses usually by informal measures.

**Informal tests to determine levels.** Teacher-made tests to determine listening levels, although not standardized and tested for reliability, can be tailor-made to the children. Sometimes children "turn off" during a standardized test if they are bored with the content or if they feel that they will fail regardless of their efforts. The teacher who knows their interests, however, can choose appropriate selections.

Construction of an informal listening test is similar to that of an informal reading inventory. In fact, an informal reading inventory may be used to determine listening levels. Instead of having children read selections written at each difficulty level to determine the appropriate level for reading instruction, children listen to the selections as they are read by the teacher. In that way the level of each child's listening abilities may be determined. The teacher may use a commercial informal reading inventory, for example, *Ekwall Reading Inventory,* by Eldon E. Ekwall (4),

---

1. *Brown-Carlson Listening Comprehension Test* (New York: Harcourt, Brace, Jovanovich, Inc., 1955); *Cooperative Primary Tests* (Princeton, N.J.: Educational Testing Service, 1967); *Durrell Listening-Reading Series* (New York: Harcourt, Brace, Jovanovich, 1970); *Sequential Tests of Educational Progress* (Princeton, N.J.: Educational Testing Service, 1972).
2. Joseph M. Wepman, *The Auditory Discrimination Test* (Chicago: Language Research Associates, 1973); *Goldman-Fristoe-Woodcock Auditory Skills Test Battery* (Circle Pines, Minn.: American Guidance Service, 1976); *Goldman-Fristoe-Woodcock Test of Auditory Discrimination* (Circle Pines, Minn.: American Guidance Service, 1970); Dale R. Jordon *JAST – Jordon Auditory Screening Test,* in *Dyslexia in the Classroom* (Columbus, Ohio: Charles E. Merrill Publishing Company, 1972).

or construct his/her own. Selections are taken from materials that are graded in difficulty (usually from basal readers). A selection is chosen from the middle of each of the readers. The length varies with the grade level, ranging from about 100 words at the primary grade levels to about 200 words at the intermediate grade levels. The teacher then writes comprehension questions that assess vocabulary (that is, the child's ability to use contextual analysis to get the meanings of words), literal meaning, and inferential meaning. Usually five to eight questions per selection are recommended to assess children's comprehension of the material. Care should be taken to construct test questions that can be answered only by listening to the selection, not by drawing on general knowledge. They should be simply worded, so that the children can easily understand the questions. Usually approximately 75 percent correct is the criterion set for comprehension at the instructional level, the level appropriate for listening in the classroom. Students scoring at the independent level, or close to 100 percent, should be tested with the next highest selection to determine the instructional level. Testing should be terminated for those scoring at the frustration level, or below 60 percent.

An example from the *Ekwall Reading Inventory* (4:91) follows on page 86a. The selection is written at the third grade level. Vocabulary questions are indicated by a *V*, fact or literal level questions by a *F*, and inferential questions by an *I*. Standards for word recognition errors would not be used in a listening test.

An informal test of listening levels may easily be combined with an informal reading inventory. Two selections are thus needed for each level, one for oral reading and one for listening. Usually teachers administer an informal reading inventory to individuals at the beginning of the school year to place students in groups and at the end of the year to evaluate progress. In addition, teachers informally listen to children read throughout the year to check progress and to note difficulties. Similarly, teachers could note progress in auditory comprehension by reading test selections to children.

With older children the teacher might save time by placing the listening selections on tape. Following each selection the questions would also be recorded. Students would then write their answers or select the correct answer to the questions on paper which later could be checked by the teacher. A tape recorder (with head phones) could be set up in a quiet corner of the room so that children could individually listen to the tape and write their answers. The teacher, however, would have to monitor the testing to start and stop the test at appropriate levels. The students also should not be permitted to rewind the tape to listen to a selection again if recall comprehension is being assessed.

Group administration, with older children, is also possible although it is not as desirable as individual administration. The teacher could read the selections and accompanying questions to the group; the students write or select their answers on paper. However, beginning selections may be appropriate for some students but too easy for others. Higher-level selections are appropriate for some but frustrating to others. Therefore, individual administration is most desirable. The teacher who has observed children during informal classwork can usually estimate the level at which to begin testing with an individual.

**Informal skills tests.** The teacher needs to know not only the instructional listening level of each student but also skill strengths and weaknesses. Appropriate instruction can take place only if diagnoses have been made. In discussing the assessment of reading skill development, we often use the term *mastery* to indicate that a child has attained a predetermined level of competence, such as 80 percent correct. The concept of mastery may be applied to most of the auditory perception skills. For example, a child can or cannot identify the two rhyming words from the four presented attaining 80 percent correct. The term *skill mastery,* however, does not seem to apply in discussing comprehension or thinking skills, since mastery may depend on the type and difficulty of the material. Although a child may seem to have mastered a given skill, he or she may not be able to apply it later in a different context. Therefore, we recommend that the teacher give the child repeated exposures to the skills in different contexts, noting proficiency as it is observed. The chart (page 86b), which includes the skills discussed earlier in this chapter, may be used as a record-keeping system. The skill categories could be expanded to fit the instructional emphasis needed. Likewise, the symbol system could be changed to indicate different types of writing (narrative, expository, descriptive) and/or different art forms (drama, movies, poetry).

Many of the skills can be observed during the informal test to determine listening level. The teacher, before giving the informal listening inventory, should note which skills are to be observed during the test. If the child consistently answers questions related to that skill, then the teacher can place a mark in the appropriate row under the child's name. For example, if during the informal listening inventory a child answers all (or perhaps all but one) of the vocabulary questions correctly, then proficiency in "Deriving word meanings from context" on test material would be noted.

The next step is to plan activities that assess and develop each of the skills that were not observed in the informal listening inventory. A double check is advisable for those skills that were assessed with only a few questions on the informal listening inventory. For older children selections written at their instructional listening levels might be taped as well as questions relating to specific skills. The test administration could be conducted in a fashion similar to that of the informal listening inventory. With younger children observations can be systematically made of individual's responses to different activities. The checklist thus becomes a guide for

Kathy had always wanted to go for a ride on an airplane. One day her father told her that she could ride on an airplane to visit her grandmother and grandfather. She was very happy and could hardly wait to get started.

When the time came to go, her father went to the ticket counter and paid for the airplane ticket. Her mother helped her get on the airplane. Then a lady told her to buckle her seat belt and she even helped her with it.

Soon the airplane was going very fast down the runway. Kathy was afraid at first but soon the airplane was in the air. Kathy peered out of the window at the ground below, where the houses and cars looked very small. The lady gave Kathy something to drink and a sandwich to eat.

**(139 Words) (Number of word recognition errors _____ )**

*Questions:*

F   1. _____ What had Kathy always wanted to do? (Go for a ride on an airplane)
F   2. _____ Who told Kathy that she could ride on an airplane? (Her father)
F   3. _____ Whom was Kathy going to visit? (Her grandmother and grandfather)
F   4. _____ How did Kathy feel about going? (She was very happy, happy, and/or she could hardly wait to get started)
F   5. _____ Who helped Kathy get on the airplane? (Her mother)
F   6. _____ What did the lady tell Kathy when she got on the airplane? (To buckle her seat belt)
F   7. _____ How did Kathy feel when the airplane started going very fast? (She was afraid)
V   8. _____ What did the word "peered" mean when it said, "Kathy peered out of the window?" (She looked, or she looked out of the window)
I   9. _____ Why did the houses and cars look small below? (Because they were up in the air, far away, or high up in the air)
F  10. _____ What did the lady give Kathy? (A drink and a sandwich) (Student must get both)

|  | Number of Word Recognition Errors | | | | | | Reading Level | |
|---|---|---|---|---|---|---|---|---|
|  | 0–2 | 3–4 | 5–7 | 8–10 | 11–13 | 14 | | |
| 0 | + | * | * | * | * | x | ⊞ Independent | ☐ |
| 1 | + | * | * | * | x | x | | |
| 2 | * | * | * | x | x | x | ⊡ Instructional | ☐ |
| 3 | * | * | x | x | x | x | ⊠ Frustration | ☐ |
| 4 | * | x | x | x | x | x | | |
| 5+ | x | x | x | x | x | x | | |

Number of Questions Missed (row labels at left: 0, 1, 2, 3, 4, 5+)

| Skills | Betty | Tom | Mary | |
|---|---|---|---|---|
| **AUDITORY PERCEPTION** | | | | |
| Auditory awareness | R | R | R | |
| Auditory discrimination | | | | |
|    Word beginnings | | R | | |
|    Word endings | | R | R | |
|    Rhyme | | R | R | |
| Auditory memory | R | R,S | R | |
| **FOLLOWING DIRECTIONS** | | | | |
|   One-step | A,Mu | R,S,Mu | R,A | |
|   Two-step | | R S A | R,A | |
|   Multiple directions | | R S A | | |
| **DERIVING WORD MEANINGS** | | | | |
| New word | | R,SS,S | S S | |
| New meaning for familiar word | R,SS | R,SS | R | |
| **AUDITORY COMPREHENSION** | | | | |
| Literal: | | | | |
|   Details | R,S | R,S,SS,M | R,SS | |
|   Main ideas | | R,S,SS | R | |
|   Sequence | S | R,S,SS,M | R,S | |
|   Comparisons | | R | R | |
|   Cause & effect | | S | | |
|   Character traits | | R | R | |
| Inferential: | | | | |
|   etc. | | | | |

Symbols:

R   Reading
S   Science
SS  Social Studies
M   Math
A   Art
Mu Music

**FIGURE 3-1. DIAGNOSTIC CHART FOR LISTENING SKILLS**

teacher observation as well as for the creation of activities.

Observations should not be limited to a language arts period. The children should be observed during content-area studies, during filmstrips, television shows, other children's presentations, and so on. If teachers have the chart before them, if they consciously formulate questions to get at the skills, if they then carefully observe individual's responses, then there is less need for structured or formal skill assessments. Teacher observation can become the primary means of skill assessment.

## INSTRUCTION

With primary grade children, once a diagnostic profile has been worked out for each pupil, grouping for instruction in listening skills can be done by looking across the chart in the row for a given skill. Children deficient in any given skill can be grouped together for instruction as part of a directed listening activity or as a special skill lesson. Demonstrations of proficiency in a skill with a given type of material can be noted in the column under the child's name.

But with preschool and kindergarten children, the emphasis is upon initial instruction with diagnosis occurring afterwards to determine who needs further instruction and who is ready for new learning. With these young children especially, time must also be spent on establishing good listening conditions conducive to learning in all aspects of the curriculum.

### Good Listening Conditions

Good listening conditions involve, as we said at the beginning of the chapter, the teacher as the model of the good listener. When a child is speaking, the teacher's eyes should be focused on the speaker, not on the other children or on the papers on the desk. The teacher's response to the speaker should draw in the other children to promote their listening. After a child has, for example, told about a pet turtle during "show and tell," the teacher's job is to lead a discussion about the main idea, sequence of events, details, and so on at various levels of Barrett's taxonomy. The children will soon realize that listening is important, since they will be questioned about the speaker's message.

Another responsibility of the teacher is to structure the classroom physically to promote good listening. Distracting noises should be eliminated if possible. However, in more "open" schools children must learn to focus their attention in spite of sounds from other groups. Chairs and desks could be rearranged during a listening period to promote good listening. A circle or a group clustered on a rug may be more conducive to listening and speaking among the children than a traditional arrangement of desks. Books, papers, pencils, and other paraphernalia should be put away, so that children are not distracted by what may be on their desks.

Children also need to learn good listening habits when working independently in groups. They need to learn "brainstorming" techniques where all ideas are heard and accepted. For example, if a group of kindergarten children is to plan independently the refreshments for a Halloween party, they need to listen to the ideas of each group member and to arrive at an agreement through discussion. One child may need to be identified as leader and recorder, possibly a role for a gifted child. Group problem-solving experiences, such as having the children identify how many ways one can make a *B* or a *4*, requires cooperation and good listening habits. Likewise other types of group work, for example at a learning center, can build respect for what other people are saying. At this early stage the teacher needs to structure small-group interaction carefully, laying the groundwork for more sophisticated group work in the primary grades.

In addition to good physical conditions that promote effective listening, the emotional and social atmosphere of the classroom influences the ability of children to attend to classwork. If a child feels threatened by the teacher or by peers, such anxieties may prevent concentration and attention. Or a child who feels an overwhelming need for attention may seek it by disruptive behavior that interferes with good listening conditions. Or a child who is hungry or comes to school upset about home problems probably will have difficulty concentrating on schoolwork. The teacher needs to deal with behavioral and personal problems of individual children in promoting good classroom conditions for learning. A warm accepting atmosphere is essential in establishing good listening conditions.

Children can help the teacher establish standards or rules for good listening. If children propose the rules (with teacher guidance), they will understand why good listening conditions are important and be more willing to implement them. The rules that the children agree upon can be printed on a chart or posted on a bulletin board in front of the room. Children can also serve as monitors. Whenever good listening conditions are being violated, a monitor can call attention to the violation. It is better to let children assume some responsibility rather than the teacher always being in the enforcement role.

One group of primary age children devised (with teacher guidance) the following set of rules:

1. One person speaks at a time.
2. Look at the speaker, not at other people or things, or out the window.
3. Listen to directions carefully. They will be given only once.

Once children agree on what good listening conditions are, they can, using creative dramatics, then participate in acting out situations portraying good and poor listening conditions. Discussion can focus on which rule is being violated in a particular situation and why the rule is important in the classroom. An activity related to creative dramatics can thus be used to reinforce the need for good listening conditions.

One source (6:317) states that four factors contribute most prominently in inattentive listening: poor motivation to hear the speaker's message, too much teacher talk, excessive noise and other distractions, and lack of a mental set for anticipating the speaker's message. The authors comment that often teacher talk is "routine oral communication." Many children, especially those who are not motivated to do well in school, soon lose interest and develop poor listening habits.

The teacher should speak in an animated fashion, presenting the material in the most interesting manner possible. Long lectures do not belong in preschool or elementary classrooms; teachers should estimate the amount of time devoted to "teacher talk" to avoid excess. The important things in making a presentation are to be brief, concise, and interesting. If children's attention begins to stray, then a change in activity is needed.

Appropriate visual material accompanying spoken material helps focus attention on the speaker, whether the speaker is the teacher or a child. For example, if a child is planning to tell about a vacation trip, pictures or postcards of scenes from travels should accompany the narration. The teacher, too, should be aware of effective visual material. An overhead or opaque projector can project information visually and help in conveying verbal material.

Some teachers have used gimmicks effectively to get children's attention. When children return from playing outdoors and are noisy, is it better to ring a bell or shout to get their attention? Usually a bell is more effective. Teachers use various signals, but the object for the children is the same — not to be the last one still talking when others have quieted down.

Other gimmicks can be used in getting children started on a new activity. Most teachers have a problem with giving directions, however. Typically, directions have to be given several times because some children don't focus their attention the first time. Directions should be given only when "all eyes" are on the teacher. A "one-time" club can be formed or stars placed on a chart, giving recognition to those who listened to and followed directions the first time. Sometimes a puppet can give directions more effectively than the teacher directly (even though it is still the teacher's voice). The gimmick should be changed frequently, however, to keep its effectiveness. Just as children will tire of hearing their teacher demanding silence, so they will also tire of a puppet or any gimmick that is overused.

Also important, as mentioned above, is providing a "mental set" (6:317) for what is going to be heard. For example, the teacher might ask some questions to guide children's listening to a story that will be read. (The directed listening activity, described later in this chapter, contains this component.) Or the teacher might ask the children to anticipate what he or she is going to say, such as what tasks need to be accomplished that day.

Once good listening conditions have been established, the teacher can concentrate on developing specific listening skills.

## Preschool and Kindergarten

**Auditory perception skills.** The most basic auditory perception skill, as presented earlier, is auditory awareness. The teacher calls attention to sounds in the environment — a truck passing by, a ticking clock, scissors cutting paper, chalk squeaking on a chalkboard. Tapes can be made to add a greater variety and complexity to the possible sounds (ice tinkling in a glass, a sewing machine running, and so on). Recordings of music can also be used; even young children can identify the sounds made by various musical instruments.

Most kindergarten children, unless they have a hearing loss or come from overcrowded homes where they have learned to "tune out" extraneous sounds in the environment, have no difficulty identifying familiar sounds. They also enjoy producing a sound for others, who have their eyes closed, to guess the source.

After children can identify sounds that ought to be familiar to them, they can begin to make discriminations among these sounds. For example, after listening to a tape recording of various animal sounds, the children can be asked to compare two particular sounds, such as those of a dog and cat, telling whether they are the same or different. Barks of different kinds of dogs can also be compared, having children judge which bark is higher or lower in pitch.

In addition to focusing on higher or lower tones, children can also be asked to discriminate between slow and fast, such as through listening to a beating drum. They can produce various sounds themselves, such as clapping hands slowly and then quickly, helping to reinforce the notion of the difference. Distinctions between loud and soft can be made through the teacher's voice and making the children aware of their own voices. Again, musical instruments are a natural way to teach the fundamentals of auditory discrimination.

Some additional activities related to music for building auditory perception skills, as prerequisite for working with letter sounds in words, follow:

1. *Direction:* Blindfolded child walks in the direction of the sound of a drum or other musical instrument.

2. *Tempo:* Children run as a drum beats quickly, skip as drum beats slow down, and walk to a slow beat with each step being taken on a beat.
3. *Rhythm:* Blindfolded children try to determine whether another child is running, skipping, hopping, or jumping. A variation would be to have a child beat a drum to correspond with the pace of another child's movements.
4. *Pitch:* Have children identify high and low notes on a piano or with a large and small cymbals.
5. *Volume:* Have children identify loud and soft tones on a tambourine versus a cymbal, or on a piano.

The teacher should be sure that children can make these basic discriminations before asking them to make discriminations in letter sounds and words. A child who is unable to perceive the differences between environmental sounds in terms of high or low, slow or fast, loud or soft, is one who should be referred for audiometric testing. Some children, however, who may be able to hear the sounds adequately may be slow to grasp the concept label — that is, the concept that the term "high" refers to a high-pitched tone. These children, perhaps limited in ability, experiential background, or familiarity with the English language, may need more experiences with auditory awareness and basic auditory discrimination before being asked to distinguish sounds in our language. A hearing problem, however, should be detected as soon as possible so that treatment and correction may be started before more formal classroom instruction takes place in the primary grades. Since auditory discrimination activities would probably produce only frustration for a child with a hearing loss, such activities ought to be suspended for that child until the hearing problem is corrected, if possible. Even after correction, the teacher must be patient, remembering that in all likelihood the child has not been able to hear well for some time and that discrimination should not be expected immediately.

Auditory discrimination activities involving the sounds of our language usually focus on discrimination in sounds in the initial position in a word, in the final position, and in rhyming words. Often names of children are used to teach beginning sounds in words. For example, the children whose names begin with the same sound as Jack's may work at the paint center.

Children can also be asked whether pairs of words begin with the same letter sound or not, as *hop* and *hit.* Initially, words beginning with consonant blends or digraphs should be avoided, so that the single consonant sounds may first be discriminated and learned. After children are able to identify whether pairs of words begin with the same letter sound, they can be asked to supply words that begin with a particular sound. A game that a small group of children enjoy is: "My father works in a grocery (or pet, department, etc.) store and he sells something that begins with /m/ (such as milk)." Care should be taken to refer to the letter sound, not the letter name, since the purpose is to teach children the likenesses and differences in sounds.

Another commonly used activity is for children to make sound books. For example, *Bb* would be printed at the top of a piece of paper along with a picture of a boy. The child is then given an old catalog, scissors, and glue, being told to cut out and paste on the paper all pictures whose names begin with the same sound as in "boy." Other pages can be made for other sounds, some of which could be illustrated by the child for variety, and then bound together in a "book." Tongue twisters, such as "Peter Piper picked a peck of pickled peppers," can also reinforce the concept of like beginning sounds.

After children can identify likenesses and differences in beginning sounds, rhyming words can be presented, at first most naturally through nursery rhymes. Children enjoy supplying rhyming words in familiar nursery rhymes, poems, limericks, and songs. A more difficult task is to have the children supply rhyming words in verses written by the teacher. Of course any rhyming word is to be accepted as correct. The children can, with some help, make up rhymes for each other to complete. Pictures of rhyming and nonrhyming words can be paired together at a learning center (for example, of a dog and log); the child decides whether the words rhyme or not. A simple version of the activity would be to place each picture on a puzzle piece; the child knows that the answer is correct if the pieces fit together. A more sophisticated version would involve an electric light board on which a light shines if the child presses the two correct choices at the same time, thereby creating an electrical connection. Children also enjoy making up lists of rhyming words, such as *cat, fat, hat*. The words from such a list could be also combined into a simple verse: "The cat is fat. He sat on a *(hat)*."

The distinction between rhyming and ending sounds is sometimes difficult for children. After children can identify and supply rhyming words, they can be asked to focus on only the final sound. At first distinctions should not be difficult, such as asking the children whether "big" and "fine" end with the same letter sound. Pairs of words that obviously end the same, but don't rhyme, can also be presented, such as *mop* and *tap*. The next step after correct identification is to have the children supply words that end with the same sound, as, say, in a child's name, for example, *Ann*. The activities presented above also could be easily adapted for teaching ending sounds.

Training in auditory memory — reproducing an auditory pattern from memory — helps children in later reading experiences, especially in phonics-oriented programs. As they sound through a new word, the sounds must be retrieved from the auditory memory in sequential order. Auditory memory may be developed by having children reproduce patterns of sounds, on a drum for example. At a more complex level children may be asked to memorize songs, nursery rhymes, and poems in which rhythm is an aid to the memory. They may also be asked to repeat simple sentences, perhaps directions, and retell familiar stories.

**Following directions.** Teachers often find that children of all ages — and even adults — have difficulty following directions. Certainly one of the reasons that we all do not attend carefully to directions is that we have learned to expect them to be repeated if we do not understand. Teachers who unwittingly give in to this expectation create problems for themselves and for the children in the future. Another reason that children sometimes have difficulty following directions is that the set of directions is too complex for the children to process. Teachers can therefore help their students learn how to follow directions by making the directions appropriate to the children.

Before directions are given, the teacher must be sure to have everyone's attention. The directions should be given simply and clearly, without elaborative explanations, one time only. With young children the teacher should begin with simple one-step directions. After the direction, the children perform the action. (For example, "Everyone take out a piece of white paper.") As the children are successful in performing a step at a time, the teacher can increase the directions to two steps. ("Everyone take out a piece of white paper and draw a tree with a green crayon.") Finally three- and four-step directions can be given as children learn to listen. They can be asked to repeat the directions to themselves as they perform the actions. The game of "Simon says" is another favorite way to teach children to follow directions and listen carefully. Auditory memory is being enhanced as well as the ability to follow directions.

**Deriving word meanings from context.** With children of all ages the most important factor in developing oral and listening vocabularies is the teacher's awareness of this task. The teacher should consciously use words that the children might not know and then have them arrive at the meaning of the word through the context. This activity should be ongoing throughout any type of activity in order for children's vocabularies to expand. This approach will yield greater benefits than specific activities offered once.

**Auditory comprehension.** Teachers ask most of their questions at the literal level, which is natural, since literal understanding is necessary to comprehension at the higher levels. With young children literal comprehension can be built primarily through questioning after listening to a story. After the teacher is sure that the children have grasped the main ideas and supporting details of the story, children can be asked to make inferences about the story. The categories in Barrett's taxonomy can be used to guide the formulation of questions. Even young children should also be asked to evaluate what they have heard. If questioning does not involve the higher levels of comprehension, children will have difficulty later on with critical reading and evaluative thinking. At the appreciation level the children are asked to place themselves in the story. How would they have felt if they were a character in the story? Would they have taken the same actions? Although all children should experience all levels of questions, gifted children should concentrate on the inferential, evaluation, and appreciation levels. Lower-ability children may need extra work on literal comprehension skills in order to grasp the content of a selection.

Teachers should not rely on their own spontaneity in asking questions. Guide questions, usually at the literal level, should be posed before reading a story to the children so that they know what to listen for. Afterwards the guide questions should be discussed as well as additional inference, evaluation, and appreciation questions. The questions should be thought out, preferably written out, before class so that all levels of questioning are employed.

## Primary Grades

Establishing a listening center is a good way to individualize instruction for skill needs. The center might contain commercial as well as teacher-made tapes. Individual headphones and cassette recorders allow the children to work individually or in groups at the listening center, depending on the activity. The material for each skill should be at several levels to permit children to work at their approximate listening levels. The important thing is that each activity is keyed to a specific skill, so that children can engage in those activities that they need.

Children should be shown how to use the listening center independently. The tapes can be labeled by skill so that the children can pick out what they need. The children will also have to be trained to use the tape recorder properly to prevent damage to the recorder or to the tapes. They will also have to be taught to work independently, if learning centers are not a regular part of the classroom. Gradually, individuals or small groups of children can work at the listening center until all children have had the opportunity to do so.

**Auditory perception skills.** The same activities suggested for young children may be used for those who have not yet mastered these skills in the primary grades. Although auditory awareness is usually assumed to have been mastered by this age, auditory discrimination activities are part of most beginning reading programs, certainly those that teach phonics as one of the word recognition skills. The more phonics is emphasized in learning to read, the more children will need to rely on auditory discrimination skills. Since today most reading programs do teach phonics more or less systematically, children need to have a strong instructional program in auditory discrimination skills as readiness for phonics and as an adjunct to phonics instruction. Indeed, one aspect of phonics instruction is to determine whether children can hear the difference between the sound being taught and other sounds.

In the primary grades, after children have mastered initial and final sounds and rhyming, they can be taught to listen for medial sounds, such as the /t/ in *butter*. Children can be asked to identify the sound they hear in a medial position as well as determine whether the medial sounds are the same or different in two words (*butter, hotel*).

As consonant blends, digraphs, long and short vowel sounds, diphthongs, and so on are introduced to children as part of their reading program, the sounds should first be introduced auditorally so that children can first hear the difference between ă and ā, for example. After children can distinguish them auditorally, they can then be taught the generalizations that determine which sound is to be used. So often teachers neglect to emphasize the auditory discrimination of a letter sound — how it is different from others. As a result, children may be able to express the generalization in parrot-like fashion but be unable to apply it.

Auditory memory activities in the primary grades can take the form of having children say number sequences forwards and backwards. (For example, if the teacher says, "5, 9, 4," the child would say "4, 9, 5.") The teacher can also ask a child to repeat a series of unrelated words or letters either forwards or backwards. Children can work in pairs with auditory memory activities prepared by the teacher. One child reads the numbers, words, or letters to another child who repeats them; the reader checks to see if the listener repeats them correctly.

While the value of auditory memory exercises is not as clearly related to the development of reading or other basic skills as, say, auditory discrimination, nevertheless these activities probably do increase children's attention span. They teach children to attend carefully and actively. One cannot daydream and be able to repeat a number sequence! Training in auditory sequencing probably also helps children as they decode words in reading, either letter by letter or syllable by syllable. They must rely on their auditory memories as they blend the sounds or syllables together to form a word. Activities developing auditory memory should also help children in learning to follow directions.

**Following directions.** Many creative and enjoyable activities can be used to teach children to follow directions. Assuming that children have mastered simple three- and four-step directions given orally by the teacher, they may enjoy working at a listening center with highly motivational material. For example, directions for making a puppet could be tape recorded and the necessary materials made available in the center. A child would then be dependent on listening abilities to assemble the puppet according to the directions given on tape.

Other types of activities that reinforce following directions may be used in a listening center. For example, directions for origami, or paper folding, may be put on tape. Directions for locating points on a grid may be placed on tape (for example, "locate the intersection of row C and column 2; place a '1' at that point"). After the tape has finished, the child connects the dots in sequence to discover the word that has been spelled or the picture that has been drawn. These types of listening center activities are self-checking in that either the product emerges correctly or it does not. The teacher is freed to work with groups of children or individuals on other instructional activities while the children at the listening center receive practice in following directions independently.

Children also enjoy an auditory treasure hunt. Instead of finding written directions, they find a tape recorder, which directs them to the next clue in the hunt for the "treasure." Most ideas presented in resource books for teaching children to follow written directions may be adapted to the auditory modality.

**Deriving word meanings from context.** In the primary grades teachers should systematically work to expand children's oral and listening vocabularies. It is especially important that words that appear in the children's reading program are familiar to children — in other words, in their listening vocabulary. For example, if a particular story in a reading book pertains to life in the city and if the children who are to read the story are rural children who have not traveled extensively, the teacher must be sure that the children first have heard and understand words that are used in the story (for example, *skyscraper, apartment,* and *escalator).* Otherwise, children will have no meaningful association for these words and may mispronounce them. These words can be presented orally in sentences, the teacher asking children to speculate on their meanings given the context.

The teacher can also offer direct instruction in words through listening by presenting them in sentences with accompanying visual material (pictures, filmstrips, movies, bulletin boards) to reinforce word meanings and concepts. Context is important, however, in helping children understand how to use the words themselves.

Further vocabulary development can occur using substitutions for particular words in one of the basic sentence patterns. Sentences following a basic pattern can be devised with a nonsense word inserted in place of a word of a particular form class. For example, the following exercise could be used orally:

Pattern:                      Sentence:
N   be   Adj.                 The boy is *floggish.*

The teacher elicits all the possible words that could be used in place of *floggish* (tall, short, fat, thin, slow, fast, nice, silly, and so on.). The important point is that words from the correct form class are used. One would not say, for example, "The boy is run." Substitutions can also be made for *boy* and *is*. Context guides the selection of the appropriate form class and helps expand children's vocabularies.

**Auditory comprehension.** The same questioning procedures before and after listening to a story that were discussed concerning young children may be employed with children in the primary grades. A few additional activities for each level of comprehension of Barrett's taxonomy are also suggested based on reading a narrative story to primary children:

**1.0** Literal Comprehension
- **A.** Use who, what, when, where, why questions to guide children before listening to a story; have them answer these questions afterwards.
- **B.** Have children identify key words, main ideas, and supporting details that they heard.
- **C.** Have the children identify the sequence of events by drawing pictures or by verbal recall.
- **D.** Have the children retell the story using flannel-board figures, puppets, and the like, representing characters in the story.
- **E.** Have the children dictate the main events of the story to the teacher who records them on a chart; the chart story can become the basis for a reading lesson using the language experience approach.
- **F.** At a learning center a child arranges a set of pictures to correspond with the sequence of events in the story.
- **G.** Give children a cloze exercise in which key words are deleted from a plot summary; for example, "After Little Red Riding Hood took a *(drink)* from the brook, she saw a *(wolf)* staring at her." The children write in the missing words.
- **H.** Have the children think of a title for the story if one has not been read to them.

**2.0** Inferential Comprehension
- **A.** Stop reading the story to the children to allow time for them to predict the ending.
- **B.** Ask children to speculate what would have happened if some detail in the story were changed.
- **C.** Have the children draw a picture of a character in the story who is not fully described. (Literal comprehension can also be checked by a child's inclusion of those characteristics that are stated.)

    **D.** Have the children draw conclusions about characters'
motives — why they acted as they did.

    **E.** At a learning center a child draws a picture portraying
the literal meaning of a figure of speech (such as
"knee-high to a grasshopper"); then the intended
meaning is written underneath ("very small").

**3.0** Evaluation

    **A.** Have the children speculate whether the story really
could have happened at any time? in the past? in the
present? in the future?

    **B.** Have the children write a paragraph explaining whether
a character was right or wrong in his or her behavior.

    **C.** Have the children try to detect the author's purpose in
writing the story. Was he/she trying to change our
thinking on some topic?

    **D.** At a learning center the child draws a slip of paper
randomly from each of two boxes; on one slip an action
is stated and on the other is a character's name. The
child writes a paragraph explaining why or why not the
action would be appropriate to that character.

**4.0** Appreciation

    **A.** Have the children tell or write what they would do if
they were a character in the story.

    **B.** At a learning center a child identifies the part of the story
that he/she thinks is the funniest, saddest, scariest or
whatever and draws a picture depicting the scene.

    **C.** Have the children discuss why the author chose certain
words in the story and what effect they have on the
listener.

    **D.** Ask the children to discuss how they would change the
story if they had been the author.

Although some of these activities may be used occasionally, depending
on the story and the abilities of the children, the main vehicle for teaching
auditory comprehension is usually the directed listening lesson.

**Directed listening activity.** The directed listening activity has the same
purposes as its counterpart in reading — the directed reading activity —
namely, to develop word recognition skills as applied in context and to
enhance comprehension and appreciation of the material. Although
children do not need to recognize words in print in a directed listening
activity, as they do in reading, they do need to recognize the meanings of
words as used in context. Comprehension and appreciation, of course, are
fundamentally the same whether the child hears or reads the material.

The directed reading activity is the teacher's major vehicle for presenting reading material using the basal reader approach. Likewise, the directed listening activity is also the teacher's major vehicle for presenting a listening lesson. Not every listening activity needs to be formal, directed listening activity; the steps in the directed listening activity can be modified — shortened, expanded, deleted — as needed. In other words, the directed listening activity is not intended to be a formal, rigid structure, but instead a model which may be adapted to the situation. The following outline summarizes the steps in a directed listening activity:

Directed Listening Activity

**I. Preparation**
 **A.** Building background
  **1.** Creating interest through relating selection to past experiences
  **2.** Developing concepts
  **3.** Introducing new words in context
 **B.** Establishing purposes for listening
**II.** Directed listening
 **A.** Listening to selection
 **B.** Questions and discussion
  **1.** Literal meaning
  **2.** Inferential meaning
  **3.** Evaluation
  **4.** Appreciative reaction
**III.** Skill instruction
**IV.** Enrichment
 **A.** Extending listening skills
 **B.** Engaging in reading, writing, and creative activities

In introducing a listening activity, the teacher first tries to capture the children's interest through a question, picture, poem, or whatever that both ties the selection in with past work and piques children's interest in the selection. For example, in connection with an ecology unit in science, if the teacher plans to read a newspaper editorial to the children on the increasing pollution of a nearby lake by a local industry, the first step might involve asking the children how many of them have gone swimming at one of the beaches on the lake. Or perhaps the children might be shown a picture of the lake, or of children swimming in it, to arouse their interest.

The next step involves the development of related concepts. If the newspaper editorial discusses, for example, the physical processes that occur during the pollution of a body of water, these processes should be explained — or better yet, illustrated by bringing some lake water to class to be inspected under a microscope. New words or familiar words used in new ways should be presented in sentences on the chalkboard to clarify word meanings. The skill of contextual analysis can be reinforced in this step as students attempt to arrive at word meanings through attention to the context.

In establishing purposes for listening, the teacher guides students to attend to the important aspects of the selection and prepares them for the skill instruction that follows the directed listening. For example, if the skill instruction is to focus on distinguishing fact and opinion at the evaluation level, the teacher might suggest that the children listen to determine whether the author is presenting facts or opinions about the lake pollution. Can the author's opinions on the subject be determined by listening to the selection? The children thus are guided in what to listen for — a very important preparatory step in promoting comprehension. Another alternative is to have the children try to establish their own purposes for listening. What do they think they might learn from the selection?

Some of the categories from Barrett's taxonomy can be used to guide the teacher in formulating questions at all levels of thinking during and after the directed listening. Questions about the literal meaning should be discussed first to clarify children's understanding of the selection. The questions might pertain to the physical process of pollution, facts about the pollution by the industry, and so on. Discussion of inferential meaning could focus on inferring the main ideas in the selection as well as on predicting the outcomes of continued pollution of the lake. Questions related to evaluation can pertain to listing facts stated and opinions stated. Parts of the selection may have to be reread to notice subtle distinctions in word choice ("The amount of pollution is increasing every day" versus "The amount of pollution appears to be increasing every day"). The students can also list the main ideas in the selection and attempt to find factual support for each of the statements made.

At the appreciation level the teacher can inquire about the children's reactions to the editorial. Were their opinions and emotions swayed by the article? What words were used to get the reader emotionally involved?

By the teacher's questions the major ideas are developed and discussed. Obviously, not all the categories of Barrett's taxonomy are used in questioning. A question from each category would become too tedious even for the most zealous teacher. But questions *at each level* should be used to develop children's thinking at all levels. The particular categories within each level should vary with the selection. For example, a question at the appreciation level about "Identification with Characters and Incidents" would be more appropriate for narrative writing rather than for expository writing, such as a newspaper editorial.

With young children the teacher may not wish to read the story in its entirety before questioning. Questions at the literal and inferential levels asked after listening to part of the story can assure the teacher that the children are comprehending and can help keep their attention throughout the story. Whether reading or telling a story, the teacher must be sure that a young audience is listening.

Skill instruction can focus on any listening skill that the children in the group need. Since diagnosis and instruction in listening skills are treated in earlier sections, now it is sufficient to say that a skill is selected in which *all* children in the group could benefit from instruction. If in this case the skill is distinguishing fact and opinion, the teacher's questions at the evaluation level already provided some instruction on the skill, using the material of the directed listening activity. The teacher can also type statements from the article on slips of paper. The children can then sort the statements into two piles — factual statements and opinions. During skill instruction the teacher also presents the skill in a different context. Perhaps advertisements from the radio and television might be recorded. The children can listen to determine whether facts are presented to substantiate the claims made for the product or whether the narrator merely states opinions about the product. The children might also listen to a radio or television commentary at home to determine whether facts or opinions are being presented.

The purpose of enrichment is to extend related skills and to increase enjoyment. Most children consider enrichment activities to be the frosting on the cake! An appropriate activity (as a follow-up to the skill instruction) would be for children to write their own editorials about any issue that concerns them. Whether the editorials are a group or individual effort, they are shared with other class members who listen to determine whether facts or opinions are being presented.

Another appropriate enrichment activity involves a follow-up to the content presented. Students might wish to do research on water pollution, survey community members for their opinions on the pollution of the local lake, write a letter to the local industry, write a letter to the editor of the newspaper in support of or in opposition to the editorial, make a model lake that simulates the process of water pollution, take a field trip to the lake to observe the effects of water pollution, and so on. Obviously, this language arts lesson could easily be one aspect of a larger science or social studies unit. All language arts skills (listening, reading, speaking, writing) could be incorporated and applied in the content area studies. The language arts skill instruction takes on more significance in the context of meaningful study, and the study of the content area is enhanced by the skill instruction that is provided.

Poor readers, particularly, can study the content areas through listening lessons. If a textbook is used, portions could be taped by the teacher, better students, or volunteer aides. Simpler, shorter reading materials could supplement the listening lessons. All students can thus apply their language arts skills at an appropriate level while learning in the content areas.

Now that you have read this chapter about listening skills and have considered the diagnosis of strengths and weaknesses in auditory skills as well as the assessment of general listening levels with instructional ideas offered for preschool/kindergarten and primary age children, it is time to assess your understanding of this information. Complete the following self-checking quiz, and reread any parts as necessary if items are missed. Good luck!

(1) Indicate whether each of the following is a good technique for establishing good listening conditions. (T or F)

_____ 1. Holding up your hand when you want the children's attention.

_____ 2. Severely scolding a child for classroom disruptions in front of other children.

_____ 3. Checking worksheets during "show and tell."

_____ 4. Having the children help in deciding on the rules for good listening.

_____ 5. Using a flannel board to tell a story.

(2) Match each learning activity to the listening skill that it most appropriately develops after the teacher has read *Over the River and Through the Woods* to the children.

_____ 6. Auditory discrimination

_____ 7. Auditory memory

_____ 8. Two-step directions

_____ 9. Multiple directions

_____ 10. Deriving word meanings from context

a. The teacher asks a child to bark like a dog and meow like a cat.

b. The teacher asks the children who "old jowler" is.

c. The teacher asks the children to supply the last word in the verse, "The horse knows the way to carry the _____."

d. The teacher jingles a set of sleigh bells three times; a child jingles another set three times.

e. The teacher asks a child to jingle a set of sleigh bells three times, pass the bells on to another child, and sit down.

(3) The children have just been told the story of "Little Red Riding Hood." For each question identify whether it required primarily

(a) literal thinking, (b) inferential thinking, (c) evaluation, or (d) appreciative reaction.

_____ 11. Why did Little Red Riding Hood walk through the woods?

_____ 12. Was it appropriate that the "bad guy" in the story was a wolf? Why or why not?

_____ 13. What would have happened if the woodsman had not rushed into Grandmother's house at the moment he did?

_____ 14. When the wolf was lying in Grandmother's bed, what did he say to Little Red Riding Hood that built up the suspense?

_____ 15. Why did Little Red Riding Hood stop to talk to the rabbit family?

(4) An activity is presented in each of the following items. Identify the step in the directed listening activity for which the activity would be most appropriate.

_____ 16. Advanced children work a crossword puzzle that contains vocabulary words found in the selection.
  a. Creating interest through relating selection to past experience
  b. Developing concepts
  c. Introducing new words in context
  d. Skill instruction
  e. Engaging in reading, writing, and creative activities

_____ 17. Very young children dramatize the following terms in the classroom: in-out, over-under, top-bottom.
  a. Developing concepts
  b. Introducing new words in context
  c. Establishing purposes for listening
  d. Questions and discussion
  e. Extending listening skills

_____ 18. The teacher asks the children if they saw a recent television show about wild animals before listening to a story about a lion.
  a. Creating interest through relating selection to past experiences
  b. Developing concepts
  c. Introducing new words in context
  d. Establishing purposes for listening
  e. Skill instruction

_____ 19. The teacher tells the children to listen for the main ideas presented by a guest speaker.

a. Creating interest through relating selection to past experiences

b. Developing concepts

c. Establishing purposes for listening

d. Listening to selection

e. Questions and discussion

_____ 20. After listening to a story about the sounds of animals, children tape record the sounds of animals around the school.

a. Creating interest through relating selection to past experiences

b. Developing concepts

c. Skill instruction

d. Extending listening skills

e. Engaging in reading, writing, and creative activities

(5) An activity is presented in each of the following items. Identify the type of assessment: (a) formal listening test, (b) informal test of listening level, (c) informal skills test.

_____ 21. The teacher plays taped selections for the whole class, following prescribed instructions and keeping within specified time limits.

_____ 22. The teacher observes how well individual children follow directions in cleaning up after an art activity.

_____ 23. The teacher reads a portion of a story to a small group of children and questions them about it.

_____ 24. The teacher asks young children to pantomime a selection that has just been read to them.

_____ 25. The teacher notes whether young children can supply words that have been omitted from rhymes.

_____ 26. The teacher receives a grade-level score on a test with known reliability and validity.

_____ 27. The teacher reads selections to children from a commercial informal reading inventory.

Answer Key

| | | |
|---|---|---|
| 1. T | 10. b | 19. c |
| 2. F | 11. a | 20. e |
| 3. F | 12. c | 21. a |
| 4. T | 13. b | 22. c |
| 5. T | 14. d | 23. b |
| 6. c | 15. b | 24. b |
| 7. d | 16. c | 25. c |
| 8. a | 17. a | 26. a |
| 9. e | 18. a | 27. b |

## RESOURCES FOR TEACHERS

Burns, Paul C. *Diagnostic Teaching of the Language Arts.* Itasca, Ill.: F. E. Peacock Publishers, 1974.

Croft, Doreen J. and Hess, Robert D. *An Activities Handbook for Teachers of Young Children,* 2d Ed. Boston: Houghton Mifflin Company, 1975.

Duker, Sam (Ed.) *Listening: Readings.* New York: Scarecrow Press, 1966.

Greff, Kasper N. and Askov, Eunice N. *Learning Centers: An Ideabook for Reading and Language Arts.* Dubuque, Iowa: Kendall/Hunt Publishing Company, 1974.

Griese, Arnold A. *Do You Read Me? Practical Approaches to Teaching Reading Comprehension.* Santa Monica, Calif.: Goodyear Publishing Company, 1977. (Note: Could be adapted for teaching listening comprehension.)

Hennings, Dorothy Grant. *Communication in Action.* Chicago: Rand McNally College Publishing Company, 1978.

Hohl, Susan and Edwards, B. Cheney. *Listening Comprehension Grades 1-3; Games and Activities.* Cambridge, Mass.: Educators Publishing Service, 1976.

Hohl, Susan and Edwards, B. Cheney. *Listening Comprehension Grades 1-3; Informal Inventories.* Cambridge, Mass.: Educators Publishing Service, 1976.

Lundsteen, Sara W. *Listening: Its Impact on Reading and the Other Language Arts.* Urbana, Ill.: National Council of Teachers of English, 1971.

Machado, Jeanne M. *Early Childhood Experiences in Language Arts.* Albany, N.Y.: Delmar Publishers, 1975.

Marbach, Ellen S. *Creative Curriculum Kindergarten Through Grade Three.* Provo, Utah: Brigham Young University Press, 1977.

Petty, Walter T., Petty, Dorothy C., and Becking, Marjorie F. *Experiences in Language,* 2d Ed. Boston: Allyn and Bacon, 1976.

Russell, David H. and Russell, Elizabeth. *Listening Aids Through The Grades.* New York: Teachers College Press, 1959.

Taylor, Stanford E. *Listening (What Research Says to the Teacher).* Washington, D.C.: National Education Association, 1964.

# REFERENCES

1. Barrett, Thomas C. "Taxonomy of Reading Comprehension." *Reading 360 Monograph.* Lexington, Mass.: Ginn and Company, 1972.

2. Bloom, Benjamin S. (ed.) *Taxonomy of Educational Objectives; The Classification Of Educational Goals. Handbook I: Cognitive Domain.* New York and London: Longman, 1956.

3. Durkin, Dolores. *Teaching Young Children to Read,* 2d Ed. Boston: Allyn and Bacon, 1976.

4. Ekwall, Eldon E. *Ekwall Reading Inventory.* Boston: Allyn and Bacon, 1979.

5. Lundsteen, Sara. "Critical Listening: An Experiment." *The Elementary School Journal* 66 (1966): 315.

6. Otto, Wayne; McMenemy, Richard A.; and Smith, Richard J. *Corrective and Remedial Teaching,* 2d Ed. Boston: Houghton Mifflin Company, 1973.

7. Spache, George D. *Diagnosing and Correcting Reading Disabilities.* Boston: Allyn and Bacon, 1976.

8. Wilt, Miriam. "A Study of Teacher Awareness of Listening as a Factor in Elementary Education." *Journal of Educational Research* 43 (1950): 626-636.

# CHAPTER 4

# ORAL LANGUAGE DEVELOPMENT AND COMPOSING

*Children – most children – learn how to talk without any difficulty at all. . . . And the more we examine the process, the more astonishing it becomes. (4)*

## WHAT IS LANGUAGE?

Language is the basis for a great many human activities. Reading and writing require language; speaking and listening require language. Since the language arts are based on language, it seems important to define the basic ingredients.

Language is a system of sounds used by a group of people to communicate and carry on their normal activities. Francis, a linguist, defines language as "an arbitrary system of articulated sounds made use of by a group of humans as a means of carrying on the affairs of their society." (6) The definition contains a number of important principles.

The first important principle is that language is *oral*. Humans use language primarily in speech. Listening and speaking are the earliest language processes a child learns. Every human society has oral language. A small minority of languages can be written down, and hence read. For example, the English language is written using twenty-six letters to represent all the sounds we use (at least forty different sounds). Many Native American (Indian) languages are not written at all.

A second important principle is that language is *arbitrary*. The symbols used are determined by the society using them, and these arbitrary symbols can be changed by the decision of those who speak them. These symbols are important, too, because the words that make up a language only represent the things they stand for. That is, the word "chair" is not the real, physical object. It stands for the object. So all words and other symbols in a language are representations of the real world. These symbols change from language to language. Within a language they change from dialect to dialect and also over time.

A third principle is that language has *system*. The rest of the chapter describes the system of sound and word patterns that is English. Every language has such an organized process for communicating. Such features as sound patterns, word endings, and word order are part of the system in English. The term "system" suggests that the patterns that occur are not

108

random or chance. These patterns recur and mean something to the users of the language.

Principle four is that language is a series of *habits* that children learn and internalize at an early age. Such habits include using the system of one's native language, learning the accepted word order, word endings, and sound patterns. Many of these habits are learned from a child's immediate environment — parents and other family members. Like other habits, language is not very easy to change, especially as the child grows older.

The final principle in the definition of language is that its purpose is *communication.* Language is useful only if it allows one person to communicate with another. This may mean speaking to someone who listens, or writing for someone to read. The listener and reader are communicating as much as the speaker and writer. But it does not seem useful for one to speak if no one is listening, or to write if no one will read. Some artists might argue that they write only for themselves, but most artists are writing to communicate with other people.

The five principles of language have only touched the surface of the topic. Language has fantastic variety and form. Its uses are many and vary with every speaker. Consider the difference between Lincoln's Gettysburg Address, a phone conversation between two teenage girls, and the confrontation between a teacher and an errant student.

A set of terminology is used to describe language. Much of this terminology will be new, so take careful note of definitions. The first major topic defined was language itself. The second major topic is *linguistics.* Linguistics is the scientific study of the processes of language. The terminology used throughout this book derives, in large part, from the recent work in language study by linguists. Because linguistics is a scientific study, language is studied in a careful, systematic way.

## The Importance of Oral Language Growth

How important is it that children's language develop from two-word sentences to the complex language that adults use? An immediate answer is that adults expect this growth and attach meaning to levels of language complexity. For example, adults who speak in short unconnected statements are sometimes judged to be of lower social class or otherwise limited in education or mental capacity. (7)

A more fundamental concern about language development stems from its relationship to thinking. There are differences within current research regarding the relationship, but all researchers consider thinking and language to be intertwined. One side of this research argument holds that:

> Human beings do not live in the objective world alone, nor alone in the world of social activity as ordinarily understood, but are very much at the

mercy of the particular language which has become the medium of expression of their society. It is quite an illusion to imagine that one adjusts to reality essentially without the use of language and that language is merely an incidental means of solving specific problems of communication or reflection. . . . We see and hear and otherwise experience very largely as we do because the language habits of our community predispose certain choices of interpretation. (13)

This view, discussed most clearly by Whorf, suggests that a person's language controls what and how he or she can think.

A different view suggests that language

provides a means, not only for representing experience, but also for transforming it. . . . Once the child has succeeded in internalizing language as a cognitive instrument, it becomes possible for him to represent and systematically transform the regularities of experience with far greater flexibility and power than before. (2)

Bruner does not agree with Whorf that language controls thinking. Rather Bruner sees language as a means for people to describe, analyze, and abstract from their immediate experience, to look for patterns and deeper meaning. This view sees language development as important in "humanizing" the child. To be truly human, one must be able to see his life in perspective, learn from past experience, make judgments about the future.

Piaget takes another and different view of the relationship between language and thought. Piaget believes that

a symbolic function exists which is broader than language and encompasses both the system of verbal signs and that of symbols in the strict sense. . . . it is permissible to conclude that thought precedes language. . . . language is not enough to explain thought, because the structures that characterize thought have their roots in action and in sensori-motor mechanisms that are deeper than linguistics. (12)

Though Piaget believes that thought precedes language, he suggests that language is an important component in the child's cognitive development. For example, as the child develops cognitively, he moves through the stage of egocentric speech, in which the child speaks to himself without intent to communicate to others, to the stage of socialized speech, in which the child's speech is intended to communicate to others. The child's development from an egocentric person to one who is concerned with other people is reflected partially in his language development.

One final view of language and cognitive development comes from the Russian psychologist, Vygotsky. Vygotsky suggests that language and thought have different roots in the child's development. "In the speech development of the child, we can with certainty establish a preintellectual stage in this thought development, a prelinguistic stage." (14) The two elements follow separate developmental lines for a period of time. Then "at a certain point these lines meet, whereupon thought becomes verbal and speech rational." (14) Vygotsky's view of language development, although different from that of Whorf, Bruner, or Piaget, nevertheless supports the importance of language development. Language must be sufficiently developed to express the rational thought of which the child (and adult) is capable.

The four views of the importance of language development given here are not mutually exclusive. None of the four has been completely accepted or rejected by linguistic researchers. Indeed, this is an area of great research activity at the present time. However, all four views are equally insistent on the importance of continuing language development in the child.

## Principles of Language Development

The process of language development, especially in young children, focuses on their use of oral language, speaking, and listening. As children mature, reading and writing become important developmental skills, but from ages three to eight oral language remains the primary focus. Readiness for writing and some early writing activities are discussed briefly near the end of the chapter. However, the concept that organizes both speaking and writing is composing. Composing is the process the child (or adult, for that matter) goes through in deciding what to say and how to say it. In this context, the difference between speaking and writing becomes one of the method of expression. The child's linguistic and thinking processes are the same, but he chooses to give expression to his composition either by using his speech mechanisms or by using his writing processes, once he develops them.

Research in language development has focused on language acquisition, the development of language in infants and small children who have no oral language at birth. The most complete review of this research to date is Dale's *Language Development,* an analysis of research and its application to an understanding of children's language. As Dale says, "The best way to begin studying child language is to find a young child and listen." The suggestion is sound for anyone interested in helping children's language develop. In practice work with a small child, preferably aged two or three, talk with him for several minutes and tape record the entire conversation. Do this three or four times, to be sure to collect a reasonable sample of the child's repertoire of language forms, then type out a transcript of the conversation and analyze the results. Look for regularities in the child's use of certain words, word forms, and grammatical structures as described here.

One principle is that children are looking for regularities in language. They rely on several sources for their information: their built-in language processing center, which is part of the brain; people around them who talk to them; and other language sources, like television and books. As a child looks for system in language, he occasionally makes mistakes. For example, it is common for two-year-olds to have concluded that past tense is marked by -ed on the verb. Two-year-olds can't verbalize the rule, but they intuitively demonstrate that they know it by adding -ed appropriately to verbs. They also add -ed inappropriately —comed, goed. When we hear comed, we can tell that the speaker has appropriately internalized the past tense marker, since -ed works a very large percentage of the time in English, but he hasn't mastered the exceptions, those irregular verbs used so much in everyday speaking. Given more time, the child will learn all the sophisticated system that marks past tense in English.

If the child has made some mistakes in common syntactic structures, it may be appropriate to talk with him again to ask whether he knows which is right or wrong in English. Is it right to say "comed" or "came," "goed" or "went"? The procedure provides a check on the data already analyzed and may help to see just where in his development the child is. You may also have an experience like the one two famous researchers had in asking their two-year-old informant:

> Interviewer: "Adam, which is right, 'two shoes' or 'two shoe' "?
> Adam: "Pop goes the weasel."

The study of child language takes great time and patience.

In research on language acquisition, the accepted form of measurement is the *mean length of utterance* (MLU), the average length of a child's utterance in morphemes. (4) An *utterance* is the words in an oral "sentence," which ends with the sound pattern we would write down as a period, question mark, or other end punctuation. A *morpheme* is a meaningful element in language. The word "girl" is a morpheme. However, some words have more than one morpheme: "girls" has two — "girl," plus the plural marker "-s." If the concept of morpheme is new, check out additional information on linguistic principles in the reading list at the end of the chapter. The process of further assessing children's language by MLU is discussed in the section on Assessment of Children's Language Development.

## Vocabulary Development in Young Children

Vocabulary development has several components. One component is the development of *meaning*, also known as *semantics*. Children gradually attach meanings to words, so that we say they "know" the word. It is important to remember here the linguistic principle that a word is not the same thing as its referent in the real world (*chair* was the example given). Instead, the word stands as a *symbol* for the real object. Young children begin to speak by naming things that are close to them — Mommy, Daddy, dog, spoon. In order to speak the English we all know, children must add to this kind of list words which don't stand for a physical object that can be pointed to:

**1.** words for actions — walk, play, run
**2.** words for being — be, have, should, can
**3.** words for describing — big, small, red, round, flat
**4.** words for relationships — before, in, under, beside
**5.** words for connection — because, and, but
**6.** words for marking — a, an, the, this

Most of these words are not concrete, but many can be demonstrated for children. Those words which are harder to demonstrate physically are the most difficult to teach a child. However, adults model language for children and show them appropriate uses of these common words.

A second component of vocabulary development is differentiation of features, the semantic features of the object. Two possibilities exist in feature differentiation: one, to begin with word meanings that are too specific, as might happen when a child says "dog" and refers only to one that is small and brown. The child must broaden this understanding of dogs to include other features (large, black, and so on). The second possibility is to define the word initially on too few features. This might explain the child who calls every man "Daddy," to his mother's embarrassment. The child is identifying meaning on features that are too general, such as short hair, deep voice, and tall. He must learn to attach specific features to the single person he calls "Daddy."

Identification of semantic features as a process of vocabulary development probably works both ways, to some extent, in each child. Therefore, teachers should be prepared to help children both to identify features precisely and to develop broader concepts.

A third component of vocabulary development is the comprehension of strings of words, or sentences. The synthesis, or integration, of several separate words into a whole is the goal of most oral language development. Indeed, "we do not listen to one sentence at a time. The process of semantic integration applies to sequences of sentences, as well as to each sentence individually." (4) This effectively combines both syntactic and semantic components of language development into the whole which we call communication. One important implication for teachers is that children need to develop comprehensible sentences and longer speeches, in addition to work on specific words and sentence structures. Context and continuous discourse are important, even for very young children.

## Cultural and Dialect Differences in
## Language Development

*Dialect* is the term commonly used to refer to language patterns different from the *standard* language. Dialects exist in all languages, and English has its share. Perhaps we should be saying standard American English, as compared to standard British or Australian English. However, we are dealing here rather exclusively with American English, so it is simply standard English. Who speaks or uses standard English? The television newscaster does; many teachers do, when they're careful; almost all textbooks do. Who speaks another dialect? In the United States, we have regional dialects: Brooklyn, Southern, or Appalachian, among others. We have social and ethnic dialects: black English, Chicano English, among others. Different professional and age groups have dialects, sometimes called jargon. Engineers, carpenters, and even teachers develop language to describe their particular work which is not easily intelligible to those outside the group.

Dialect, as far as can be determined, is a naturally occurring phenomenon. Dialects have all the characteristics of language described earlier, including regularity and system. If we carry the definition of dialect to its logical extension, we find that each speaker of a language is a little different from all the others and therefore speaks his *own* dialect, or idiolect. This point is important to teachers of young children. As children develop language, they are molding it after the language they hear from the important people in their lives, most notably the family and later the community. Teachers must be familiar with the dialect children bring to school, be tolerant of the language they live with, and seek to expand their ability to handle language of varying levels.

Should teachers allow students to use their own dialect in the classroom? Or should they demand standard English at all times? Recent research suggests that young children should be encouraged to use the language they bring with them to school, as much as possible, as they adjust to the new social world of the classroom. Because their language represents their culture, home, and security, it is threatening to their self-concepts to suggest they change to a new and "foreign" language. As Burling says,

> Nothing can ever fully take the place of the language that we learn from our parents and from our earliest friends. For each of us, this language has special emotional connotations, and I would like to work toward the time when we can all respect one another's varied linguistic heritage. Of course, a man's language will grow and change as he encounters new people and as he studies new subjects. No one continues to speak like a five-year-old all his life. But we learn most successfully and we move most easily into new experiences when we can build upon what we already know. If teachers

could appreciate the child's own language and recognize its irreplaceable value, they would be able to work together with the child, helping him and helping his language to grow and develop . . . . (3)

The question of dialect and how to deal with it is most important as it relates to reading and reading readiness in young children. It is also important as it relates to writing and writing readiness, which will be discussed more fully later in this chapter. The issue of standard English versus dialect is both complex and provocative.

## ASSESSING THE LANGUAGE DEVELOPMENT OF YOUNG CHILDREN

Teachers of young children recognize that helping children develop adequate oral language is a critical part of their work. The development of oral language is fundamental to all other language skills described in this book and to intellectual and social development in general.

It follows logically, then, that the teacher will feel it necessary to assess each child's language to see how well the basic components — vocabulary and sentence structure — have been mastered and how well the child can articulate the language. A large variety of tests, formal and informal, is available to assess language development. We will consider formal and informal assessment techniques, with the goal of developing a practical classroom assessment procedure.

### Formal Tests of Language Development

A number of tests have been developed and standardized with the goal of assessing the language development of young children. Since children's language development has been recognized as an important factor in academic success, intellectual and social development, and especially reading readiness, researchers have continued to search for a single standard assessment procedure, preferably easy to administer and interpret, that teachers can use to gather information on their children's language. No such test has yet been developed. However, a few tests are used fairly widely. Results of these tests may be reported on children's records for teachers' use in setting goals and preparing instruction.

*The Peabody Picture Vocabulary Test* (PPVT) is a simple test of vocabulary. The child must point to one of four pictures after the tester says a word. This test is well standardized, but it views language development solely as a function of the size of the child's vocabulary. It is sometimes used as a general intelligence test, since vocabulary is an important component of intelligence. However, it remains a partial view.

The *Illinois Test of Psycholinguistic Abilities*(ITPA) reflects the newer psycholinguistic views of language development. It has twelve subtests, and the full test is not always used because it is long and cumbersome. The test places heavy emphasis on auditory and visual processing and less assessment of other areas, like syntactic patterns.

Several tests are available for articulation and discrimination. Generally, such tests are structured to test specific sounds in initial, medial, and final positions. These tests are most often administered by a specialist in speech problems. Results are reported in the form of sounds which a child makes or doesn't make successfully.

Tests focusing on syntactic development have been appearing in recent years. Though none is fully accepted as being well standardized, several are in regular use to assess children's syntactic development. *The Northwestern Syntax Screening Test* is perhaps the best known. It asks children both to point to the picture (of a pair) that depicts the sentence given by the examiner and to say the correct sentence when the examiner points to a picture. Sentences are paired to show specific contrasts in syntax: "The girl will drink" versus "The girl is drinking."

It is likely that research on tests of language development will continue and additional tests claiming to test language development successfully will be published. Teachers of young children will continue to be faced with questions about how to use results of such tests and which tests to use in language assessment. Several important problems remain with such tests. The first problem is that the tests developed to date represent white, middle-class language as the standard. To the extent that teachers recognize dialect in their children's language, they will not feel confident that any of the tests given here represent fully their children's language development.

A second problem is that none of the tests published to date covers all language development effectively. Tests focus on vocabulary or syntax or articulation. In order to provide a complete picture of a child's language, a teacher would need to give several tests, a very time-consuming process.

A third problem is that a teacher using these tests needs a broad understanding of linguistics and tests and measurement in order to choose the tests wisely and interpret them appropriately. It is dangerous for a teacher with limited knowledge in these areas to give and interpret the tests listed here. However, it is possible that teachers will find the results of such tests reported on school records. The careful teacher will seek out the specialist who gave the test to ask for explanation and interpretation of the results. The process of teaching, especially setting specific goals for each student, requires that the teacher understand fully the diagnostic information available on each child. The teacher must ask for more specific information than a simple age or grade equivalent in language development.

### Informal Assessment of Young Children's Language

If formal techniques have not yet been fully perfected in the assessment process, neither have informal techniques. However, informal tests have several distinct advantages. The primary one is that they measure the child's developing language in a natural setting, usually conversation, rather than providing isolated words, phrases, or pictures for the child to respond to. The context which characterizes informal assessment is important, because it is closer to the way the child uses language normally. For example, the *Northwestern Syntax Screening Test* asks the child to discriminate the present progressive from the future tense ("The girl is drinking" versus "The girl will drink") without identifying who, when, and where. The picture stimulus is a line drawing. In an informal assessment, the teacher listens to a child's language (or looks at a transcript of it) and checks whether these constructions are present during a fifty - to one hundred-utterance sample. The constructions, if present, are used naturally by the child in the course of conversation.

This situation presents one of the limitations of informal assessment, as well. In order to be sure of capturing all the constructions a child can make, the teacher will need relatively more language and may spend more time than would be required to give one of the tests described earlier. Thus, using informal assessment procedures requires a significant time commitment by a teacher and also requires careful planning.

Planning is required to structure situations in which the child feels comfortable and is willing to speak and in which the child reveals most of the constructions and vocabulary at his or her command. Any conversation between a teacher and a child may be analyzed for developmental patterns. The sample of utterances used may come from several short conversations over a period of days, especially for very young children, as a teacher collects enough of the child's language in enough different situations to produce an appropriate sample for analysis. The tape and transcript analyzed in the beginning section of the chapter is an example of such a sample.

What does a teacher look for in an analysis of language development? Simply put, for both syntactic and vocabulary development and for articulation of the phonemes used in English.

**Syntactic milestones.** There are no absolute age levels by which a normal child develops a given language pattern. As with all developmental processes, language develops differently in different children. There is regularity, however, in the developmental sequence. In addition, sufficient research has been completed to give us a global view of the points at which critical linguistic features begin to appear regularly in children's language. Even though age levels are not absolute, it is useful to know approximately when certain language events occur. Following is a list of critical language events, as a function, very broadly, of age.

## SOME SUMMARY FEATURES OF DEVELOPMENT OF
## THE SYNTACTIC SYSTEM

| Emerging Process or Structure | Approximate Age in Months |
|---|---|
| When the child produces single words, these are sentence-like in meaning because he applies different intonation contours. Also, the words he chooses represent the topic of the situation he find himself in; e.g., he may say "light out" and point to the bulb but "on" as he points to and wants to turn the switch. | 12-20 |
| When he uses two- or three-word utterances, the words already form categories, and their combination is systematic. The categories are not yet like adult form classes — they have, in the main, semantic delimitation — but the behavior is the same. Two-word utterances have intonational contours of declarative, imperative, question, and negative sentence types. | 28-33 |
| Sentences take the subject + predicate form (.e.g. "big boat" becomes "that a big boat"; "eat cake" becomes "John eat cake"). | 28-36 |
| The predicate expands to verb + object ("Don't touch me"); verb + adverb ("Put it here"); verb + prepositional phrase ("put it on table"). | 28-36 |
| The subject becomes expanded into a noun phrase through addition of modifiers like articles, quantifiers, possessive nouns and pronouns, or adjectives (e.g., "Daddy new coat"; "some more milk"). | 30-36 |
| The noun phrase becomes a movable structure — it is used in both subject and predicate position. | 30-40 |
| Negative form ("I not here"); interrogative ("Is he coming?"); wh- questions ("How he do that?") appear. | 30-40 |
| Past tense appears ("I broke my car"; "it's broked"). | 33-45 |
| Plural marker appears ("See those kittens?"). | 33-45 |

## SOME SUMMARY FEATURES OF DEVELOPMENT OF
## THE SYNTACTIC SYSTEM (Cont.)

| Emerging Process or Structure | Approximate Age in Months |
|---|---|
| Progressive (-ing) form appears ("turning round"; "I going drop it"). | 33-40 |
| Forms of "to be" appear, first in verb role ("what is that?", "that's a truck"), later as auxiliary ("we are working hard"). | 35-42 |
| Verb agreement appears ("I don't see him"; "he doesn't know"). | 35-45 |
| Possessive marker appears ("mommy's bag"; "those are mine"). | 35-45 |
| Verb complement appears ("I want to play"). | 35-45 |
| Some auxiliaries appear ("I did see him"; "we can do this"; "I won't play"). | 36-45 |
| Relative clause appears ("I don't know what is missing"). | 55+ |
| Reflexive ("washed himself"); passive ("got spanked"; "was sent home"); adjective comparison ("the biggest of all"). | 60+ |
| Auxiliary "have" ("I have been thinking"), various conjunctions ("if," "so," "because"); nominalization ("she does the shopping"); participle complement ("I like playing"). (Compiled from 4, 8, 9) | 60-72+ |

All the syntactic events given can occur at different levels of "correctness," especially if that is viewed traditionally. Generally, children learn new constructions over time and only gradually gain control over them. A good example is given by Dale (4) in the development of questions. Note the differences in the age of the children at the given MLU, as well as the progressive control of question forms:

| MLU | NAME AND AGE (months) | EXAMPLES |
|---|---|---|
| 1. 8-2.0 | Adam 28 | No ear? |
| | Eve 18 | Where Daddy going? |
| | Sarah 27 | |
| 2. 3-2.9 | Adam 32 | You can't fix it? |
| | Eve 22 | Who is it? |
| | Sarah 32 | Why not he eat? |
| 3. 4-3.6 | Adam 38 | Can't you get it? |
| | Eve 25 | Does turtles crawl? |
| | Sarah 38 | Why you caught it? |
| | | What did you doed? |
| | | What lives in that house? |

The development of question forms is important in English. It is also complex and sophisticated. The linguist can distinguish between a large number of different types of questions. The teacher of young children, ages three to five, probably is not concerned with the specifics of many types of questions, but instead that children can use questions to communicate and gradually gain control over the forms required. For example, it may be appropriate for a three-year-old to say "What did you doed?" showing ability to use the *wh-* question form. The incorrect form of the verb is an indication that he can't control the reorganization of the verb phrase and the *do-* form of the verb his question requires. If that same child is making the same mistake in verb form six months later, the teacher should be concerned and may decide that specific attention to the verbs in questions is appropriate.

It is useful for the teacher of young children to have some sense of the normal developmental sequence of important syntactic elements. The basic sentence patterns, such as questions, are critical features of English syntax. Children work toward control of these patterns from the one-word sentence stage and usually gain this control by the time they are five to six. The chart given here is a summary of four critical sentence patterns as they develop. This is a practical application of the developmental changes in syntax given earlier. For example, in the declarative sentence examples, the child uses the present tense early ("Rick go"), but it is much later that he controls the present progressive tense completely ("Rick is going").

**TABLE 4-1.   STAGES IN THE DEVELOPMENT OF DECLARATIVE, NEGATIVE, QUESTION, AND IMPERATIVE SENTENCES**

| | A<br>*Early* | B<br>*In Between* | C<br>*Later* |
|---|---|---|---|
| Declarative | That box<br>Big boat<br>Rick go | That's box<br>That big boat<br>Rick going | That's a box<br>That's a big boat<br>Rick is going |

TABLE 4-1.  STAGES IN THE DEVELOPMENT OF DECLARATIVE, NEGATIVE,
QUESTION, AND IMPERATIVE SENTENCES — CONTINUED

|  | A<br>*Early* | B<br>*In Between* | C<br>*Later* |
|---|---|---|---|
| Negative | No play<br>No a book<br>No fall down | I no play<br>That not book<br>(a) I not falling<br>    down<br>(b) I'm not fall<br>    down | I won't play<br>That's not a book<br><br>I'm not falling down |
| Question | See shoe?<br>Truck here?<br>Where baby? | Mommy see shoe?<br>Truck's here?<br>(a) Where baby is?<br>(b) Where's baby is? | Do you see the shoe?<br>Is the truck here?<br>Where's the baby? |
| Imperative | Want baby!<br><br><br>No touch!<br>Have it! | | I want the baby<br>or<br>Give me the baby?<br>Don't touch it!<br>Give it to me! |

Paula Menyuk, THE ACQUISITION AND DEVELOPMENT OF LANGUAGE, ©
1971, pp. 106. Reprinted by permission of Prentice-Hall, Inc., Englewood Cliffs,
New Jersey.

In summary, teachers of young children want to assess students'
syntactic development and determine where they fit into the broad
categories given here. However, they will be careful not to expect every
child to meet a restrictive timetable of development. Faith in the normal
developmental processes suggests that except for children who are
markedly different from the normal children described here, teachers
should choose to stimulate as much language use as possible, in as
comfortable and supportive a context as possible, with maximum
opportunity for expansion of each child's language. Children with marked
differences in syntactic development should be referred to the speech
clinician for careful diagnosis.

**Vocabulary assessment.** Except for the *Peabody Picture Vocabulary Test,*
assessment of children's vocabulary is usually informal. Because
vocabulary is so dependent upon experiential background, dialect,
culture, and other social variables, the teacher should develop informal
assessment techniques that reflect the particular background of the
student.

Vocabulary assessment is of two major kinds. The most basic assessment
is of experience. Can the child name people, objects, places in the
environment? Can he or she use the words showing relationships ("over,"
"under," "out")? Verb forms to show differences in time ("He did it
yesterday," "he will do it tomorrow," "he does it every day")? Descriptive
words ("the big box," "the red barn")? Generally, this basic assessment

requires the child to be able to describe his or her own life and surroundings in words.

The second major kind of vocabulary assessment is of those words which reflect aspects of the world that are not part of the child's immediate environment. This kind of vocabulary building is particularly important in later academic success and in broadening the child's opportunity to understand and control his world. The same types of words make up this wider vocabulary, but they deal with places, objects, events that the child comes to know through books, television, movies, and other experiences outside his own family and culture. It is in this area of vocabulary that disadvantaged children are especially weak. Compensatory experiences to help broaden the child's understanding and use of words may be needed, if assessment shows him to be weak in this area.

Informal vocabulary assessment may be done in two general ways. One is to list the words, by function, found in the transcript of the child's language used earlier. Catalog the kinds of words the child uses naturally: nouns, adjectives, adverbs, verbs; function words to show relationships (over, under), for use with verbs (has, can, should), or for use with nouns (a, the, this). Look at the inflections he uses: Does he form correct noun plurals, verb tenses, other word endings? Identify any words that do not come from his immediate environment, but instead show his broadening vocabulary beyond his own experience. A chart like the one in Figure 4-1 will keep a record of the child's vocabulary at a given time. Comparison of the results from two separate analyses six months or one year apart should show developmental change.

The second way to assess vocabulary follows the first. If analysis shows that the child does not use a particular word or type of word, the teacher can set up a specific informal testing situation aimed at that type of word. It may be that the child knows the word, but the conversations recorded for analysis just don't call for it. Rather than conclude that the child doesn't know that word or word type, the teacher should check his ability to use it directly.

For example, if the child does not demonstrate understanding of the use of "over" and "under," the teacher can place books on a table in the classroom, with blocks underneath. Then he asks the child, "What is under the table?" "What is over the blocks?" "What is on the table?" If the child answers correctly, the teacher can say that the child understands, or comprehends, the words. A second level of questioning requires the child to use or produce the relationship words: Where are the blocks? Where are the books? The child's correct answer should be "under the table," "on the table." Complete sentences are not necessary to demonstrate that the child can produce the right relationship words.

Another way to check on developing vocabularies is to use a word list like the Dolch list, which lists words commonly used in American English.

NAME _____   MLU _____

AGE (Months) _____   NUMBER OF WORDS (TOTAL) _____

List words by function:   NUMBER OF DIFFERENT WORDS _____

Nouns

Verbs

Adjectives

Adverbs

Function Words

    used with nouns

    used with verbs

    relationships

Words **not** from school/home environment

**FIGURE 4-1.  RECORD KEEPING CHART FOR VOCABULARY ASSESSMENT**

Ask the child to use the words as the teacher pronounces them, or to show the teacher what the words mean. For example, if the word is *round,* tell the child "Point to something *round.* Where is something round?" If the child does this task correctly, the teacher knows that the child understands *round,* even though she or he doesn't yet know that the child can use the word independently.

Effective use of informal assessment in the classroom requires that the teacher use the regular objects and materials in the classroom to set up situations for language use. The child feels comfortable when using familiar things in familiar surroundings. Creative use of everyday items makes the most effective situation for specific language assessment.

**Articulation.** The child's ability to pronounce speech sounds progresses developmentally, just as syntax and vocabulary do. It follows that the teacher must know what to expect in children's speech patterns. Following are some broad age references for the sequence and normal age of mastery of speech sounds (adapted from [9] and [15]).

TABLE 4-2. SEQUENCE OF SPEECH SOUND MASTERY

| AGE | SOUND | EXAMPLE |
|---|---|---|
| By age 3 | b | *b*aby |
| | m | *m*ama |
| | n | *n*o |
| | f | *f*ine |
| | w | *w*ater |
| | h | *h*orse |
| By age 4 | p | *p*en |
| | d | *d*og |
| | g | *g*o |
| | k | *k*iss |
| | y | *y*es |
| | l | *l*amb |
| By age 5 | t | *t*op |
| | v | *v*an |
| | š | *s*ee |
| | ž | *z*oo |
| | č | *sh*ow |
| | z | a*z*ure |
| By age 5½ | c | *ch*urch |
| | r | *r*un |
| By age 6 | j | *j*udge |
| By age 6+ | th (voiced) | *th*en |
| | th (voiceless) | *th*in |

All the vowel sounds are normally produced by age 2.

Most children develop speech sounds successfully, in the order given here, and in generally the same time frame. Of the children who do not develop certain sounds in the time given, a good number will develop them successfully, but it will take them longer. Careful teachers, then, listen to students' developing articulation patterns, knowing what sounds they should be making at their particular ages, and concern themselves only with those children who are clearly not articulating at appropriate levels.

Careful classroom assessment of articulation includes the following steps:

1. Teacher listens carefully to children working in small groups, noting the sounds that particular children are having trouble with.

2. Teacher checks developmental speech sounds lists to see whether children of this age should normally be making those sounds correctly.
3. Teacher identifies children somewhat behind the developmental schedule for making particular sounds; she sets up an informal testing situation and asks those children individually to pronounce words using the sound in question. The list should include words using the sound in different positions (r as in *run*, *car*) and in context as well as in isolation.
4. If a child is markedly behind schedule or if the teacher suspects a serious physical or psychological problem, she refers the child for careful diagnosis by the speech clinician and school psychologist. Children so referred will return to the classroom with specific suggestions for the teacher to use in working with that student. If referral is not appropriate, the teacher can set up systematic practice with particular sounds and blends (such as bl-, sn-, -ng, -lt) as children seem to need such practice.

It is important to indicate the danger of overemphasis on the correction of children's pronunciation. It is possible to create problems by constantly nagging children to say words correctly, especially if they are not developmentally ready to do it. The decision to work with children's articulation overtly should be made only after some consultation with specialists. Most of the time, the teacher's best course of action is to say the word correctly for the child, without calling attention to the child's error. This means that whenever the child is speaking to the teacher, he will be hearing the sound said correctly. Since a child who is not ready to make the sound may not be able to hear the difference between his own sound and the one the teacher is making, hearing tests (especially of auditory discrimination) are important precautionary measures.

Another danger in overcorrection lies in the effect on his *home* language. If the child speaks a dialect other than standard English, it will probably contain some pronunciation patterns that differ from standard English. The teacher should beware of trying to force a child to say words differently in school from the way they are said out of school. The same concerns apply in correcting articulation that apply to any other aspect of the nonstandard English a child brings to school. Accepting and supporting the child's use of language is more important than correction in these early years. However, the teacher must still be sure that the child's development is progressing appropriately. That means knowing the child's dialect well enough to answer this question: When John says "*l*uck" as "*w*uck," is that a feature of the dialect or of his personal language development? If it is dialect-related, the teacher's goal is to provide continuous models of standard English but not to correct him overtly. If it is *not* dialect-related, the teacher can proceed as with any other articulation problem.

## Informal Language Assessment in the Classroom

The summary of this section on language assessment provides general guidelines for informal assessment in the classroom.

**1.** Look carefully at all the aspects of language: syntax, vocabulary, articulation.

**2.** Use an informal setting to collect primary language from children, but structure it to get the kinds of language needed for assessment.

**3.** Follow up with informal, specific tests to verify data gained from the informal language sample.

**4.** Decide on one of the following courses of action:
— Refer the child for specialists' diagnosis;
— Develop careful classroom practice work aimed at a specific problem;
— Continue to provide language model and attend to the child's developing control over the specific language feature in question;
— Keep careful records so changes over time can be assessed.

Informal diagnosis goes on every time the teacher and child talk together.

## ORAL COMPOSITION: HELPING CHILDREN TALK TOGETHER

### Goals for Oral Language Development

One of the most widely accepted goals for education is to help children develop the communication skills needed for success in adult life — speaking, listening, reading, writing. These skills form a large part of any basic curriculum. Research and teaching practice both agree that before students are asked to read and write (the literacy skills), they should have well-established skills in speaking and listening. The major goal for teachers of young children, then, is to develop these two skill areas as part of reading and writing readiness and as important skills in their own right.

Once a teacher has assessed the level of oral language of her class, she must prepare activities that will provide systematic use of oral language and allow continued assessment. Several more specific goals for oral language development are widely accepted.

**1.** To develop fluency. Fluency may be defined as a willingness to use language, resulting in gradually increasing amounts of language. Being able to produce language in appropriately increasing amounts remains a critical feature of language development through maturity (8, 11).

Fluency is developed only gradually, but its development should be a major goal of teachers of young children. To do so, teachers must:

a. Set up speaking situations that children understand and can relate to.

b. Allow freedom for the child to respond from his own experience and in his own language.

c. Provide support and encouragement as children speak.

d. Encourage children to speak to each other, singly or in groups, as well as to the teacher, so that the child's peer group is his audience much of the time, rather than the teacher.

2. To encourage syntactic development. Much syntactic development occurs naturally as children model their language after their parents and other adult and peer speakers. Most children use and understand all the basic English sentence patterns before they reach kindergarten age (4). However, certain syntactic relationships need systematic encouragement, especially for children who demonstrate no knowledge of them by age three or four.

The features most often in need of encouragement and reinforcement are those abstract ones like relationships (before, after, when), connection (and, but, because), and describing (big, small, red). After assessing a child's use of various linguistic structures, the teacher should focus on activities to assist students in developing the necessary language abilities. Teachers must:

a. Structure games and situations in which children will naturally use the desired language features.

b. Provide mutiple models of the desired features (teacher, other adults and peers, records).

c. Assess carefully for continuing development.

d. Assess the ways the child's own language (dialect) differs from the standard used by the teacher, so that the new features the teacher encourages are as little different as possible from the child's language.

3. To encourage broad vocabulary development. Children will add new words to their vocabulary any time they are introduced to new ideas or information. The more natural the context in which the new word occurs, the more likely that it will be remembered. In order to add the word to their permanent vocabulary, children must use it and hear it in different contexts. Reinforcement for their and peers' correct use of the word and modeling of the word by the teacher are important processes. For continuous vocabulary development, teachers must:

a. Structure learning experiences in science, social studies, arithmetic, health, and daily living skills to include a specific list of vocabulary new to the children.

b. Be sure there are few enough new words that children can assimilate them quickly.

c. Build follow-up experiences in which these words occur naturally to provide reinforcement for the words and help develop full concept meanings.

4. To integrate language use with daily life, in and out of school. Good language use must not become a school-only activity. The separation of "school language" from the language the child hears outside of school encourages the feeling that school and "life"or the "real world" are not related. This dangerous idea has its roots in young children's school experiences, especially if they feel that their language, home, community, or culture is being systematically "put down" by the teacher and other school people. In order to avoid this problem, yet still provide children with positive models, the teacher must:

a. Structure learning experiences in which the child describes life outside of school (activities, places, and things of his own life).

b. Encourage children to share with other children and adults their reactions to and feelings about what happens in and out of school.

c. Include community members and events in the planned learning experiences of the classroom.

5. To encourage self-expression, both for specific communication purposes and for its own sake. Children must see the classroom as a place that welcomes them and all their emotional reactions. The socializing process going on during the first years of school must not be allowed to repress children's responses to what happens inside and outside the classroom. Thus, self-expression becomes a way of responding on a personal basis and also a way of learning to communicate with others. The processes of discussion and interaction with others are heavily emphasized in young children's school experiences. Social processes involved in discussion are dealt with more fully in Chapter 3. Here the emphasis is on creative self-expression. To develop self-expression, the teacher must:

a. Remain accepting and supportive of the child's feelings and responses.

b. Set up situations that encourage creative responses and the use of imagination.

c. Set aside time and space for children to think and imagine, quiet and nonthreatening.

6. To encourage the use of language as a way to organize thinking,

as an aid to cognitive development. Adults use language largely to express ideas, to record events and to organize life experiences in some meaningful way. School experiences demand this kind of language use more and more exclusively as children grow older. Hence it is imperative that teachers of young children begin to provide structured experiences for such language use. In addition, this kind of language use will probably receive less emphasis at home than others mentioned earlier. The teacher must, therefore:

a. Structure learning experiences in all content areas to encourage the use of language in problem solving, reporting, comparing/contrasting, and evaluating.
b. Set up experiences in which children work in teams of two to four to encourage natural use of language.
c. Require constant feedback and verbal interaction between teacher and student as learning activities proceed.
d. Provide opportunities for both formal and informal reporting procedures.

### Techniques that Work with Preschool Children

What follows is a brief catalog of techniques that work with children five years old and under. Every teacher needs a large store of techniques like these, and the current list is meant to be suggestive. As these techniques are tried and discussed, adaptations and variations will come to mind. These should be written down, developed, tried out, and evaluated (as good teaching requires in all areas). Each technique responds to the goals given above, with most techniques responding to more than one goal.

1. Reporting Activities. Very young children respond well to requests for "show and tell." Some children need to bring in a toy or object to describe or tell a story about (narrate). Others can use a picture (photograph or their own drawing). Others can describe an event without props (Christmas morning, a vacation, a funny happening, a favorite place or event). Reporting involves something that really happened or exists, rather than imaginary things. Developing a sense of what is real and what is imaginary is a major developmental goal for children during these early years. Not all children will be able to distinguish them clearly by age five, but teachers need to remind children continually of the distinction.

2. Inventing stories. The teacher can label narrative situations as imaginary or invented, helping to clarify the distinction described earlier. Inventing stories is both fun and valuable as an extension of self-expression and creative thinking. Learning experiences may

need to be structured: "Pretend you're an astronaut. What do you look like? Where are you going?" These inventions can spring from current events, content area learning in social studies, science, or health, or real life. Children can respond to things that are real in the world but which the child has never experienced firsthand — like the astronaut — or to things that are totally imaginary — like the Grinch or an imaginary animal or place. Teachers should choose roles or situations based on these criteria:

   **a.** Familiarity to child's economic, social, geographical situation.

   **b.** Whether the teacher's objective is real-world description, fantasy, narrative, or another form.

   **c.** Whether the child can act out the situation or must rely on words.

These two techniques, reporting and inventing stories, together provide teachers with multiple opportunities to develop fluency and self-expression in children.

   **3.** Acting out activities. Activities that ask children to act out situations or events require that they not only understand the situation but can express it in action to the teacher or other students. The difference between inventing stories and acting out is primarily in the action required. Acting out can be simple and wordless, as in charades, or it can be fairly complex, as in acting out "What do you do in the morning?" or "What do you do when you play a game?" or "What happens when you argue with your brother or sister?" More discussion of dramatic play is given in Chapter 7.

   **4.** Responding to pictures. Pictures are the source material for several different types of oral language activities. Children can respond to a single picture by describing what is in the picture or by telling a story about what (or who) is in it. This is a specific application of 1 and 2 above. The teacher structures the language activity by the question asked of the child. "What (or who) do you see here?" requests description. "What is happening here?" asks for a narrative.

A sequence of pictures, as in a comic strip, gives rise most naturally to a narrative response from the child. A teacher who wants the child to practice sequencing pictures may give the child a picture sequence that tells a complete story. If the child is to consider consequences, as in cause and effect, or to invent alternative endings, the teacher can give the child a sequence with no obvious ending and ask the child to invent a conclusion. Such an open-ended activity is more creative and asks children to use their own experience and imagination. The choice of stimulus depends on the teacher's objective.

After children have experienced these ways of responding to pictures, they can create their own pictures for other children to respond to. One way of structuring such an experience is to have a group of children create pictures in response to a story read by the teacher. These children can then retell the story with their illustrations to another group of children. Another structure for such response is for children to create a series of pictures detailing events in one of their experiences, like a visit to the Grand Canyon, which they can use as they describe the experience orally to the others in the group. They can, of course, substitute photographs or memorabilia for their own drawings.

> **5.** Word games. Very young children especially enjoy word games, which ask them to name objects pictured on cards or boards. They can name objects, people, familiar places, and actions. This becomes an important activity for developing reading readiness, since older children can move naturally from naming things orally to reading the word labels next to the picture.

A more complex word game involves the child repeating a finger play or song like "The Eensy Weensy Spider" or reciting favorite rhymes. Real competition can be introduced as children try to guess the speaker's word from his description of it or, in a "Twenty Questions" format, from his answers to questions. These games move naturally to word games which involve reading the word and guessing it from the picture or reading the clues to the identity of the mystery word.

A different kind of word play asks children to name words which begin with the same sound: "The key word is *sunny.* Now everyone think of a word that begins with the same sound as *sunny.*"Then each child in the group contributes a word to the list. With very young children, the group can repeat the word after each child's contribution. For older children, closer to beginning reading, the teacher may choose to put the key word and each child's contributed word on the chalkboard. Variations on this word play are easy to develop. The important process here for oral language development is the systematic repetition of a particular sound or sound pattern, such as -ly, -ness, or un-. More emphasis can be placed on similarity of prefixes and suffixes as children grow older, so that the progression is from beginning sounds (*sunny*), to ending sounds (*ring*), to vowel sounds (*boot*), to prefixes and suffixes (*undress, clearly*), and finally to sequences of words with similar features (*green grass*), and sequences with different beginning sounds (*green acres*). In this last variation, the child's response is a two-word sequence beginning with the same two sounds as the stimulus phrase. Thus, with the stimulus *green acres,* the child's response could be great *air* or gruesome *aid*. Using the stimulus green *grass*, the response could be tall *tale*, or big *boy*, the objective being to give a two-word phrase with the same initial sound on both words. These word plays that emphasize sounds and sound patterns are clear previews of work with phonics which is a large part of many beginning reading programs. A teacher who is preparing children to enter a program heavy with phonics will probably want to spend a substantial amount of time on word plays like these.

6. Giving directions. Another specific technique that combines oral language with cognitive development involves the child giving instructions to other people. The audience is important, since the child's directions to another child may be quite different from those he gives the teacher or another adult. The child knows instinctively what people close to him already know and responds candidly to requests to explain something that is already known. As one five-year-old said to his mother, who had asked him to tell how he played football for the benefit of an interviewer, "Don't you 'member nothin'?" Therefore, it's important for teachers to structure situations of real interest and value to children. This may involve having the child develop the situation, along with the teacher, so that it represents something the child knows well and also something he knows the other children don't already know. It should be easy to make a list of things and processes that require directions, from the simple things, like how to build with blocks or Lincoln Logs or Playdough, to more complicated processes like playing an instrument, building a bird house or a model, putting a puzzle together, or making cookies. Demonstrating the process as the directions are given is the most natural way to do it, but it may be fun sometimes to ask children to describe a familiar process completely with words and without any props. It quickly becomes clear to children that some processes that seem simple, like tying shoelaces, are very difficult to describe orally, leading to the conclusion that some things must be seen to be understood — an important perspective for children to develop. Language has its limitations as well as its possibilities, and one of its limitations is its abstractness. Young children don't need to know that term to understand the limitation it places on language.

When the teacher searches for the structure for experiences in giving directions, then, she must remember to involve the child in the selection. Almost every child can come up with a set of directions from home to school, perhaps also to grandparents', to church, to some special place in the community. Children can also develop directions from the classroom to other parts of the school: the gym, the cafeteria, the playground, to give to visitors or new students. Children can also be asked to choose a place they have visited that other children probably have not and to develop a set of directions for other children to follow. A creative version of this activity, more useful perhaps for older children, is to have children develop an imaginary destination and a set of directions for reaching it. The principal concepts on which this exercise is based are (1) the logical thinking and problem solving necessary to develop the sequence of directions, and (2) the oral language facility to express the sequence clearly enough for hearers to follow them.

## Techniques for Working with Primary Grade Children

When children enter formal schooling, in kindergarten or first grade, they are not very different from the children we were discussing in the last section. The same techniques will work with kindergarten children, providing that the teacher is sensitive to changing and developing sentence structure and social organization.

When children enter school, however, the movement toward reading and writing is intensified. It is important for teachers to consider their students' language activities in light of their need to move in that direction.

**Word games.** Word games continue to be appealing. With children's growing social ability, competitive games can be introduced. For example, charades: teams of three or four children; one child acts out his word for his teammates; each child on both teams takes his turn, and the team with the lowest total time is the winner. It is easy to play this game without the competition aspect, if the teacher prefers. Many other "guessing" games with words are possible.

**Words as labels.** Preschool children work frequently with pictures to which they can attach words as labels: "Who (what) is in this picture?" Primary children can label pictures of more academic content: animals, people, places; kinds of rocks, buildings, cars, trees; places on maps of the world, their town or state, the universe, outer space, or imaginary worlds like the Land of Oz or Pooh's world. These labeling processes are good ways to extend the child's vocabulary, but they are also extending his conceptual understanding of diverse academic areas: science, social studies, math.

Consider, for example, the labeling of geometric forms: square, triangle, circle, and the learning of labels for numbers. Being able to count the number of sticks, blocks, or toys is training in arithmetic; being able to use the correct word for each number is a function of language. It is also a function of language to say "there are more blocks in this pile." Later a child must learn that four is greater than three (and less than five). When the child moves away from the blocks (the concrete) and manipulates only the numbers (the abstract), he is totally dependent on symbols: 5 >4 >3 is the same as "four is greater than three and less than five." Making this movement away from concrete objects and developing the ability to operate with symbols only is the essence of elementary school education. Gifted children make this movement more easily than others. Some children will never make the transition at all. But whether we like it or not, academic success requires that teachers continually encourage children to move toward greater dependence on words, on language, on symbols, and less on concrete objects.

**Reporting activities.** "Show and tell" is still an important part of school for primary children. These children should be encouraged to share experiences with others, rather than simply displaying an object and describing it. Or they may choose to give a more complete explanation of how something operates or why it is important. Teachers can encourage greater depth in the reporting by asking children some questions as they speak:

> If it's an experience, tell us where you went, what and whom you saw, what happened to you, and other interesting events. If it's an object, tell us how it works, how it's made, what it does, why it is important, who needs/uses it.

Teachers must help children develop their reporting ability by asking them for a little more information each time they speak.

It is important that children's reporting be on topics they choose, if at all possible. This kind of language activity should be based on interest. In a general classroom activity, children can share whatever they choose. In a more structured unit in science or social studies, the teacher can provide a large group of topics from which children can choose one to report on. Teachers should always allow children to propose their own topic, if they wish, within the unit framework. Creative and/or gifted children need the freedom to explore widely and report their explorations to the group.

What can a teacher do about a child who is shy or otherwise unwilling to talk in front of others? Forcing such children to speak before the whole class can be very damaging. As with preschool children, these five-to eight-year-olds should be encouraged to talk with the teacher or another student first. Gradually, they should be willing to talk before groups of two or three, perhaps even five or six children. Oral language use is just as effective if done before a few children as before the whole class.

Moffett (10) suggests that children should question the child who is "holding forth," so that natural dialogue will develop and the speaking child will become aware of the audience. Questioning the child will help him or her to anticipate what the audience (small group, class, or individual) wants to know, and the child will give the audience what it wants before they ask questions.

Moffett also suggests that as children become familiar with the "show and tell" process the teacher should structure their speaking by specifying the kind of talk. He suggests that the teacher ask for "something that (1) has a good story behind it, (2) they made or grew, (3) especially means a lot to them, or (4) moves or works in a funny or interesting way." (10) Such assignments, and others like them, give children experience in narration, exposition and explanation. This is really oral composition, because the speaking has a purpose and structure which the speaker must generate.

**Invented stories.** It's a short step from reporting real experiences to reporting invented experiences, ones made up by the speaker. These "made up" stories can be about animals or people from real life or from books. They can be set up by situations or left totally to the child's imagination.

Most children will invent stories naturally, but they sometimes fear that invented stories are "lies" or are otherwise immoral. To counter this fear, teachers can introduce invention in a humorous way. Tell a humorous and exaggerated tale so the children get the idea. Then let them volunteer to tell one of their own. Or give the children an exaggerated situation, and ask them to respond: Pretend you landed on Mars and found some Martians. What happened to you?

Children also enjoy total nonsense. Put lots of pictures of things (from magazines) in a box. Each child draws out three or four items at random and makes up a story using the ones he drew. Or have each child in a group of six draw one item from the box. The first child starts the story, using his picture; the second child must continue the story using his picture, and so on until all children have added to the story.

The idea of group composition can be used in many ways, especially with childen who are reticent. Try poetry. The first child makes a statement. The next one adds a line, then the third, and so on. The teacher can set the stage by helping the children think of a topic and, perhaps, helping with the first line. A good preparation for composing poetry is for the teacher to read some simple poems to the children. The rhyme and rhythm are appealing and easy to imitate. If necessary, the teacher can start the first line.

**Giving directions.** Preschool children can give directions from their house to school or to a special friend's house. Primary children can provide more complex directions. As their experiences have expanded, they have developed many more interests and much greater knowledge about those interests. It is important for them to gain experience in relating their knowledge to others who don't share it. That is, they must learn to anticipate the other person's needs and to structure their explanation so it can be understood by someone unfamiliar with the topic.

Primary grade children have had diverse experiences not shared by their peers. So the process of telling other children *how to do it* is the direction-giving process that is important here. Here are some examples possible for second- and third-grade children:

How to feed gerbils (fish, dogs)
How to ride a bicycle
How to skate (ski, toboggan)
How to play baseball (football, soccer)
How to grow tomatoes (corn, flowers)
How to put together a puzzle (a model, a train set)
How to conduct a science experiment
How to take a bus (subway, train, plane)
How to sell cookies (holiday cards, newspapers)

The list can be expanded. The key is that the child is explaining how to do something that he knows how to do and the other children don't. That gives practice in organizing things clearly and also demonstrates that the child is unique. Here again, other children's questions will help the speaker learn how to anticipate what the listeners need to know and in what order they need to hear it, so allowing children to question the speaker (respectfully) is important.

**Acting out.** Acting out means showing others what happened, demonstrating the events, rather than reporting them. Acting out is closely related to creative drama, which will be discussed in Chapter 7. When a child acts out something that has happened, or when two children develop a dialogue showing the event, they are imposing structure on the experience. They must be able to sort out the order of events and to anticipate what the audience needs to know. In other words, acting out is like *reporting,* except that it requires showing physically what happens.

The acting out process also shows that these children understand the position and reactions of the character they are portraying. They must put themselves in the character's mind, to at least a limited extent, a valuable developmental process.

Acting out can include children portraying other people, animals, or imaginary things as long as they must speak and express orally what is happening. The teacher must set the situation for the children or to help them formulate the situation for themselves. For example,

What happened at breakfast this morning? (at dinner last night?)
What happened on the school bus?
What happened in the art room (music room, gym)?

These situations should allow children to choose the one that makes them feel comfortable. The situations should also be structured to direct the children to realistic or imaginary situations. Imaginary situations might include:

You're the first person to land on Mars. What happens to you?
You have been elected president of the United States. What do you do on your first day in office?
You are principal of our school. What happens when you talk to a parent?

These situations should bring to mind the situations given for reporting activities. Indeed, the same situations work well in both instances, but the differences are important:

Reporting is telling about, describing, explaining.
Acting out is showing, demonstrating.

The child acting out can not describe or tell about actions; he must show them.

As acting out activities are planned, the teacher should remember that puppets, marionettes, and masks can be useful tools. Children can sometimes "put on" other characters more easily when they have some physical item to hang on to. Shy and reticent children will feel more comfortable with masks or puppets, but all children should have the liberating experience of moving outside themselves through these devices.

A great deal more on acting out is given in Chapter 7. The teacher must remember that each creative situation is an opportunity for language use and, therefore, for language development.

## WRITTEN COMPOSITION: THE BEGINNING OF WRITING

### Goals for Writing Development in Young Children

Children in primary school are ready to begin the process of writing down what they can say. This principle is important to remember. Young children can learn to write down what they can say. Oral language development and composing orally must precede the beginning of writing, just as listening and understanding oral language precede reading. Therefore, the teacher of young children should be careful to introduce writing only after children have demonstrated basic competence in composing orally. The major goals in writing development for young children include:

**1.** Develop basic transcribing skills.

The child is encouraged to write down what he can say. Initially it will be very simple statements of daily events and experiences. As children's writing fluency increases, they can write more of what they feel and see. As they write more, structure gradually emerges, and the children gradually gain control over their writing. It is important for teachers to encourage children's emerging writing skills by providing many opportunities to write and by being supportive rather than critical of children's writing attempts. The emphasis should be on developing fluency, rather than correctness. As children become more fluent and comfortable with writing, they will be willing to consider spelling, punctuation, and other regularities of the written language.

It is particularly important to follow this principle in working with children whose language is not standard English. These children will need to feel that the teacher accepts their language and appreciates what they have to say. If they need to move toward writing in more standard English, that can wait until they are conscious of the differences and gain control over their own language.

**2.** Integrate writing into daily life.

This goal aims at helping children realize that writing is a natural and useful part of daily life, in school and out. A number of the techniques given later are aimed at this goal. Children who come from families in which writing is used frequently will find it relatively easy to identify with writing tasks aimed at real life experiences. However, children who have no models for writing at home will need to find examples in school — the teacher and the other children. Now that television is such a common part of children's life, teachers must be especially concerned to demonstrate the value of writing in the world outside. The kinds of oral composing situations that relate to the real world can be used as situations for stimulating writing.

**3.** Encourage syntactic development in writing.

Earlier we described oral syntactic development as a natural development, one which can be supported but probably not changed dramatically. The same seems to be true for written work. The best way yet suggested to encourage syntactic development is for children to write a great deal. Primary children are not ready for systematic instruction in grammar or language structure, but they can appreciate writing in different forms — narration, or telling a story; description; explaining, or telling how, what, and why something is; and evaluation, or telling how good or bad, useful or useless something is. As children write for different purposes, they will be compelled to use different syntactic structures, sometimes stretching their syntactic capacities to include higher levels.

**4.** Encourage wide use of vocabulary.

This goal is similar to the last one. Children must write frequently in response to many different stimuli in order to stretch their vocabularies to new and higher levels.

The developing written vocabulary of primary children will normally lag behind their oral vocabulary. They will be able to use more words orally than they can in writing. The movement to a larger written than oral vocabulary, one mark of a well-educated person, does not happen until later in a child's life. Therefore, the teacher who works to increase oral vocabulary is indirectly working to increase written vocabulary.

It is still useful to help children to see the written form of words they know orally. This process can be systematic, as in teaching the new written vocabulary in a unit of social studies or science, or it can be incidental, as when the teacher helps a child with a specific word he is struggling to write. The teacher's role again is to encourage and support children when they try to use a new word, rather than putting them down or correcting them in a negative manner. Children must learn to "hear" the correct usage of new words as they use them. Indeed, it is often necessary to have them read the sentence aloud, so that their more advanced listening skills can tell them that they haven't used the word quite right.

5. Encourage writing for specific purposes.

This principle should underlie all situations a teacher develops for students' writing. Each piece of writing has a purpose and an intended audience. Six-year-olds won't understand this consciously, but they can learn to ask why they are writing and who is to read it. Unless the teacher is careful, the audience quickly becomes the teacher, so that the teacher is the reader for whatever the children write. This is similar to writing on the job only for the boss. That is, the writing is directed to the authority figure. The careful teacher, then, organizes writing situations in which the audience differs:

> Letters to other people, in school or out.
> Notes and explanations to other children.
> Letters and reports to parents.
> Journals to himself!

There are many other possible audiences, which the teacher and children can help develop.

Purposes for writing vary with the assignment. Sometimes the purpose is just for self-expression or release, as in a daily journal. Sometimes the purpose is action, as in a letter to the principal about the lunchroom. Sometimes the purpose is to explain something to someone who doesn't know it, as in explaining a vacation trip to other children. But sometimes children must write for academic purposes — to demonstrate that they have learned or discovered something that they didn't know before. Purposes vary and are worth discussing with children. What is important is dealing with purpose clearly and seriously.

6. Encourage writing as a means of self-expression.

Writing can be a liberating process. Novelists and poets tell us that writing releases things within them that they can't say orally. The same thing works for children. Poetry, descriptions, even stories, allow children to say things that can't otherwise. Self-expression is a particular purpose, which needs emphasis mostly because a lot of school-based writing is not designed for self-expression. The teacher wishing self-expression must not just tell children to write and express themselves. They need some stimulus, some structure to get them started (some children need more than others). Reading poetry aloud and then giving written copies to children can help them get started with poetry. The same can be done with stories and descriptions. Or the teacher can stimulate oral discussion of a problem or situation and ask children to write their responses to it afterward. If the purpose is self-expression, children should be given as much freedom as possible in determining the form, structure, and content of their writing. Again here, teacher support is essential, that warm, comfortable feeling that says the teacher accepts whatever the child writes.

## Techniques that Work with Primary Children

Techniques for primary grade writing are extremely varied. The imaginative teacher can create many different situations to stimulate writing. A few tested techniques are given here, primarily to provide ideas and stimulate teachers' thinking.

One thing is not included here: worksheets and workbooks full of fill-in-the-blanks and other practice exercises. The suggestions given here emphasize the children's composing process, their demonstration of their ability to develop language (in this case, written) in their own minds. Practice with various aspects of language may be justified in other contexts, but when the context is composition, it is appropriate for children to compose.

The composing situation is important, too. The supportive classroom atmosphere has been mentioned before. In addition, teachers should be sure that children have plenty of thinking time as they begin to write. Once the stimulus is given and the writing situation is set, children need time to think about what they will write, plus time to do the physical writing. Some children will use more time than others, so the teacher should structure class time to permit some children to spend longer than others. That means providing other activities for children who finish earlier or whose attention span is shorter. Encouraging children to spend more and more time writing, gradually increasing it over a year's time, is important. It's also important not to rush children who spend a great deal of time writing.

**Writing centers.** One answer to this difference is to develop a writing center in the room, a place for children who choose to write often to sit and write comfortably, relatively separate and more quiet than the rest of the classroom. Ideas for writing are available in such a center, along with paper, dictionaries, and other stimulus materials. During regular class writing sessions, children who take longer to write can use the center and be less disturbed when the rapid writers are finished.

These writing centers can focus on writing situations related to a current unit in science or social studies. One third grade teacher developed the "Writing Rocket" to use during a science unit on the solar system titled "Things in Our Space." The "rocket" is a stack of coffee cans with cardboard pockets attached on all sides. The rocket sits in the middle of the writing center, with each pocket holding a different writing assignment for children to choose. In this unit, the teacher required that children complete a creative writing assignment five times in two weeks' time.

Writing centers can be places to display children's writing, too. Displaying different responses to the same assignment or responses to several different assignments can be motivating to children who are less inclined to write.

**Journals.** Children learn to write by writing. But not everyone has something to say on every topic. So it's a good idea to introduce the journal early in the primary years. Everyone can record what has happened to him that day. The journal can be helpful in starting off children who don't have good writing models at home or who are otherwise reluctant to write.

A child's journal should be kept in a notebook "just for that." The journal is private and not necessarily open to the teacher. So the teacher needs permission to read it. This has several purposes. Children are more fluent writing in journals when their audience is only themselves. They are less constrained by propriety and the need for privacy. A public journal, one that is designed for the teacher and others to read, will look quite different from a private journal. Since one writing goal is fluency, it's important for the child to have a place in which to write just what he or she wants to. That is the journal.

Topics for the journal can be anything. Children who have difficulty getting started can be asked to think about what has happened to them since they last wrote: what they did, whom they saw, who visited, and other things they might want to remember some day. They can write about their feelings, their wishes, their fears. Indeed, Fader (5) even suggests that his adolescent nonwriters start by copying into their journals things they have read that they'd like to keep.

The idea of a journal can be introduced first as a group project in which a small group of children writes a daily account of activities and events in the classroom. Each child can contribute one sentence or they can dictate their journal entries to a scribe who transcribes them as a record.

**Letters.** Letters are easy to introduce and use in many different ways. They are realistic and easy to apply to the real world. Letters have one restriction: they must be sent. They must have a definite audience and must be sent to that audience in order to complete the process. In addition, there should be some expectation that the letter will be answered. A letter is a two-way communication device. Phony letters to no one do not provide much motivation for the letter writer to attend to the task.

To whom can children write letters? Their parents and other relatives, their siblings, neighbors, and other people in their community; the principal, other teachers, their classes, the librarian, the custodian, the lunchroom supervisor, local officials, and other government figures deserve letters; manufacturers, advertisers, television stations all deserve letters. The teacher can develop innumerable situations in which writing a letter is an appropriate response:

A request for information about a problem or topic.
An expression of the writer's opinion about something.
An appeal for support of something the child supports.

Children develop better writing processes when they have experienced a variety of situations and purposes for writing.

**Words and pictures.** Just as children can describe pictures orally, they can do it in writing. Asking children to write descriptive words and phrases about a picture is one way to focus on description. Very early writing situations may include writing a word or phrase about a picture, usually stating what is in the picture. As children develop, the description should grow more elaborate, using more specific words to describe the picture or building a story around the events in the picture or writing a poem in response to the picture.

Pictures in sequence can be used to stimulate writing, as well. The young child can write the captions to pictures in a sequence and discover that the result is a story — the beginnings of narrative writing. Children may be able to draw their own pictures, then after discussing them with the teacher, write a simple story describing the pictures. The composing process here includes the oral discussion, the composition of the picture, and finally the written statement — a complex process but useful for second and third grade children.

**Reporting.** Reporting in writing is just talk written down. All the situations described under oral composition fit here — show and tell, describing events, explaining how to do or make something, and so on. The teacher of primary children should be careful not to expect as much in writing as she or he expects orally. However, children can begin early to think about how to get across their message. The best way to alert children to what readers need to know is to have other children, as well as the teacher, read and react to their writing. Questions such as "What do you mean by this?" and "What happened here?" will begin to indicate to the writer that something is missing. The teacher or another adult needs to be involved in this group process, to ensure that it doesn't become negative and defeating for any one child. The size of the group responding to each other's writing can vary from two to as many as five or six.

Initial reporting for academic purposes can begin in second or third grade. Such reports should be short and very specifically focused. The content of the reports is important. In a social studies unit, the child can write short reports in response to oral discussions, films, demonstrations, or short reading assignments. In each case, the objective should be related to developing fluency and the ability to organize thoughts and put them down on paper. Children who find writing difficult and the combination of thinking and writing impossible should not be forced to attempt formal reporting. These children should continue to write informally and personally until their writing and thinking skills develop sufficiently for them to try the reporting process.

**Inventing stories.** Writing down invented stories can be an exciting adventure for children whose writing skills are fairly well developed. For children whose skills are not yet well developed, writing can be a frightening and frustrating experience. Such children should be encouraged to write, but not required to create stories and write them down all at once. Sometimes composing orally is an important preliminary to writing: children can be encouraged to invent stories orally, then to write them down.

Inventing stories in writing, without intervening oral telling, may not arrive for all children before the end of third grade. For those who can do it, teachers should provide the same kind of writing space described earlier — a center or quiet place for concentration and thinking. The teacher's role should remain one of support and encouragement, developing creative stimulus situations, which can be responded to either orally or in writing, and allowing children some choice in which situation they choose. Reading stories orally to children, providing stories for them to read, encouraging them to view movies and television as stories — all together these stimuli will create the atmosphere in which children can write successfully.

## RESOURCES FOR TEACHERS

Dale, P. S. *Language Development, Structure and Function,* 2d Ed. New York: Holt, Rinehart & Winston, 1976. A comprehensive review of research, readable but technical. Specific references: Language Acquisition — Chapters 1, 2, 5; Vocabulary Development — Chapter 7; Dialect and Cultural Differences — Chapter 10; Assessing Oral Language Development — Chapter 11.

Hildebrand, V. *Introduction to Early Childhood Education,* 2d Ed. New York: Macmillan Publishing Co., 1976. Chapters 10 & 11.

Lamb, P. (Ed.) *Guiding Children's Language Learning,* 2d Ed. Dubuque, Iowa: William C. Brown Co., 1971. Chapter 4 deals with oral English, especially preprimary language development. Chapter 9 deals with language; Chapter 6 with writing.

Leeper, S. H., Dales, R. J., Skipper, D. S., and Witherspoon, R. L. *Good Schools for Young Children*, 3d Ed. New York: Macmillan, 1974. Chapters 11 & 12.

Menyuk, P. *The Acquisition and Development of Language*. Englewood Cliffs, N.J.: Prentice-Hall, 1971. Informative about development patterns in syntax.

Moffett, J. *A Student-Centered Language Arts Curriculum, Grades K-13: A Handbook for Teachers*. Boston: Houghton Mifflin Co., 1973. Part One, Kindergarten through Third Grade, describes all the language arts for primary students. Chapter 4 deals specifically with oral language activities.

Pasamanick, J. *Talkabout, an Early Childhood Language Development Resource*, Books 1 and 2. Little Neck, N.Y.: Center for Media Development, 1976. Activities and techniques for language development.

Tiedt, S. W. & Tiedt, I. M. *Language Arts Activities for the Classroom*. Boston: Allyn & Bacon, 1978. A compilation of many classroom activities. Chapter 4 deals with oral language activities; Chapters 6, 7, and 9 also deal with concepts mentioned in this chapter.

Todd, V. E. & Hefferman, H. *The Years Before School: Guiding Preschool Children*, 3d Ed. New York: Macmillan Publishing Co., 1977. Chapter 11.

Shine, R. E. & Freilinger, J. J. *Practical Methods of Speech Correction for the Classroom Teacher*. Davenport, Iowa: Teaching Aid Co., 1962. A good reference for careful classroom processes with articulation problems.

Smith, J. A. *Adventures in Communication: Language Arts Methods*. Boston: Allyn & Bacon, 1972. Chapter 6 deals with oral expression; Chapter 12 deals with language with emphasis on K-3 children.

Ward, Marjorie E., Cartwright, G. P., Cartwright, C. A., and Campbell, J. *Diagnostic Teaching of Preschool and Primary Children*. Report No. R-54, The Computer Assisted Instruction Laboratory, University Park, Pa.: The Pennsylvania State University, 1973.

## REFERENCES

1. Brown, R. and Bellugi, U. "Three Processes in the Child's Acquisition of Syntax," *Harvard Educational Review* 1964, *34*, 135.

2. Bruner, J. S. "The Course of Cognitive Growth," *American Psychologist* 1964, *19*, 4.

3. Burling, R. *English in Black and White.* New York: Holt, Rinehart & Winston, 1973, pp. 160-61.

4. Dale, P. S. *Language Development, Structure and Function,* 2d Ed. New York: Holt, Rinehart & Winston, 1976, pp. 1, 107, 109.

5. Fader, D. *The New Hooked on Books.* New York: Berkeley Publishing Corp., 1976.

6. Francis, W. N. *The Structure of American English.* New York: Ronald Press Co., 1958, p. 13.

7. Labov, W. *The Study of Nonstandard English.* Urbana, Ill.: National Council of Teachers of English, 1970.

8. Loban, W. *Language Development: Kindergarten Through Grade Twelve.* Urbana, Ill.: National Council of Teachers of English, 1976.

9. Menyuk, P. *The Acquisition and Development of Language.* Englewood Cliffs, N.J.: Prentice-Hall, 1971.

10. Moffett, J. *A Student-Centered Language Arts Curriculum, Grades K-13: A Handbook for Teachers.* Boston: Houghton Mifflin Co., 1973, p. 66.

11. O'Donnell, R.C., et al. *Syntax of Kindergarten and Elementary School Children: A Transformational Analysis.* Urbana, Ill.: National Council of Teachers of English, 1967.

12. Piaget, J. "Language and Thought from a Genetic Point of View," in *Six Psychological Studies,* trans. A. Tenzer. New York: Random House, 1967, pp. 91, 98.

13. Sapir, E. "Language and Environment," in D. G. Mandelbaum (ed.), *Selected Writings of Edward Sapir in Language, Culture, and Personality.* Berkeley: University of California Press, 1958, p. 162.

14. Vygotsky, L. S. *Thought and Language,* trans. by E. Hanfmann and G. Vakar. Cambridge, Mass.: M.I.T. Press, 1962, p. 44.

15. Ward, M. E., et al. *Diagnostic Teaching of Preschool and Primary Children,* Report No. R-54, The Computer Assisted Instruction Laboratory. University Park, Pa.: The Pennsylvania State University, 1973, pp. 277, 281, 282, 283.

## TEST REFERENCES

Dunn, L. M. *Peabody Picture Vocabulary Test.* Circle Pines, Minn.: American Guidance Service.

Lee, Laura. *Northwestern Syntax Screening Test.* Evanston, Ill.: Northwestern University, 1969.

# CHAPTER 5
# HANDWRITING

Handwriting, the art of writing by hand, is a tool of communication, a means of sharing thoughts, where the emphasis is on what is written. Handwriting instruction, focusing on how the message is written, is mainly concerned with legibility and the efficient production of symbols. Attending to both "what" and "how," the primary goal in handwriting programs today is to help children produce a free flow of ideas or easily read thoughts onto paper with a minimum of attention to mechanics.

Researchers who have studied language arts programs for young children (10) contend that the readiness phase for handwriting has received little attention in instructional programs and in the professional literature. Reports that are available (5, 3, 2) suggest that the development of readiness for handwriting often seems to play a secondary role in its relationship to the development of other academic areas and that when combined with other areas, actually receives little attention. Some researchers (8, 6, 9) emphasize the need for integration in the instruction of listening, speaking, reading, and writing skills, but are ready to state that no statistical research exists to show that using the solely integrated approach makes for better penmanship. The relationship of handwriting skill to reading is not often addressed in research literature, but it is contended that the readiness phase for handwriting is as important as a sound readiness program in reading (1).

The material in this chapter concerns the design and implementation of handwriting programs for the beginning handwriters. Included are a general overview of handwriting, identification of tools and techniques for assessing handwriting, and activity suggestions for handwriting practice. Readiness and beginning writing are explored.

## THE WRITING PROCESS

Since the goals of education concern growth and development of the whole child, educators are concerned with the cognitive, affective, and

146

psychomotor behaviors of children. Educators are more aware of cognitive and affective behaviors observable in children and therefore are better prepared to structure learning experiences to bring about desirable changes in children's behaviors in these two learning domains. More recently, however, attention has been given to movement behaviors that comprise the psychomotor domain. Understanding of this domain serves to increase educators' appreciation of meaningful movement for the development of the child. It provides the essential framework to early childhood readiness programs, which are predominantly movement oriented. Writing by hand is a process categorized as belonging to the psychomotor learning domain, since concern with manipulative skill and perceptual abilities is primary.

The readiness period of the handwriting process consists of three hierarchically arranged stages of muscle control and perceptual skill through which children progress. In the first stage the children make random arm and hand movements. As they play, handling dolls, pushing trucks, and bouncing balls, they develop motor skills that depend on coordination of the larger muscles in the shoulders and upper arms.

The second state of the handwriting readiness period begins when the child makes controlled movements that resemble writing. Arm and hand movements made while handling drawing and painting tools strengthen the muscles that are guiding tools for writing. The finer muscles of the hand and fingers develop control and coordination with eye movements as children string beads and play with clay. Through games that exercise large body muscles and play activities that serve to develop fine hand muscles, children practice making controlled straight, curved, and circular motions of the shapes that later combine as letters and numerals.

In the third stage of readiness for handwriting children develop the ability to copy. They perceive the image and reproduce it. Perception of the image is an essential first step in performing a motor act. It is the process of becoming aware of objects, qualities, or relations by way of the sense organs. The perceptual and motor components combine to produce the act of handwriting. With copying skill and muscle control developed, prewriters move to a point of preparation for the formal school writing lessons presented as part of most primary grades.

## The Components of Handwriting

At some point in children's development it becomes necessary to prepare them for actual letter and numeral formation through experiences aimed at teaching the components of handwriting. A program introducing children to basic handwriting strokes; letter formation, size, and proportion; and to spacing, alignment, and line quality should foster growth in readiness for the more formal handwriting programs of elementary school children. Young children do engage in activities that serve to prepare them for writing by hand, but the development of readiness for handwriting often seems to play a secondary role in its relationship to the development of other academic areas. Concern over the deterioration of handwriting quality suggests that it may be necessary to stress the importance of developing the child's awareness of the components of handwriting.

The strokes basic to handwriting are horizontals ⟶ verticals ↓ diagonals ╱ ╲ and circulars ⊂ ⊃ and (7). As manuscript writing is made up of vertical, horizontal, and slanted lines, plus circles or parts of circles, awareness of letter formation instilled through activities emphasizing the basic handwriting strokes promotes a simple and easily learned way of writing. Therefore, guidance should be provided to help children recognize the fine differences between the letter forms through practice with the basic strokes and to develop a strong visual image of the correct form of each letter.

A second handwriting component, size and proportion, develops as the beginning writer matures in visual discrimination skill, that is, the ability to distinguish correctly between items of difference or recognize similarities. Early visual experiences occur as part of the infant, toddler, and young child's world of physical objects including the people around him. Following experiences with concrete manipulative objects, children begin to be able to recognize varying or similar appearances in symbol forms. Developing visual skill and becoming aware of basic line and shape patterns is accompanied by the capacity to identify sameness or difference in signs like our printed letters and numbers.

Spacing and alignment, too, depend on the writer's visual discrimination skills. Spacing is the most difficult element of manuscript writing because attention must be given to correct spacing not only between letters, but between words, sentences, and lines of writing. Proper alignment occurs as writers check their work to see that letters all rest on a baseline, and that letters of the same size are even in height.

Often math, reading, and science programs, whether specifically planned or spontaneously occurring, regularly engage children in exercises to develop their concepts of sizes and shapes. Along with these, young children need participation in activities that instill awareness of sameness and difference in proportion, spacing, and alignment.

A final component, line quality, is achieved by producing a written line of consistent thickness. Even pressure on the writing instrument — the result of correct hand and body position —will result in even line quality. Steadiness of a line is also checked. A wavering line can be the result of tension and cramped finger position.

To prepare children for being able to produce writing with even line quality, emphasis is placed on activities designed to promote muscle development of the arm, hand, and fingers. Stroking practice with large basic strokes, perhaps at the chalkboard, should occur to strengthen large muscles before beginning writers are asked to handle small tools or work within the confines of small paper. Programs of muscle development exercises contribute to the child's ability to control the writing tools comfortably and produce even line quality.

## Pressure, Speed, and Quality

Legibility is usually considered to be the primary objective of handwriting instruction. The most important thing to look for in children's handwriting is that it is legible even though various forms of certain letters are evident. Among the factors contributing to legibility of handwritten material, the problem of pressure plays an important role. Along with regulation of sitting position, paper position, and pencil position, the amount and points of pressure exerted by the writer affects product legibility.

Pressure in handwriting is observable at three points of contact:

**1.** Pressure of the finger upon the writing instrument,
**2.** Pressure of the writing instrument upon the writing surface, and
**3.** Pressure of the arm and hand resting upon the writing surface.

To promote the development of writing habits that produce legible results with the least amount of effort by the writer, early attention is given to children's sitting, paper, and pencil positions. A table and seat of appropriate height for the writer that allows feet to rest flatly on the floor and enables the child to sit erect with forearms comfortably resting on the table are conducive to promoting good writing position. The hand not holding the writing instrument should be free to hold the paper straight for manuscript writing so that its bottom edge is parallel to the edge of the desk. The paper should be far enough onto the table to force the child's arms to rest lightly on the table surface. Left-handed writers may tilt the paper up and toward the right.

The pencil hold should be relaxed as the pencil is held loosely by the thumb and second finger. The first finger rests more toward the pencil point than the thumb. A comfortable size writing tool rests on the third finger, while the fourth and fifth fingers rest lightly on the writing surface.

The practice of initiating instruction in handwriting for all children regardless of their degree of fine motor control of the hand and drilling for uniformity in pressure and speed among writers should not occur. Children forced to move away from their normal writing tempo write with pressure points varied from regularity which causes decreased legibility. Increases in writing speeds occur appropriately when children practice on individually prescribed or small-group programs where speed changes are encouraged in small steps.

## Sex Differences, Instruction, and Remediation

The development of handwriting skill is closely related to the development of the individual. Studies of handwriting legibility show what appears to be a generally accepted point — there are maturational differences among all students and between males and females. From birth the skeletal development of girls is generally superior to boys, and from birth on females tend to mature earlier than males. It is important, therefore, that programs of beginning handwriting be planned appropriately to meet individual differences and differences between males and females of the same chronological age groups.

Children entering a group situation usually cannot all begin formal handwriting at the same time. Males generally need readiness exercises longer than females due to slower rates of motor development and shorter attention span than girls of the same age. Readiness activities should be planned which engage children in prewriting experiences appropriate to their individual physique, character, personality, age, mental ability, and perceptual maturity. Careful observation of children's levels of operation and working capacities is necessary to help prevent repeated experiences of frustration or failure.

Recognition of the value of individualization in planning pre- and beginning writing programs is not new to education. Some years ago, evidence from research favored individualized analysis and program planning, especially in the area of handling remediation of handwriting difficulties.

Handwriting lessons are of two types — teaching lessons and practice lessons. Children are introduced to new letters through directed lessons taught by an adult who will later prescribe practice lessons. Practice lessons enable the children to rehearse the formation of those letters that they found difficult to form during the teaching lesson. As the handwriting teacher, your responsibility is to guide the cycle of teaching, observe student difficulties, and prescribe practice. Careful observation and analysis of difficulties contribute to helping children in need of remediation to improve handwriting skill, thereby increasing legibility.

Just as children are not all ready to begin meeting writing formally at the same time, not all children will need practice on the same letter forms for the same length of time. Growth in writing by hand occurs most when programs include teaching, observation, evaluation, and practice for individuals or small groups formed by common need.

## The Beginner's Handwriting Tools

Traditionally, the tools used by the beginning writer are the large kindergarten pencil and paper that is either unlined or lined at intervals of one and one-half inch. Research presently available suggests that neither of these special supplies is absolutely necessary for beginning writers. Some investigators claim that children write best when using a primary pencil, while others argue in defense of the standard school pencil. Tradition dictates the use of varying sizes of paper, while research gives no justification for requiring beginners to use paper that is different from the kind they will use as adults. In contradiction to current and past practice, the standard adult-sized pencil and paper with half-inch spacing are satisfactory tools for use by young children as they begin the task of learning to write by hand. Until further evidence is available, it appears satisfactory to allow beginning writers to select and use the tools they find comfortable for manipulation and control.

## Copying Versus Tracing

After children show ability to write basic handwriting strokes by handling tools acceptably, they begin to practice forming letters of the alphabet. Following practice of individual letters, children combine letters to form words for the eventual purpose of communicating through writing.

Alphabet letter-formation practice can occur in two forms — letter tracing and letter copying. Whether copying or tracing is the better method of practice is an area of concern and controversy to persons responsible for children's handwriting instruction. Studies, primarily focusing on the issue of letter formation when letters must be reproduced from memory, reveal that copying produces better learning than tracing.

## DIAGNOSIS AND EVALUATION

An important component in any educational program is the evaluation of the work students are doing. In the teaching of handwriting, evaluation of the students' work occurs prior to instruction, during the teaching, and after practice of the writing element being taught. Prior to instruction, teachers must observe and evaluate their pupils in order to plan appropriate lessons. During the teaching, observation of the pupils occurs to assess their execution of the tasks at hand. After practice, evaluation is done again to recognize the pupils' success of practice while diagnosing problems that require additional instruction or remediation.

Teachers responsible for handwriting education find informal and formal evaluation tools available for assistance in making observations of children's writing. *Informal* tools are checklists, rating scales, and anecdotal record sheets designed for identifying children's handwriting behaviors. Such tools usually serve to measure the child's individual progress, noting and comparing today's abilities with the student's own earlier achievements. *Formal* evaluation tools are those tests commercially developed to measure the students' achievements in comparison to a set standard. In handwriting, the formal measures match the child's writing to a model.

Informal and formal observation and handwriting evaluation instruments are grouped according to the general level of abilities they seek to assess. The first group includes tools for assessing readiness for handwriting. These measures are usually administered with preschool and kindergarten children, but may be used with older children experiencing handwriting difficulties. Once children have demonstrated handwriting readiness and begin lessons on letter and numeral formation, they are periodically given tests to assess their writing abilities and attention to the major handwriting components. These tests appear as a regular part of the elementary school child's program.

The following sections more specifically identify the preschool and kindergarten readiness measures and the primary grade writing achievement tests and scales.

## Tools for Assessing Readiness

Informal assessments of readiness for handwriting take the form of checklists, rating scales, or anecdotal records. Checklists are designed to allow quick marking of whether or not the persons being observed possess the skills in the list. Such lists require a "yes" or "no" reply concerning the child's ability to execute a specific task or exhibit a specific behavior. (See Figure 5-1.) Rating scales depend on similar lists of tasks, abilities, or behaviors but allow the observer to identify a degree of execution rather than a simple "yes" or "no." Rating scales are designed to require the observer to identify that a child can execute a task "always-frequently-occasionally-seldom-or never." (See Figure 5-2.) A third assessment form, the anecdotal record, is designed to allow observers to write down what the child is doing and use the collected discourse to evaluate achievement after the observation and recording period. (See Figure 5-3.)

Checklists, rating scales, and anecdotal record-style observation forms require observers to select or develop lists of tasks, abilities, or behaviors unique to the area being assessed. For handwriting programs, the first use of such lists occurs in the assessment of children's readiness for handwriting.

When are children ready to write? Anecdotal records of the child's exhibitions suggesting readiness for handwriting include notes about the

---

CHECKLIST

Observer:_____ Date:_____

Skill:   writes horizontal stroke (—) from left to right

               Students                      Yes—No

1.

2.

3.

4.

5.

Note:   Check each child several times during the term to determine if growth has
taken place.

---

FIGURE 5-1.   SAMPLE CHECKLIST FORM

---

RATING SCALE

Observer:_____ Date:_____

Skill:   uses acceptable positioning of body and writing tools

Students

Never     Seldom     Occasionally     Frequently     Always

1.

2.

3.

4.

5.

---

FIGURE 5-2.   SAMPLE RATING SCALE FORM

"hieroglyphics" brought to school from home, attempts demonstrating desire to write names, and the ability to copy simple shapes and designs. Note also the child's use of tools that resemble writing instruments, muscle development, and general eye-hand coordination.

The following list is suggested (4) for assessing readiness for handwriting. Does the child have:

1. A mental age six and one-half to seven,
2. Interest and desire to write,
3. Adequate visual acuity and discrimination,
4. Understanding of left to right directionality,
5. Adequate muscular coordination,
6. Proper arm bone development,
7. Hand dominance,
8. Social and emotional maturity,
9. Language maturity, and
10. A school writing program suitable to his maturity?

Another source of items for handwriting readiness checklists and scales is the information included on scope and sequence charts from commercial handwriting companies. Most companies suggest that some attention be given to the child's ability to:

1. Produce horizontal, vertical, slant, and circular lines,
2. Follow directions,
3. Work with simple sequencing,
4. Manipulate handwriting tools,
5. Make visual discriminations, and
6. Exhibit some degree of visual memory.

Teachers often prepare their own checklists. Teachers preparing checklists appropriately select items by giving attention to the components of handwriting. Based upon the components of handwriting, a checklist such as that in figure 5-4 is proposed (see page 156).

Formal assessments of readiness for handwriting exist usually in the form of subtest components of general readiness tests. Such components are labeled as copying tests and require the children to copy a printed design presented to them. One such test is the copying section of the Metropolitan Readiness Test (Level II) administered to children who are completing kindergarten or beginning first grade.

Not specifically prepared to predict success in handwriting, the Metropolitan Copying Test is designed to enable teachers to observe pupils' abilities to write their names and to copy a simple sentence. Each pupil writes his own first name and then copies the sentence as much like

```
┌─────────────────────────────────────────────────────────────────┐
│                        ANECDOTAL RECORD                           │
│                                                                   │
│  Student Observed_____     │
│                                                                   │
│  Date of Observation_____      │
│                                                                   │
│  Time of Observation  _____      │
│                     Notes of reminder to the observer:            │
│  1.  Determine in advance what to record; be alert for behaviors. │
│  2.  Observe and record enough to make your record meaningful.    │
│  3.  Record observations as soon as possible.                     │
│  4.  Limit each anecdote to a brief description of one incident.  │
│  5.  Keep your description and interpretation separate.           │
│  6.  Record both negative and positive incidents.                 │
│  7.  Collect a number of anecdotes on a pupil before drawing any  │
│      inferences about typical behavior.                           │
│                                                                   │
│  OBSERVATION: _____      │
│                                                                   │
└─────────────────────────────────────────────────────────────────┘
```

**FIGURE 5-3.   SAMPLE ANECDOTAL RECORD FORM**

the model as he can. This skill is an indication of eye-hand coordination, a visual-perceptual, motor-development skill important for success in beginning reading and mathematics. Teachers also get information about their pupils' handwriting skills already acquired, handwriting skills to be taught next, and the general level of coordination of visual discrimination and fine motor skills.

Another test not specifically designed to render information predicting success with handwriting, but examining components related to writing, is the Perceptual Forms Test. The Perceptual Forms Test, for individual or group testings of children six to eight and one-half, intends to discover the child who lacks that degree of eye-hand coordination considered requisite for beginning school tasks. Children taking the Perceptual Forms Test draw seven figures presented to them and finish incomplete forms shown.

## Tools for Assessing Handwriting

Continuously throughout instructional handwriting programs, it is necessary to assess the pupils' accomplishments. Identifying the skills that children use satisfactorily allows teachers to plan and prescribe appropriate future lessons. Informal assessment of handwriting abilities occurs as part of daily programs. Formal assessments are generally used less frequently during a school year. Informal assessments seek to examine the individual's improvements over previous work, while formal measures

| HANDWRITING READINESS student names ⟶ | | | | | |
|---|---|---|---|---|---|
| makes verticals on upright surface | | | | | |
| makes horizontals on upright surface | | | | | |
| makes diagonals on upright surface | | | | | |
| makes circulars on upright surface | | | | | |
| makes verticals on horizontal surface | | | | | |
| makes horizontals on horizontal surface | | | | | |
| makes diagonals on horizontal surface | | | | | |
| makes circulars on horizontal surface | | | | | |
| makes strokes of even line quality | | | | | |
| makes strokes with comfortable speed | | | | | |
| has adequate eye-hand coordination | | | | | |
| understands left-right directionality | | | | | |
| understands general handwriting vocabulary (line, space, writing position, and so forth) | | | | | |
| understands directional handwriting vocabulary (left/right, up/down) | | | | | |
| understands visual discrimination handwriting vocabulary (larger/smaller, straight/curved, open/closed) | | | | | |
| understands spatial relations handwriting vocabulary (above/on/below, side, bottom, top/bottom) | | | | | |

FIGURE 5-4. CHECKLIST FOR HANDWRITING READINESS

compare the students' writings with standard scales or commercial models.

During the first year of handwriting instruction children begin to practice the formation of letters and numerals. Each letter is introduced individually with direction concerning the letter's stroke and sequence pattern. Teaching lessons, followed by practice lessons, give instructors time to observe students' abilities to form each letter taught. Checklists, rating scales, and anecdotal records are tools appropriate for recording pupil progress on letter and numeral formation.

| LETTER FORM ASSESSMENT | name | | | | | |
|---|---|---|---|---|---|---|
| A / a | | | | | | |
| B / b | | | | | | |
| C / c | | | | | | |
| D / d  etc. | | | | | | |

**FIGURE 5-5.   SAMPLE CHECKLIST FOR ASSESSING LETTER FORMATION**

Letter form assessments are completed to record progress in children's practice lessons or to keep account of their letter forms exhibited in daily usage.

Lists like that in Figure 5-5 may also include the categories identified as components of handwriting. Check should continue throughout writing programs as to whether or not children regularly attend to proper spacing, alignment, size, proportion, and the presence or absence of slant. In addition, proper pencil, paper, and body writing position should be encouraged. Adding positional items to the checklist insures that they, too, be watched.

As in the assessment of readiness for handwriting, examination of writing scope and sequence charts from commercial handwriting companies acquaints teachers with items to be included in assessment lists. Along with noting the completion of individual letter stroke sequences, most handwriting companies suggest that assessors identify the particular strokes within the letters which seem to cause each individual difficulty. With such information, practice can be prescribed on the vertical, horizontal, diagonal, or circular stroke causing problems. Program planning can focus on meeting individual needs.

For informal assessment, the standard of acceptance is established by the classroom teacher. Sometimes, school curriculum developers decide on local standards, but it is the teacher's task to decide what work by pupils is satisfactory. Remembering that the focus of handwriting is the production of legible material, teachers use informal observations to assess children's improvement from one lesson to the next. Major concern is for helping individuals grow from where they are to an acceptable, legible standard.

Formal assessment of the handwriting by children is made by comparing children's work with normative scales or models. Along with the normative samples provided by most commercial handwriting programs, scales published apart from handwriting programs are available.

The Thorndike Scale for Handwriting (1910-1912), developed by E. L. Thorndike, was the first scientifically calibrated instrument for the measurement of an educational product. Designed to be used with writers in grades two through eight, the Thorndike Scale includes handwriting at fifteen different quality levels with scoring for speed and equality.

In 1912 a second scale was developed to evaluate handwriting of children in grades two through eight. The Ayers Scale, revised in 1917 and known as the Ayers Measuring Scale for Handwriting: Gettysburg Edition, was designed as a measuring device rather than a standard. The Ayers Scale measures speed and quality at eight quality levels.

A five-quality level scale for each of grades one to eight was provided in 1915 by Freeman. The Freeman Scale placed emphasis on legibility and form with some attention to the components of handwriting.

Unlike some of the earlier scales, the Evaluation Scales for Guiding Growth in Handwriting (1958) are easy to score. Presenting seven scales at each level of grade from first to ninth, the evaluation scales are most useful as a self-diagnostic device for focusing the pupil's attention to handwriting form.

Teachers using measurement and evaluation scales to assess handwriting should consider what use will be made of the collected scores before using these instruments with children. Since legibility is the key to handwriting for communication purposes, a simple observation of the readibility of children's writing may adequately serve assessment purposes. Scales are most appropriately used as diagnostic tools, allowing teachers to make accurate prescription of writing components children are to practice.

## INSTRUCTIONAL STRATEGIES

Child growth and development theories identify three basic kinds of responses exhibited by children. Earliest in life, children make *reflex responses,* those that occur automatically as a result of stimulation. Later, *maturational responses,* those within the child, and *learned responses,* those resulting from training, are made too. As learning environments are created and instructional programs are designed, consideration is given to children's use of these kinds of responses.

In the years before school and the early school years, children's programs promote learning by providing an environment in which children are encouraged to respond. Encouragement occurs through the intelligent placement of materials with which children can interact or through the conversations and questions discussed. Material and human interactions permit reflex, maturational, and learned responses.

To accommodate varying response types, an environment created to foster growth in children's handwriting abilities should include materials and activities on which children can work individually or cooperatively. Some experiences ready a child for writing simply through the manipulation of tools. Other experiences develop readiness as children are directed through exercises specifically designed to develop the skill of writing by hand.

The following suggestions are activities to include in children's environments prepared to foster growth in areas related to handwriting.

## Practice on Basic Handwriting Strokes
### Basic chalkboard practice with circular and straight lines.

*Purpose:*

To move the arms, hands, and fingers in circular and straight line patterns.

To practice drawing the strokes basic to handwriting.

*Materials:* Chalkboard and chalk or similar surface and tool.
*Procedure:* Have the childen stand facing the chalkboard to make:

**1.** Repetitive circular motions with chalk held in the dominant hand moving from the ten o'clock position

**2.** Circular motions with both hands moving from outside of the body to the outside

left hand      right hand

**3.** Repetitive circular motions with the chalk held in the dominant hand moving from the two o'clock position

**4.** Circles with both hands moving from the outside of the body to the inside

left hand      right hand

Have the children facing the chalkboard use both hands to:

**1.** Make two lines from up to down

**2.** Make lines with one going up and one going down simultaneously

**3.** Make lines horizontally from inside out

**4.** Make lines horizontally from outside in

**5.** Make lines diagonally from outside in (up to down)

**6.** Make lines diagonally from inside out(up to down)

*Variations:* See the following sections concerning basic strokes on upright surfaces.

**Vertical strokes on upright surface.**
*Purpose:*

To move the arm, hand, and fingers in vertical motions, emphasizing the downward movement.

To draw vertical downward strokes with various tools on varying surfaces.

To make downward vertical strokes on surfaces in an upright position such as chalkboard and easels.

*Materials:* Container of water and chalkboard surface.

*Procedure:* Have the children stand facing the chalkboard. Direct them to wet the index finger of their dominant hand and draw vertical lines of wetness on the board. Emphasize making the strokes downward, pulling from top to bottom. The lines will evaporate as drawing continues or children may blow dry the board. Games of counting or drawing to rhythm may accompany the stroke practice.

*Variations:*

    **1.** Use the index finger of both hands to make two vertical downward strokes simultaneously.

    **2.** Use paintbrushes of varying widths to paint with the water.

    **3.** Use chalk of varying colors for the stroking practice.

    **4.** Paint outdoors as well as inside.

**5.** Provide fingerpaint to be used on easels, murals, waxed paper, foil, and other surfaces.

**6.** Suspend yarn in front of the children and have them pull a hand from the top to the bottom of the suspended piece.

**7.** Provide balls or corks on elastic which children can pull down, stretch, and release.

**8.** Wipe the chalkboard or a piece of dark paper with a dusty chalkboard eraser and allow the children to make vertical downward strokes with their fingers.

**9.** Put drops of water at the top of the chalkboard and encourage children to follow them with their index fingers.

**10.** Trace the fingers along vertical lines in the environment (mortar between bricks, door and window frames, room corners).

### Horizontal strokes on upright surface.
*Purpose:*

To move the arm, hand, and fingers in horizontal motions, emphasizing the left-to-right movement.

To draw left-to-right horizontal strokes with varying tools on various surfaces.

To make left-to-right horizontal strokes on upright surfaces.

Use the same materials, procedures, and variations for practicing the stroke as were used for practice of the vertical strokes on upright surfaces. Focus now is placed on the left-to-right movement.

### Diagonal strokes on upright surfaces.
*Purpose:*

To move the arm, hand, and fingers in diagonal motions, emphasizing the downward movement.

To draw diagonal downward strokes with various tools on varying surfaces.

To make downward diagonal strokes on upright surfaces.

Use materials, procedures, and appropriate variations for practicing these strokes as were used for practice of the vertical strokes on upright surfaces. Focus is placed on the downward slanted movement.

### Circular strokes on upright surfaces.
*Purpose:*

To move the arm, hand, and fingers in circular motions, practicing circles drawn clockwise and counterclockwise.

To draw circular strokes with various tools on varying surfaces.

To make circular clockwise and counterclockwise strokes on upright surfaces.

Use the materials, procedures, and appropriate variations for practicing these strokes as were used for practice of the vertical strokes on upright surfaces. Focus is directed toward clockwise and counterclockwise movements.

*Additional variations:*
1. Place a large game-type spinner in the chalktray or leaning against a wall and have the children push the spinner around with their fingers.
2. Tack one end of a string to the bulletin board. With a cork on the other end of the string allow the children to hold the cork and move it with circular motions around the tack.
3. Trace circular lines inside stencils of various sizes. Focus on the motion, not the construction of perfect circles.
4. Erase with circular motions on a dusted upright surface such as chalkboard or dusty easel.
5. Twirl a three-foot length of crepe-paper streamer in large circles to the rhythm of music being played.

**Handwriting strokes practiced on horizontally positioned surfaces.**
*Purpose:*
To move the arm, hand, and fingers in vertical, horizontal, diagonal, and circular motions, respectively emphasizing the downward, left-to-right, top-to-bottom, and clockwise/counterclockwise movements.
To draw the basic handwriting strokes with various tools on varying surfaces.
To make basic handwriting strokes on surfaces in the horizontal position such as tabletops and floors.

*Materials:* Use materials appropriate to the items mentioned within the variations section below.
*Procedure:* Using the various materials and ideas below focus on having the children:

1. Draw a set of horizontal lines stroking back and forth, later just left to right.
2. Draw a set of vertical lines stroking up and down, later just top to bottom (reaching away from the body and pulling toward the body).
3. Draw diagonal lines starting away from the body and stroking toward the body.
4. Draw circular lines, one set from the ten o'clock position and one set to the two o'clock position.

*Variations:* For practice making handwriting movements on horizontally positioned surfaces try the following:

1. Box lids containing sand about one-quarter inch deep.
2. Fingerpaint, pudding, or shaving cream on waxed paper, foil, mirrors, or similar surfaces.
3. Chalkdust on dark paper.
4. Chalk on wet paper, wet chalk on dry paper.
5. Brushes stroking through liquid tempura paint mixed with other substances to provide varying textures (salt, oatmeal, rice, egg shells, soap flakes, coffee, sawdust.)
6. Brushes on powdered tempura paint mixed with condensed milk, buttermilk, or liquid laundry starch to produce, respectively, shiny, chalky, or creamy paint.
7. Practice the basic strokes with various hand-held tools (bottle caps, popsicle sticks, spools, vegetables).
8. Stretch clay from a ball in the straight line-stroke directions.
9. Stretch elastic that has one end fastened to a board in the straight line-stroke directions.
10. Push small toys such as cars along paths on a map containing vertical, horizontal, diagonal, and circular roads.

## Rhythmic Responses

As children gain proficiency in producing the strokes basic to handwriting, it is possible to begin practice which focuses on line quality and speed. Correct, even line formation is the goal, not rapid production. Development of a writing rhythm that yields lines of equal darkness, written and not sketched slowly, may be fostered through exercises requiring responses to rhythm. Making the strokes to musical accompaniment allows for varying the pace to accommodate the writer with the intention of increasing tempo as speed develops along with accuracy of line formation. The goal is to reach a production rate that comfortably allows the writer to produce accurately formed lines of even pressure.

Recordings or piano music may be used to help children practice making horizontal, diagonal, and circular lines. As they listen or sing along, a chorus of "Here We Go Round the Mulberry Bush" or "This Old Man" might make the often tedious stroking practice a pleasant exercise. Circular motions for going around the bush and vertical downward strokes to represent the old man permits practiced strokes paced rhythmically to eliminate sketching.

Traditional nursery rhymes and preschool verses also allow practice through regulated speed. Consider Humpty Dumpty and his historic fall. As recitation occurs these accompanying strokes may be practiced:

Humpty Dumpty sat on a wall

O O — — —

Humpty Dumpty had a great fall

O O — — — —

All the king's horses and

/ / / / / /

all the king's men

| | | |

Couldn't put Humpty together again.

O O O  O O

A model of the strokes to accompany the rhymes may be shown by a leader, or children may be left to select their own strokes to practice. Some observation and direction by a leader should occur, though, to insure correct direction of the stroking.

*Purpose:*
> To make vertical, horizontal, diagonal, and circular strokes to the varying rhythms of songs, verses, and rhymes.
> To write strokes basic to handwriting with line qualities of equal pressure.

*Materials:* Writing surface and tools.

*Procedure:* Have children practice making vertical, horizontal, diagonal, and circular lines to varying rhythms of songs, verses, and rhymes. Work toward a speed that yields accurately formed strokes of equal pressure and written, not sketched. Use the following rhymes and lines, then design others to children's poems and recordings.

1. Fall, fall rain from way up high,

| | | | | | |

Fall from the dark and cloudy sky.

| | | | | | |

2.  Buses, trucks, and cars have wheels

    O  O  O    O

    To ride the interstate

    ▬▬  ▬▬  ▬▬

    Along the road and down the hill

    ▬▬  ▬▬      \  \

    Hurry, don't be late.

    O  O  O

3.  These little lines are fun to make.

    ▬▬  ▬  ▬  ▬  ▬  ▬  ▬▬

    I'll make them all day long.

    ▬  ▬▬  ▬▬  ▬  ▬  ▬▬

    I'll always pull from left to right,

    ▬  ▬▬  ▬  ▬▬  ▬  ▬  ▬▬

    Then I'll be right, not wrong.

    ▬▬  ▬  ▬  ▬▬  ▬  ▬▬

4.  A big balloon went floating by,

    OO    O  O

    I saw that it was yellow.

    O  O  O

    I reached to pull it from the sky,

    |    |    |    |

    But couldn't reach the fellow.

    |    |    |

5. A sliding board is lots of fun,

\ \ \ \

I'd like to slide on a great big one.

\ \ \ \

I'd climb the ladder carefully

— — — —

And slide right down with a great big WHEEE!!

\ \ \ \

## Visual Control — Eye-Hand Coordination and Left/Right Directionality

Many activities available in a young child's environment are appropriate for fostering growth in eye-hand coordination. The following list suggests those exercises generally available for developing visual motor control.

| | |
|---|---|
| bouncing a ball | pasting |
| building with blocks | puzzles |
| modeling with clay | rhythm exercises |
| climbing | sand and water play |
| coloring | sewing |
| cutting | stringing beads |
| dot-to-dot exercises | throwing activities |
| drawing | tool manipulation |
| fastening activities | tracing |
| easel work | woodworking |
| painting | |

Along with activities usually provided, the following ideas may be helpful in developing children's visual control, eye-hand coordination, and awareness of left to right directionality.

*Purpose:* To track moving objects with the eyes.

*Materials:* Collection of strings about twenty inches long with a ball, cork, or similar item attached to one end.

*Procedure:* Have the children use the strings to:

**1.** Stand, swing the object back and forth in front of their body, and follow the movement of the ball with their eyes.
**2.** Swing the object forward and backward while tracking.
**3.** Swing the ball in circular motions while tracking.

*Variations:*

1. Place a star or other cutout design on the end of the minute hand of a toy clock. Turn the hands while children track the movement of the cutout.
2. Slide objects down sliding board or other inclined plane with children watching the item move.
3. While children lie on their backs on a carpeted floor swing a ball on a string over them in varying directions as they track the moving object.
4. Place several different solid-colored marbles in a box lid, shake the lid gently, and ask children to focus on a particular color marble.
5. Inflate a large balloon, release it, and have children follow its movement by watching from where they are seated.

*Purpose:* To manipulate objects while watching their movements, thereby exercising coordination of the eyes and hands.

*Materials:* Small objects that children can pick up. Use the materials appropriate to each activity listed in the variations below.

*Procedure:* Provide games and activities that require the children to handle small objects by picking up particular ones, reordering them, or placing them into containers. Such exercises develop the coordination between children's eye and hand movements.

*Variations:*

1. Provide a box of assorted solid-color beads or marbles from which children select only those of the color named to them.
2. Provide a box of Ping Pong balls along with an empty box. Direct the children to move the balls from box to box, one at a time, to the rhythm of the music which can be played.
3. Have children use their dominant hands to put pegs in a pegboard. Suggest they remove pegs with the opposite hand.
4. Supply ten corks on strings hung side by side spaced three inches apart. Direct the child to push each cork lightly, beginning on the left and progressing right. Vary directions to maintain the child's interest by suggesting:
   tap every other cork
   count as you tap
   tap to the rhythm of music or rhyme
   tap with the subdominant hand
   alternate hands
   tap with one hand; stop the cork with the other hand
5. Allow children to play at stacking and construction activities with small pieces of sponge or foam rubber, varying the piece sizes for consideration of children's various hand sizes.

*Purpose:* To have the child's eyes follow an object as it moves from left to right.

*Materials:* Movable objects that children can track with their eyes. Use the materials appropriate to each activity listed in the variations below.

*Procedure:* Have the children sitting an appropriate distance from an object so that they can track its left-to-right movement with their eyes. At first, allow children to move their heads as they follow the movement. Later, encourage only eye movement as the head remains still.

*Variations:*

1. Shine a flashlight beam to the left side of the room in front of children. Move the beam slowly to the right. Turn off the flashlight and go back to the left side and begin again. Lines may be horizontals or diagonals, straight or wavy, but always left to right.

2. Roll balls, marbles, and similar round objects of varying sizes in the chalktray or piano book rack. When the objects get to the right end of the tray, carry them to the left and repeat the exercise.

3. Pull a truck attached to a string across the room in front of the children. Almost any blocks, boxes, toys, or child's plaything can be moved left to right in this manner.

4. While children watch a small animal run through a maze, have them raise their hands when the animal goes in a left to right direction. To eliminate confusion have all children watch from the same side of the maze. This exercise allows the teacher to observe children recognizing a left-to-right movement among movements in other directions.

5. Provide paper strips with a green starting dot on the left and a line traveling right to a red dot signaling stop. Lines may be straight, wavy, or composed of connected diagonals.

## Handwriting Vocabulary

As children begin the practice of writing by hand, they not only face the difficulty of manipulating essential writing tools but are also asked to handle a set of vocabulary words that take on new meaning as they relate to writing. For the beginning writer, the task of finding the top of a tree or toy truck is certainly different from finding the top of a piece of paper. Even though going down the steps and going down a page sound much the same, spatially they are different. Children have learned that doors, windows and jack-in-the-boxes will open and close, but imagine their questions when first experiencing open and closed curved lines. As in other subject areas, young children may grow in their readiness for handwriting by having experience with the vocabulary and concepts unique to the art before formal handwriting instruction begins.

The terms and concepts that appear in beginning handwriting lessons seem to fall into groups identified below. The vocabulary from each group and activities for children's experiences with those words follows the group listing.

1. General handwriting vocabulary
2. Directional handwriting vocabulary
3. Visual discrimination handwriting vocabulary
4. Spatial relation handwriting vocabulary

*Purpose:* To discuss general handwriting vocabulary through manipulation of objects.

*Materials:* Use materials identified in the variations below.

*Procedure:* Direct the children in activities designed to provide experiences in hearing and using general handwriting vocabulary. Discuss, demonstrate, and provide activities that help children develop understanding of the following concepts:

| | |
|---|---|
| a line | alignment |
| a space | size |
| spacing | proportion |
| slant | writing position |

*Variations:*

1. Place objects (magazine pictures, paper cutouts, felt shapes) on a flannel board or cardboard poster, attaching the objects in a row or column and discuss their placement in positional relationship to each other. Have children arrange pictures in rows and columns, spacing them evenly to avoid overlap. Discuss the spacing, alignment, and sizes of the objects.
2. Draw lines on cardboard or use string or yarn as a guideline for placing objects in rows, placing objects left to right, stressing placement on the line.
3. When placing objects or pictures on guidelines, put them in groups representing letters in words. Discuss the spacing between these groups, trying to draw relationship to printed word and sentence form. Discuss the slant or absence of it in the placement of the objects.
4. Provide children with materials to practice identifying the lines and the spaces. Unlined paper such as paper bags, wrapping paper, butcher paper, or purchased plain paper may be folded and used along with various types of commercially lined papers. Ask

children to trace the lines with their fingers or a crayon and color in the spaces. Discuss the concept of lines and spaces as they pertain to writing paper.

5. Discussing and pointing out certain occurrences in the environment will also demonstrate the concepts of alignment and spacing to children. Observe birds sitting on a telephone line, clothespins on a laundry line, or parking meters along the sidewalk as well as cars parked at the football game, trees growing beside the road, or windows in a large building. The child can see objects he recognizes and talk about lined or evenly spaced objects and those of equal or varying heights. Drinking glasses arranged in the kitchen cupboard or shoes aligned in the closet are examples of these concepts in the child's home surroundings.

6. Use pictures, games, and demonstrations to discuss proper position for sitting when preparing to write. Experiment in the three bears style with table and chair sets that are too big, too little, and just right.

*Purpose:* To discuss directional handwriting vocabulary through manipulation of objects.

*Materials:* Use materials identified in the variations below.

*Procedure:* Direct the children in activities designed to provide experiences in hearing and using directional handwriting vocabulary. Discuss, demonstrate, and provide activities that help children develop understanding of the following directions as they relate to writing on paper.

left — right
up — down

*Variations:*

1. Provide a floor sheet or butcher paper with a green left edge, black middle line, and a red right edge. Children may stand single file on the black line so left/green and right/red are appropriate. Following the leader's command, the children can side-step left to green or right to red.

2. Put a green line on the left and a red line on the right of the inside of a box lid. Give the child a marble to put in the lid, and instruct him to roll the marble to the side named by the leader. Later, paste a piece of writing paper to the inside of the lid so the child can see the marble rolling to the left and right of writing paper, too. A small toy car may replace the marble for variation. The same box can be turned so green is up and red is down.

3. Prepare a supply of papers with a green/left edge, a black line down the middle, and a red/right edge. Crayons, magic markers or

colored stars can be used to mark the papers' edges. Direct children to draw green diagonals from the center line to the left/green edge and red diagonals to the right/red edge. Try red and green fingerpaint diagonals pulled from the center line to the edges.

**4.** With paper containing a colored line, row of dots, stars, or other design across the top and a different color across the bottom, direct children to go to the color at the top and roll a crayon or similar cylindrical object down to the other colored line. Pick up the crayon, go back to the top color, and roll it again. Be sure to name the color of the line as well as the terms up and down. Change the movable object and play games for variation while stressing up and down.

**5.** Supply paper containing a row of pictures, designs, or stamps across the top and bottom and a column of items on the left and right edges. Each row and column should be different from the other row and column. Place a dot in the center of the page. Give the children directions to draw from the dot going left to the picture, start up at the star and draw to the dot, and so on. Focus attention on the vocabulary.

*Purpose:* To discuss the visual discrimination vocabulary related to handwriting.

*Materials:* Use materials identified in the variations below.

*Procedure:* Direct the children in activities designed to provide experiences in hearing and using visual discrimination vocabulary. Discuss, demonstrate, and provide activities which help children develop understanding of the following concepts.

| larger | — | smaller |
| straight line | — | curved line |
| open curve | — | closed curve |

*Variations:*

**1.** For practicing the use of larger and smaller as they relate to designs on a printed page, supply pages containing two line designs identical in all respects except size. Put two paper rectangles with each page and direct children to hide the designs by covering them with the rectangles. Discuss the comparative relationships using the terms larger and smaller.

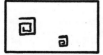 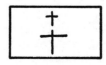 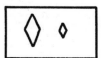

**2.** Supply a collection of string-like materials (yarn, thread, pipe cleaners, shoe laces), and help children make and discuss straight and curved lines.

**3.** Provide a set of papers each with one straight or curved line. Ask children to put string on the lines in the same shape as drawn on the papers.

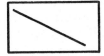 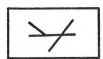 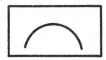 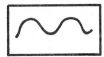

**4.** Do variations two and three above using and discussing open and closed curves.

**5.** Using decks of cards prepared with straight or curved lines, ask the children to group the cards into line types. Repeat the exercise using open- and closed-line cards.

*Purpose:* To discuss the spatial-relation vocabulary related to handwriting.

*Materials:* Use the materials identified in the variations below.

*Procedure:* Direct the children in activities designed to provide experiences in hearing and using spatial relation vocabulary. Discuss; demonstrate, and provide activities that help children develop understanding of the following positions as they relate to writing on paper.

above — on — below
on top of — at the bottom
side
middle

*Variations:*

**1.** To help children develop awareness of these terms as they refer to locations on paper, introduce each place by discussing its location in respect to the parts of a house. Give children a paper with a picture of a house to put on the table in front of them as they listen to the names of the parts of a piece of paper. (See house on next page.)

Following the discussion, give the children pieces of another house to match to the one pictured in front of them. Directions

might include, "Put the roof on the top of the house. See how it goes almost to the top of your paper. Put your finger on the top of the house. Is your finger also near the top of the paper?"

2. Use a paper plate to make a mask while discussing the addition of features above, below, in the middle, and so on. Discuss the terms while children work with the plate resting on the table, not held up in the air. When writing, the paper is usually resting on a horizontal surface.

3. Give each child a paper and collection of paper shapes or small toys. Give directions for placement of the shapes or toys on the paper. Showing a model of what the design would look like if directions are followed correctly, help the children correct their designs. Sample directions might include, "Put the toy boat in the middle of your paper. Now place the yellow fish below the boat." Try making up stories to accompany the directions.

4. Using a piece of paper as a placemat and cut out eating tools, direct children to set a pretend table by putting the pieces as indicated by the terms used by the teacher. Possible suggestions include, "Put the glass above the plate. Put the fork on the napkin." Cut-out pictures of food can be added, too.

5. Direct children to use the piece of paper provided to them as a work space to place colored cubes above, below, on, and next to one another. Have them use the words and make placements at the top, middle, bottom, and side of the work space.

## Beginning Formal Writing

When prewriters have shown readiness to begin the lessons typical of elementary school writing programs, it is necessary to plan lessons which focus on three elements of beginning handwriting. Beginning handwriting lessons should include introduction to the stroke and sequence patterns for letter formation, exercise in making the transition from writing on unlined paper to writing on lined paper, and practice in attention to the handwriting components as they relate to letters on lines.

**Letter formation.** In order for young children to write for communication, they must learn to form the letters which eventually they will combine into words and sentences. Prior to or along with study of the form of individual letters, it may be beneficial to help beginning writers become aware of several rules that can be applied to correctly forming letters of the alphabet. Although some variations exist among the commercial handwriting companies' letter formation stroke and sequence charts, the application of these rules will help children form manuscript letters in a style acceptable to most programs.

Suggested stroke and sequence rules to apply in letter formation:

- of the strokes needed for each letter, make the verticals first, horizontals next, then diagonals and circular strokes
- within the order of the above rule, make the left-most stroke first and progress right

(left vertical, right vertical, left diagonal, right diagonal)
- where applicable make top strokes first and progress downward

(vertical, top circular, bottom circular)
(circular, halfstroke)

- make half strokes last

*Purpose:* To examine, explore and discuss the shape and formation of letters of the alphabet.

*Materials:*
Varying size sandpaper shapes of the letter
White drawing paper for each child
Pipe cleaners or popsicle sticks
Crayons
Box lid containing sand

*Procedure:* Draw the letter being taught while the children watch. Discuss the sequence and strokes required to form the letter. Distribute sandpaper shapes of the letter for children to feel. Direct the children to put white paper over the sandpaper letter and rub over it with crayon. Discuss the appearing shape. Repeat the crayon rubbing using varying colors and letter sizes. Next, distribute pipe cleaners and/or popsicle sticks with which the letters can be formed by placing the sticks and/or pipe cleaners on the crayon rub model.

Finger-traced letters in the sand provide exercise in making the letter being studied. Discuss the letter's formation by using handwriting vocabulary introduced in earlier activities.

*Variations:*

1. Give the children a model of a correctly formed letter followed by attempts to reproduce it, some correctly done, others incorrect. Ask children to find those that correctly match the model. For handwriting purposes, the focus is not on the name of the letter, but rather the strokes required to form that letter.
2. Allow the children to use their bodies as straight or curved lines and combine with other children to form the letters by resting on the floor.
3. Give children a model of a correctly formed letter followed by an incomplete reproduction of that letter. Direct the children to finish the reproduction so it is formed like the correct letter model.
4. Draw a letter as a model while discussing its form. Have the children model that letter with clay. A salt clay recipe mix may be used to provide modeling clay, which may be left to harden and be painted. Letters may be modeled free form or by placing clay pieces on a paper model of the letter.
5. Discuss the number of strokes and the shape and arrangement of the letter lines of letters that are available in the environment.

**Transition from unlined to lined paper with focus on the handwriting components.**

*Purpose:* To write letters on lined paper while experimenting with slant, spacing, size, alignment, and proportion of letters.

*Material:* Use the materials appropriate to each activity as identified in the variations below.

*Procedure:* Supply paper prepared to guide children's transition from writing on unlined paper to writing on lined paper.

*Variations:*

1. Give children a set of cut-out letters and paper with several lines drawn edge to edge. Discuss and direct placement of some cut-out letters on the top line and suggest that children copy the letter forms on the next line.
2. Prepare papers that permit children to copy the letter models in each box. Supply letters of varying sizes with each letter sitting on a base line.
3. Have children trace the lines on standard size writing paper to call attention to those lines. Direct them to color the spaces between each line. Suggest that they try coloring every other line only.

Show letters the children are learning to write, and suggest that these letters be copied in the uncolored spaces. Direct correct letter formation, stressing equal sizes, touching the base line, and printing without slant.

4. Supply standard size lined paper and direct writers to trace the lines. Using a different color pencil, have children draw down the paper from line to line, creating a page of boxes. Allow children to color lightly in the boxes while discussing the spaces they are coloring. Next, suggest children copy letters displayed by the leader into some of the boxes. Discuss the alignment, proportion, and spacing varieties possible.

5. Produce charts showing a row of one letter copied several times. Have some letters formed correctly and others out of proportion, off the base line or exhibiting some other error. Ask children to find those correctly formed by matching the letters to the model at the beginning of each row.

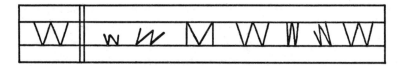

Give children paper on which they may practice forming a row of the letter just analyzed. Stress equal spacing, size, and proportion as well as placement on the line.

## Program Goals Beyond Letter Reproduction

The young child's beginning handwriting lessons are primarily aimed at developing the neuromuscularity and eye-hand coordination necessary for tool manipulation and the production of printed symbols. Along with the readiness-oriented activities and the formal school exercises of letter reproduction, attention should be given to helping children develop an acceptable attitude toward writing and the habit of analyzing and correcting their own work.

*Purpose:* To create a learning atmosphere in which children may develop acceptable attitudes toward handwriting.

*Materials:* Use the behaviors and materials necessary to help children feel comfortable in their writing attempts.

*Procedures:*

1. As the writing teacher, keep a good attitude about the task yourself.
2. Offer personal comment and praise to individuals and groups of writers.

3. Provide writing lessons appropriate to each child's level of attention and interest.
4. Focus on legibility rather than perfect reproduction of models.
5. Use teaching and acceptance standards appropriate to individuals rather than expecting one set of standards for the whole group.
6. Be creative when planning practice lessons.

*Purpose:* To create a learning atmosphere in which children may develop the habit of analyzing and correcting their own work.

*Materials:* Use the behaviors and materials necessary to help children develop the habit of self-correction.

*Procedures:*
1. Demonstrate and discuss checking your work. Use various media for teaching (charts, chalkboard, overhead projector).
2. Work with each individual to provide personal guidance.
3. Supply commercial and teacher printed models for comparison. Save good work done by the children as models of their own standards to maintain.
4. Following practice, allow time specifically for children to analyze and correct their work.
5. Provide examples of writing with different degrees of legibility and discuss the importance of correcting work after it is analyzed.

## RESOURCES FOR TEACHERS

Recordings available from Educational Audio Visual Inc., Pleasantville, New York 10750, on rhythm and rhyme easily lend themselves to the uses suggested in the previous section of this chapter.

*Nursery Rhymes* — C1R 191 LP, rhyming folk songs for the very young and for use in special education.

*And One And Two* — C1R 607 LP, Ella Jenkins sings and plays games with preschool students.

*Rhythms for Today* — C6RR 132 Set-2LPs, a set divided into more than fifty sections, including natural and body movements, travel, animals, and nature; each section with music and sound effects.

The following recordings aimed at developing motor skills are available through Educational Record Sales, 157 Chambers Street, New York, N.Y. 10007.

*Individualization in Movement and Music* — LP, action songs, chants, games, dances, story, drama, and so on. Activities stress rhythms, movement, and music involving perceptual development, basic locomotor activities, directionality, body control, and readiness.

*Developing Body-Space Perception Motor Skills* — LP, a series of records that stress the development of body-space perception, fosters motor skills, and stimulates the sensory-motor performance that is basic to all subsequent learning.

*Exploring Perceptual-Motor Needs of Primary-Level Children* — LP, an album, that provides a sequentially developed training program to help pupils establish necessary perceptual-motor skills. From three to eleven exercises are included for each aspect of the program. The training includes the sequential development of the following: agility, balance, locomotor-agility, turning, and others.

Materials for giving children exercise in making visual discriminations are available in varying forms of media, from multiple sources, for preschool and primary grade children.

Audio Tapes— Random House School & Library Service
457 Madison Avenue
New York, N. Y. 10022

Learning Machines
Box 511
Portales, New Mexico 88130

Charts and Posters — Milton Bradley Co.
74 Park Street
Springfield, Massachusetts 01101

Film Strips — Hudson Photo, Ind.
Irvington-On-Hudson
New York, N. Y. 10533

Coronet Instructional Films
65 E. South Water St.
Chicago, Illinois 60601

Encyclopaedia Britannica, Inc.
425 N. Michigan Ave.
Chicago, Illinois 60611

Educational Developmental Labs
Division of McGraw-Hill
Huntington, N. Y. 11743

Kits — Kendry Mfg. Co.
P. O. Box 629
San Mateo, California 94401

Manipulatives — Dennison Manufacturing Co.
300 Howard St.
Framingham, Massachusetts 01701

The Macmillan Co.
866 Third Ave.
New York, N. Y. 10022

The following resources are identified as sources of ideas and activities for the development of readiness and practice of handwriting. These references include experiences for children that are different from those included in this chapter.

Braley, W. T., Konicki, G., and Leedy, C. *Daily Sensorimotor Training Activities.* Merrick, New York: Achievement Aids, 1968.

Cratty, Bryant J. *Movement, Perception and Thought.* Palo Alto California: Peek Publications, 1969.

## REFERENCES

1. Barbe, Walter B. and Lucas, Virginia H. "Instruction in Handwriting: A New Look." *Childhood Education,* February 1974, *50,* No. 5, 207-209.

2. Bolen, John E. "A Study of Manuscript Writing and Spelling Achievement in the Third Grade." Dissertation Abstracts 1965, *25,* No. 11, 6422.

3. Byers, Loretta. "The Relationship of Manuscript and Cursive Writing to Accuracy in Spelling." *Journal of Educational Research,* October 1963, *57:* 87-89.

4. Donoghue, Mildred R. *The Child and the English Language Arts.* Dubuque, Iowa: William C. Brown, 1971.

5. Herrick, Virgil E. "Handwriting and Children's Writing." *Elementary English* 37 (April 1960): 248-58.

6. Mackay, David, Thompson, Brian, and Schuab, Pamela. *Breakthrough to Literacy: Teacher's Manual: The Theory and Practice of Teaching Initial Reading and Writing.* London: Longman Group Ltd., 1970, pp. 49-55.

7. Rubin, Dorothy. *Teaching Elementary Language Arts.* New York: Holt, Rinehart and Winston, 1975.

8. Spalding, Romalda B. and Spalding, Walter T. *The Writing Road to Reading: A Method of Phonics for Teaching Children to Read.* 2d rev. ed. New York: William Morrow, 1969, pp. 45-75.

9. Vukelich, Carol. "Language Arts In Early Childhood Education." *Elementary English,* February 1974, *51,* No. 2: 300-315.

10. Wright, J. P. and Allen, Elizabeth G. "Ready to Write." *Elementary School Journal,* April 1975, *75,* No. 7: 430-435.

# CHAPTER 6

# TEACHING SPELLING IN THE EARLY YEARS

*Our Queer Language*

*When the English tongue we speak*
  *Why is "break" not rhymed with "freak"?*
*Will you tell me why it's true*
  *We say "sew" but likewise "few";*
*And the maker of a verse*
  *Cannot cap his "horse" with "worse"?*
*"Beard" sounds not the same as "heard";*
  *"Cord" is different from "word."*
*Cow is "cow" but "low" is low,*
  *"Shoe" is never rhymed with "foe";*
*Think of "hose" and "dose" and "lose";*
  *And think of "goose" and not of "chose";*
*Think of "comb" and "tomb" and "bomb,"*
  *"Doll" and "roll," "home" and "some";*
*And since "pay" is rhymed with "say,"*
  *Why not "paid" with "said," I pray?*
*We have "blood" and "food" and "good";*
  *"Mould" is not pronounced like "could";*
*Wherefore "done" but "gone" and "lone"?*
  *Is there any reason known?*
*And in short it seems to me*
  *Sounds and letters disagree.*

*Source Unknown*

A character in a familiar comic strip announces to a friend, "I got an A in spelling. When I grow up, I'm going to be a speller!" This comment illustrates the way in which spelling is often isolated from the other language arts and separated from its meaningful context, written language. The major goal of spelling instruction is to teach children to spell the words they want and need to do their own writing. Conforming to correct spelling conventions enables writers to share their thoughts with others. Creative spellers are not welcomed by those readers who attempt to gain meaning from what is written!

What is spelling? Lundsteen describes spelling as an alphabetic writing code that represents the words that we say according to convention or standard usage. (10)

The English code is written with only twenty-six letters which are combined to form more than forty sounds that may be represented in writing in more than one way, with some in as many as twelve different ways. For example, some looks like home but is pronounced like sum. "Meat, great, and threat rhyme with suite, straight, and debt." (10:325)

Why does the English language seem to have many irregularities in the spelling of words? Some words or parts of words reflect their sources in other languages such as French, Latin, German, Greek, and Scandinavian. For example, borrowed words from the French may retain a French-like pronunciation and French spelling such as chauffeur and rendezvous. Many of the prefixes and suffixes are Latin-based. Additionally, changes in the spoken language are not reflected in the records of accepted spellings (dictionaries).

Initial efforts to standardize English spelling are credited to printers. A uniform spelling system contributed to an easily readable product and improved the appearance and appeal of the product. This consistency in the writing system is standard across dialects. Their efforts were strengthened by the publication of the first English dictionary, "A Dictionary of the English Language" by Samuel Johnson in 1755. This was followed by Noah Webster, an American, who published a book known as "Webster's Spelling Book" in 1783, the famous "blue-backed speller" which was used in many of the early one-room schoolhouse classrooms.

## GENERAL IMPLICATIONS FROM CURRENT RESEARCH

Research efforts during the last decade have established that the English spelling system is more regular than it was believed to be earlier. Three important observations have come forth from this current research on the English spelling system:

1. Alphabetical systems don't operate on a letter-to-sound basis. They involve complex pattern relationships.
2. English spelling is, in general, regular (rule-governed), but the rule system is very complex.
3. Spelling is fixed and standard across dialects (18:247).

Extensive research concerning various spelling instructional strategies has also been conducted. Some of the most significant results that are supported by the findings of noted researchers in the field of spelling instructional strategies include: (1) the best method for testing spelling is the word-list format (16, 15); (2) the test-study-test plan for improving spelling achievement is the most effective approach (11, 16); (3) many words must be learned as whole words (14, 19); (4) there are some spelling generalizations that have few exceptions and should be learned by each student (16, 14, 5, 19); and (5) an appropriate time allotment for directed spelling instruction is seventy-five minutes per week or approximately fifteen minutes per day (6, 16, 19). These implications are further discussed in the paragraphs that follow.

## Word-List Testing Format

This format is time-efficient and concentrates on the major objective of learning to spell the lesson or assigned words. According to E. Horn:

> Research has consistently shown that it is more efficient to study words in lists than in context. Words studied in lists are learned more quickly, remembered longer, and transferred more readily to new context. Occasional lessons may be justified in which words are presented in context for the purpose of encouraging children to do certain types of writing, such as writing invitations, thank-you notes, and letters to classmates who are ill at home (7:27).

If you want to inject variety in the testing procedure on occasion, you may consider dictating sentences or a small paragraph containing several or all of the assigned spelling words. The difficulty with this variety in test form is that words that were not on the assigned list might be included when the sentences or paragraphs are formulated.

## Test-Study-Test Plan

This procedure is definitely superior to the study-test plan. A pretest helps the individual and the teacher to focus on the immediate instructional needs of each student and to avoid wasting time on the study of words that can already be spelled. After the testing has been completed, students should have the opportunity to correct their own test responses. This immediate feedback converts the test situation to a learning experience and enables students to see what they have spelled correctly and to note inappropriate spelling pattern and option responses. Self-correction activities may help prevent reinforcement of spelling errors that were made. As a misspelled word is identified, the student writes the word in correct form above or next to his pretest response. The misspelled words become his word list for the weekly spelling activities.

Some teachers spell the words out loud as the students correct their own papers. Most teachers follow a more effective self-correcting procedure which includes the distribution of the words in a list written in good manuscript or cursive form as a model for the students. This visual aid to self-correcting seems most helpful to students.

## Whole Word Study

Lundsteen describes the profile of a good speller: "Exceptionally superior spellers are frequently people with superior visual perception and memory. They may be able to produce total recall in the form of a picture in the mind's eye of a whole, lengthy word" (10:339). As a result of their research activities Fitzsimmons and Loomer recommend that it is preferable to learn words by the whole word method as opposed to learning them by syllables (4:121).

The general procedure for studying a spelling word includes two phases—impression and recall. The image or impression phase usually involves visual, auditory, and kinesthetic impression. The recall phase usually suggests "visualizing" the whole word in the mind and then writing it down. It is also important for children to know the correct pronunciation for the words they are visualizing.

## Selected Spelling Generalizations

Only those generalizations that occur in a considerable number of words and have few exceptions should be included in spelling instruction. The generalizations are presented by an inductive learning approach. Spelling words that demonstrate the generalization are presented. Students can then observe the pattern and with the help of the teacher state the observed generalization and internalize it. Only one generalization is presented at a time. Any exceptions can be noted. Many opportunities to note the application of generalizations are important as are plans for frequent review.

The following generalizations are appropriate for introduction in the spelling program (16):

1. The letter q is followed by u in common English words.
2. The guidelines for adding suffixes: changing y to i, dropping final silent e, not dropping the final silent e, and doubling the final consonant.
3. Most adjectives formed from proper nouns and proper nouns start with capital letters.
4. Guidelines for the formation of plurals.
5. Guidelines for the omission of letters in contractions.
6. Guidelines for the use of the apostrophe.

## Time Allotment for Spelling Instruction

It is not necessary to devote more than seventy-five minutes per week to have an effective spelling program. This time should be distributed on a daily basis to approximately fifteen minutes per day. In spelling, distributed practice seems to be more effective than mass practice. Practicing a troublesome word for five to ten minutes twice a day may be more useful than massed lengthy sessions.

## ASSESSING AND DIAGNOSING FOR SPELLING INSTRUCTION

### Preschool and Kindergarten — Informal Measures

Although much information is available regarding spelling readiness, it is not possible to make sweeping conclusions about when a child is ready for formal spelling instruction. Readiness for spelling differs with individuals just like readiness for reading or any other school subject. In addition to the level of language development variable, others include interest, age, word awareness, interest in print, experiential background, auditory and visual perception and discrimination. For additional information about how language develops and how the teacher can informally assess the level of language development in children, refer to Chapter 4 in this text.

Informal observation checklists can assist the teacher in assessing various other indicators of spelling readiness. A checklist to note whether chidren are developing the concept of "word awareness" includes some of the following behaviors (11:8):

- listens to stories
- questions pronunciations and meanings
- repeats words and phrases heard in conversation, on television, and elsewhere
- recognizes labels, signs, posters, and some words
- realizes that letters stand for something

Children may be expressing an interest in print and the printed word for the purpose of writing if you notice a combination of these or similar behaviors (11):

- develops proficiency in printing or handwriting
- tries to combine words learned to express ideas
- speaks with accuracy
- notes that ideas can be shared through writing

In addition to the spelling readiness factors of language facility, word awareness and interest in print, the areas of auditory and visual perception and discrimination should be observed. Farnett and others have prepared a helpful checklist for teachers of young children to use (2). Examples of some of the items used are:

*Visual Perception and Discrimination – examples*
- knows colors and shapes
- knows the letters in own name
- can match upper and lower case letters of the alphabet
- can recognize his written name
- recognizes visual similarities and differences
- is able to reproduce visual sequential patterns
- can interpret pictures

*Auditory Perception and Discrimination– examples*
- uses complete sentences
- can answer questions
- can follow directions
- repeats simple nursery rhymes
- understands opposites
- discriminates sound similarities and differences
- discriminates beginning word sounds
- can rhyme words
- can repeat a sequence of five words
- can verbally count in sequence from one to ten
- is able to retell a short story including plot, main ideas, and characters

For additional assessment ideas in the area of auditory perception and discrimination, refer to Chapter 3 of this text.

As you probably noticed, most of the skill areas that are classified as spelling readiness are also generally included under general readiness for formal schooling. Thus, the informal assessment activities can be incorporated into the daily routine and won't need to take place in isolation of the daily readiness curriculum.

## Preschool and Kindergarten — Formal Measures

Formal assessment measures for spelling readiness at the preschool-kindergarten level are nonexistent; however, many of the readiness factors discussed in the informal measures section of this chapter are formally measured in reading readiness test batteries. Some of these formal measures are:

1. *Harrison-Stroud Reading Readiness Profiles* by M. Lucille Harrison and James B. Stroud (Houghton Mifflin Company). Areas related to spelling readiness — auditory discrimination and visual discrimination.
2. *Clymer-Barrett Prereading Battery* by Theodore Clymer and Thomas C. Barrett (Personnel Press, Inc. — A Division of Ginn and

Company). Areas related to spelling readiness — visual discrimination, auditory discrimination, letter recognition, word matching, and sentence copying.
3. *Search* by Archie A. Silver and Rosa A. Hagin (Waker Educational Book Corp.). Areas related to spelling readiness — visual memory, visual recall, auditory discrimination, and letter recognition.

Many other readiness batteries include subtests that formally measure some of the spelling readiness factors mentioned earlier. It is important to remember that children who are prereaders are not ready for any kind of formalized spelling program. A combination of the informal and formal assessment measures can provide preschool-kindergarten teachers with important diagnostic information about a child's progress toward acquiring spelling readiness skills. Again the areas of diagnosis include: word awareness, interest in print, experiential background, auditory and visual perception, auditory and visual discrimination, and letter knowledge.

## Primary Grades — Informal Measures

Assessment of progress in spelling in the primary grades should be related to the major goal of a spelling program as stated in the introduction of this chapter: "The major goal of spelling instruction is to teach children to spell the words they want and need to do their own writing." Informal assessment measures can help teachers judge children's progress toward this goal.

Informal measures in a primary spelling program include weekly, monthly, and perhaps end-of-the semester tests. Words included on these tests should be words that the children have studied or learned previously or words selected from lists used earlier and/or during the semester.The weekly procedure includes a pretest and a final test. Words missed on the final test can be included as review words on the following week's test.

In addition, teachers may want to use a standard spelling scale to compare the spelling of a class with the spelling of children of the same grade level as noted in the scale. An example of this type of scale is *The New Iowa Spelling Scale* (Bureau of Educational Research, University of Iowa). The scale lists 5,500 words and states the percentage of children in grades two to eight who spelled each word correctly (16).

Just as you as a teacher may keep progress charts of each child's spelling work, you may consider having pupils record their own individual progress. Students may do this in several ways. Progress charts may show individual progress on weekly final tests or progress on written activities — the number of words misspelled per 50 or 100 words written as periodically checked and recorded. As students correct their own tests, they may keep a record of the type of errors they made.

Student spelling errors may be classified into several general areas (20):

1. Doubling — doubling a single letter in a word where it's not needed or not doubling a single letter in a word where it should be.
2. Omissions — any syllable or letter omitted in a word (except failure to double).
3. Homonym — when there are two forms for a word, the spelling of the wrong or inappropriate one.
4. Insertions — any syllable or letter appearing in a word where it should not (except doubling or transposition).
5. Letter substitutions — applying a generalization to words or syllables with irregular spellings.
6. Transpositions — when two adjacent letters that should appear in a word are placed in reverse order.
7. Confusions due to incorrect pronunciation.
8. Unclassified words — words that are unrelated or omitted, words that include more than one kind of error, or errors not applicable to the general classifications stated.

You may want to develop a check sheet that lists the spelling error types and can be used to diagnose the specific spelling needs of each pupil in the class.

Another type of informal diagnostic check sheet may include items about the student's ability to spell correctly in a writing situation. Examples of items on this type of checksheet include: (1) student uses generalizations, (2) student uses dictionary, (3) student proofreads written work, (4) student proofreads spelling assignments, and so on.

Finally, you may choose to prepare a diagnostic chart that includes a list of contributors to accurate spelling as described by Personke and Yee (15):

1. Skills of auditory discrimination;
2. Personal, adaptable study skills for learning how to spell words;
3. A store of memorized words, word meanings, and generalizations;
4. Awareness of accurate spelling; and
5. Useful dictionary skills.

## Primary Grades — Formal Measures

There are a few formal spelling-assessment measures presently available. Some formal measures assess the child's ability to spell certain words that represent specific spelling patterns; other formal measures assess the child's ability to recognize correctly spelled words; and others measure the child's ability to recall and spell from dictation. It is important to remember that standardized tests include only a sampling of the words from our written language and do not control for the vocabulary knowledge of the individual taking the test. Some of the formal spelling measures include:

1. *Gates-Russell Spelling Diagnostic Tests* by A. I. Gates and D. H. Russell (Teachers College Press, Columbia University). Nine subtests are included; the results indicate a speller's strength and weaknesses.
2. *Wide Range Achievement Test* by J. F. Jastak and S. R. Jastak (Guidance Associates). Spelling — recall and spell from dictation.
3. *Durrell Analysis of Reading Difficulty* by Donald D. Durrell (Harcourt, Brace, Jovanovich). Spelling-related areas — visual memory of word forms; visual discrimination; auditory discrimination of word forms; and spelling — phonetic and word list activities.

Spelling assessment plans should combine the results of formal and informal measures. A student's spelling ability should be assessed by observing his/her spelling skills in isolation, as on weekly lists, and by observing his/her spelling in the context of writing assignments.

## INSTRUCTIONAL STRATEGIES

### Preschool, Kindergarten, First Grade

As children listen to the reading of alphabet books and "help" by pointing to the featured alphabet letter on the page, they experience first awarenesses of the fact that words are made up of separate elements called letters. This awareness continues as children observe parents or other adults writing grocery and shopping lists and letters or cards to family and friends.

Word and print awareness can be facilitated in preschool, kindergarten, and first grade children by providing experiences with the following activities or similar ones.

1. Read alphabet books to and with children individually or in small groups. Have a child point to the alphabet letter on the page as the words are read. Point to the words on the page as each is read.
2. Read books that include a few words that are repeated throughout, such as *The Eye Book* by Theo LeSieg, or that include a language pattern such as *Brown Bear, Brown Bear, What Do You See?* by Bill Martin, Jr., to and with children individually or in small groups. Be sure the listeners can see the words as well as the pictures as you read.

3. Let children observe you as you write the letters to form their names on pictures they draw, puppets they make, pictures they paint, and other projects.
4. Let children observe you as you write down the names of things and ingredients the group will need to bake cookies for Halloween. Say each word as you write it down. You may want to draw a little picture next to the word to illustrate its meaning.
5. Make signs to identify various objects in the classroom, and attach the signs to the objects.
6. Let the children observe you as you write a thank-you note to a person who has visited the classroom.
7. When you give directions to children, write them down on a chart or the chalkboard using key words and numbering them in sequence.

Visual perception and discrimination activities are also an important aspect of the spelling readiness program for preschool-first grade children. The following ideas for developing visual perception and discrimination are suggestions and not meant to be all-inclusive. A child must first be able to recognize likenesses and differences in form, shape, size, and so on in order to recognize likenesses and differences in letters and words for reading or spelling (19).

1. Show pictures of three to four objects that are alike and one that is different. Have the student choose the one that is different. Magazine pictures or gummed stickers may be used.
2. Show pictures of things with missing parts. Ask the child to tell what's missing.
3. Play color games — sorting colored beads, finding specific colors in the classroom, sorting colored circles into egg cartons.
4. Picture-domino games — make or buy picture domino cards. Each card has two pictures, for example, a square on one end and a circle on the other end. The game is played like regular dominoes except that pictures rather than dots are matched.
5. Classify objects such as blocks according to shapes such as rectangle, circle, triangle, arch, and so on, or by color.
6. Letter matching — make a simple worksheet with a letter in a box at the top of the page. The remainder of the page (sized not larger than half of an 8½ x 11 sheet) contains a variety of letters. The student marks *only* the ones that are the same as the letter in the box.
7. Letters card game — make approximately fifty cards, each one with a letter of the alphabet on it. Each letter can be represented two to four times. The game is played like Old Maid with students

matching cards with the same letter. The one who matches the most cards correctly wins.

8. Word matching — use the same format as with letter matching. Start with one word on a half sheet of paper, then work up to using a whole sheet of paper with four to five rows, one stimulus word per row.

9. Letter cluster matching — use same format as with letter matching and word matching, using letter clusters as the stimulus.

10. Phrase matching — phrases may be placed on a large chart or the chalkboard. Duplicate phrases are prepared on large cards. A student chooses a phrase card and matches it to a phrase on the chart or chalkboard. A similar activity could be used with short sentences.

Auditory or sound discrimination is another important spelling readiness skill for preschool-first grade children. We know that childen know the sounds of English, so as teachers we begin with what they know by helping them move from oral language, which they hear and speak, to the written language they will learn to read and write. Below are a few of the numerous activities that can be used to help children refine their auditory discrimination skills.

1. Same or different words — pronounce words in pairs. The student can respond in one or two different ways according to your directions: (a) the student can tell you if the word pair is the same word or two different words, or (b) the student can respond by clapping hands or with some other designated response if the word pairs are different (no response if they are the same).

2. The same activity can be done with phrases or short sentences.

3. Add-a-word — say two or three words that begin with the same initial consonant and ask each child to add a word to the list.

4. Rhyming words — have the children listen to a poem (read by you or on a tape recorder) and ask them to repeat the rhyming words that they heard.

5. Rhyming words — pick a color word that describes something and rhymes with it— for example, red sled, green bean — and ask the children to make up some.

6. Rhyming words — say a word and ask the children to help you think of words that rhyme with it, for example, cat — fat, mat, skat — and then try to make up a sentence or poem with the words, such as A fat cat skats on a mat.

7. Beginning sounds — make a worksheet with picture pairs. The student marks the picture pairs that begin with the same initial consonant.

8. Ending sounds — follow the procedure described under beginning sounds. Students mark picture pairs that have the same final consonant sound.

9. Nonrhyming words — say a series of three to four words. Include three that rhyme and one that doesn't, and ask children to listen and tell which word does not rhyme with the others.

10. Have children help you write rhymes using the names of people that rhyme with the names of items or foods, for example,

| | |
|---|---|
| I saw Jean, | I saw Bill, |
| Eat a bean. | Take a pill. |

or write rhymes using starter lines, for example,

| | |
|---|---|
| I have fun | Dad will get |
| When I _____. | An erector _____. |

Finally, a spelling readiness program for preschool-first grade children should include some experiences with the alphabet and letter recognition. Some of the experiences that you may plan for the children include:

1. Music-singing the Alphabet Song does help children become familiar with the alphabet letter names is a positive way.

2. Use commonly found letters in the environment when teaching the letter names, such as A&P, R. C. Cola, CBS, ABC, NBC, U. S.

3. Using nouns to illustrate the sounds of the alphabet letters still helps children. Prepare large cards with key pictures and the alphabet letters to help children remember the letter names and see how the letters are formed, for example, card with the picture of a dog and this sentence under the picture, "D is for dog."

4. Alphabet pretzels or cookies — each week a new letter is studied, the children can make an alphabet pretzel or cookie. Before eating it, they must say its name and a word that begins with that sound.

5. Upper and lower case letters— make worksheets for students to match upper and lower case letters, or make a center where children can manipulate cards that have either an upper case or lower case letter on the front. After the student matches the cards into sets, the cards can be turned over for the student to "self-check" his responses.

6. Alphabet books — each booklet is made in the shape of the letter the class is studying. Children may cut pictures from magazines or draw pictures that represent the sound of the letter, for example, The "B" alphabet book —

Make the cover from oak tag or construction paper. On the first page each child writes the upper and lower case "b," and on the remaining two or three pages pastes or draws "b" pictures.

7. A class alphabet book — follow same idea as for individual alphabet books. The class booklet could be much larger in size than individual ones.

8. Alphabet foods — each week when a new alphabet letter is introduced, select a day to serve an alphabet food snack, for example, during the "d" week, the snack could be doughnuts; during the "n" week, the snack could be nuts, and so on.

9. Alphabet sequence practice — alphabet dot-to-dot activities are fun and provide an opportunity for this type of practice.

10. Alphabet recognition practice— select or make up pictures that are keyed to certain alphabet letters. Write out instructions for the students to follow when coloring the picture puzzle, for example,

Make the A's red.
Make the B's green.
Make the C's yellow.
Make the D's brown.

By helping childen experience activities such as the ones described in this section, you are facilitating the spelling readiness skills of word and print awareness, auditory and visual perception, auditory and visual discrimination, letter recognition, and an interest in print.

## Primary Grades

Formal spelling instruction generally begins near the end of the first grade or at the beginning of second grade. There seem to be several valid reasons for this timing. In the reading process, words are worked with as units of whole thought in sentence form; the words appear in printed form to be recognized. Reading gives attention to the development of meaning of word units. To read or recognize words, primary attention is focused on the beginning and ending of words in addition to considering the context in which the words appear.

Emphasis on spelling should be delayed until students have made a strong start with reading because habits and behaviors of learning to spell conflict with those used in learning to read. Unlike the reading process described in the previous paragraph, spelling requires the student to select and put together the correct letter units in the right order to form a word. Spelling requires a conversion from sound (phoneme) to letter (grapheme), which is the opposite of the reading process.

Fernald states (3) that the words a child should study are indicated by the level of linguistic maturity rather than by grade level alone. She suggests that a child is ready to learn to spell a word after there is evidence that the word: (a) can be read by the child, (b) is understood by the child and used in oral language, and (c) is needed by the child when writing.

A number of research studies have investigated children's writing to determine a core spelling/writing vocabulary. The most comprehensive studies were conducted by Ernest Horn, Henry Rinsland, and Ves Thomas. The major finding of these studies and many others was that there appears to be a somewhat consistent core writing vocabulary for children and adults. The most commonly used of these high-frequency words should be included in the elementary spelling program. A comprehensive spelling program, additionally, includes words needed by individual children or small groups of children. Misspelled words from personal writing are good additions to each child's individual word study list. The word lists from the Horn and Rinsland studies are included in this chapter for your reference.

Thus far, we have discussed when, in the primary years, a formal spelling program can be organized, what words children should study, and guidelines for judging when a child is ready to learn to spell a specific word. A suggested procedure for studying and learning to spell a word follows (16, 20).

1. *Look* at the word in isolation.
2. *Pronounce* it clearly, looking at it as it is said.
3. *Think* about the word, try to visualize the way the word is written.
4. While covering the correct spelling of the word, *write* the word, pronouncing it to yourself as you write.
5. *Check* your own spelling immediately after writing the word.
6. If the word was spelled correctly, go on to the next word. If the word was misspelled, go back to Step One.

Some practices to *avoid* when teaching the spelling of words include (10, 16):

1. Copying a spelling word several times over usually does not aid recall of the word.
2. Spelling words orally does not aid recall of the word. The oral pronunciation of the letter names seems to interfere with the process of visualizing the word. Perhaps in a "spelling bee" type situation, students could write the word on a piece of paper or the chalkboard.
3. Having students cross out silent letters in words distorts the spelling pattern of the word; instead, suggest that students underline the particular spelling pattern that forms the sound in that word.
4. Looking at the "hard spots" in words is usually more confusing than helpful. Students should be aware of the spelling patterns

with which they have difficulty as individuals and make special note of words that contain those patterns.

**5.** Additional cautions include: *(a)* Writing words in the air for practice is not really a tactile experience; it's better to use sand or the chalkboard; *(b)* condemning or punishing children for asking how to spell words or by having them copy words over and over are practices that do not improve spelling skills and do not promote positive attitudes toward spelling.

Now that we have considered all the specifics for organizing a spelling program in your classroom, which include: *(a)* words to study, *(b)* time per week for word study, *(c)* study format and word study guidelines, *(d)* readiness for spelling and for studying specific words, *(e)* common spelling generalizations, and *(f)* practices to avoid, it is important to look at the spelling program within the context of other classroom language arts learning experiences. An isolated spelling program probably will not be too successful.

According to Zutell, young children need opportunities "to systematically examine words and to freely generate, test, and evaluate their own spelling strategies" (21:847). A supportive language arts classroom environment provides opportunities for children to apply and strengthen spelling skills through the following experiences:

**1.** Opportunities to explore thought through their own writing. Early writing experiences in the first grade begin with a dictation activity. The child thinks about what he wants to say and how he wants to say it, and the teacher writes it down. The child observes the letters and words as they are formed, but the teacher does the writing and the spelling. At first, the teacher may ask the students to help with spelling a word by providing the initial consonant. Later the teacher will ask the students to help spell a whole word.

As children are ready, the teacher prepares the dictated sentences on the chalkboard or a paper, leaving appropriate space for students to copy directly beneath the teacher sentences. A class word chart is developed, which includes words the children most frequently use in dictating stories. A child's first spelling words are the ones the child needs to communicate a special thought or idea.

As children in the second and third grades create and examine their writing, they have opportunities to think about what they said and how they said it. As children prepare their written products for sharing with others, the teacher has an opportunity to begin teaching the skill of proofreading. Personke and Yee (15) believe that children do not learn the skills of proofreading without teacher guidance. They suggest that children be taught to underline any word that they

### TABLE 6-1. WORDS OF HIGHEST FREQUENCY USE:
#### First 100 Words in Order of Frequency*

| | | | | |
|---|---|---|---|---|
| 1. I | 21. at | 41. do | 61. up | 81. think |
| 2. the | 22. this | 42. been | 62. day | 82. say |
| 3. and | 23. with | 43. letter | 63. much | 83. please |
| 4. to | 24. but | 44. can | 64. out | 84. him |
| 5. a | 25. on | 45. would | 65. her | 85. his |
| 6. you | 26. if | 46. she | 66. order | 86. got |
| 7. of | 27. all | 47. when | 67. yours | 87. over |
| 8. in | 28. so | 48. about | 68. now | 88. make |
| 9. we | 29. me | 49. they | 69. well | 89. may |
| 10. for | 30. was | 50. any | 70. an | 90. received |
| 11. it | 31. very | 51. which | 71. here | 91. before |
| 12. that | 32. my | 52. some | 72. them | 92. two |
| 13. is | 33. had | 53. has | 73. see | 93. send |
| 14. your | 34. our | 54. or | 74. go | 94. after |
| 15. have | 35. from | 55. there | 75. what | 95. work |
| 16. will | 36. am | 56. us | 76. come | 96. could |
| 17. be | 37. one | 57. good | 77. were | 97. dear |
| 18. are | 38. time | 58. know | 78. no | 98. made |
| 19. not | 39. he | 59. just | 79. how | 99. good |
| 20. as | 40. get | 60. by | 80. did | 100. like |

Words 1-3 account for 10 percent of all words written in English.
Words 1-10 account for 25 percent of all words used in the writing of adults.
Words 1-100 account for over half of the running words written by adults.

*From Ernest Horn, *A Basic Writing Vocabulary: 10,000 Words Most Commonly Used in Writing.* University of Iowa Monographs in Education, First Series, No. 4, Iowa City, Iowa, 1926.

### TABLE 6-2. 100 WORDS USED MOST FREQUENTLY: FROM RINSLAND'S STUDY*

| | | | | |
|---|---|---|---|---|
| 1. a | 21. eat | 41. in | 61. our | 81. there |
| 2. all | 22. for | 42. is | 62. out | 82. they |
| 3. am | 23. girl | 43. it | 63. over | 83. this |
| 4. and | 24. go | 44. just | 64. play | 84. time |
| 5. are | 25. going | 45. know | 65. pretty | 85. to |
| 6. at | 26. good | 46. like | 66. put | 86. too |
| 7. baby | 27. got | 47. little | 67. red | 87. three |
| 8. ball | 28. had | 48. look | 68. run | 88. two |
| 9. be | 29. has | 49. made | 69. said | 89. up |
| 10. big | 30. have | 50. make | 70. saw | 90. want |
| 11. boy | 31. he | 51. man | 71. school | 91. was |
| 12. but | 32. her | 52. me | 72. see | 92. we |
| 13. can | 33. here | 53. mother | 73. she | 93. went |
| 14. Christmas | 34. him | 54. my | 74. so | 94. what |
| 15. come | 35. his | 55. name | 75. some | 95. when |
| 16. did | 36. home | 56. not | 76. take | 96. will |
| 17. do | 37. house | 57. now | 77. that | 97. with |
| 18. dog | 38. how | 58. of | 78. the | 98. would |
| 19. doll | 39. I | 59. on | 79. them | 99. you |
| 20. down | 40. I'm | 60. one | 80. then | 100. your |

These words comprise about 60 percent of all children's written word usage.
*From Henry Rinsland, *A Basic Writing Vocabulary for Elementary School Children,* New York: Macmillan, 1945.

**TABLE 6-3.  RINSLAND'S LIST A:**
**253 Words of Highest Frequency Use**

| | | | | | |
|---|---|---|---|---|---|
| a | Christmas | going | lots | pretty | through |
| about | close | good | love | put | time |
| after | cold | got | | | to |
| again | come | grade | made | ran | today |
| all | coming | great | make | read | told |
| along | could | | man | red | too |
| also | country | had | many | right | took |
| always | | happy | me | room | town |
| am | daddy | has | men | run | tree |
| an | day | have | milk | | two |
| and | days | he | more | said | |
| another | dear | heard | morning | Santa Claus | until |
| any | did | help | most | saw | up |
| are | didn't | her | mother | say | us |
| around | do | here | much | school | |
| as | dog | him | must | see | very |
| asked | doll | his | my | she | |
| at | don't | home | | should | want |
| away | door | hope | name | sister | wanted |
| | down | house | never | snow | was |
| baby | | how | new | so | water |
| back | each | | next | some | way |
| ball | eat | I | nice | something | we |
| be | every | if | night | soon | week |
| because | | I'm | no | started | well |
| bed | father | in | not | summer | went |
| been | few | into | now | sure | were |
| before | find | is | | | what |
| best | fine | it | of | take | when |
| better | first | its | off | teacher | where |
| big | five | | old | tell | which |
| black | for | just | on | than | while |
| book | found | | once | that | white |
| boy | four | know | one | the | who |
| boys | friend | | only | their | will |
| bring | from | large | or | them | wish |
| brother | fun | last | other | then | with |
| but | | let | our | there | work |
| by | gave | letter | out | these | would |
| | get | like | over | they | write |
| called | getting | little | | thing | |
| came | girl | live | people | things | year |
| can | girls | long | place | think | years |
| car | give | look | play | this | you |
| cat | glad | looked | played | thought | your |
| children | go | lot | please | three | |

The 253 words listed above comprise more than 70 percent of all children's written word usage.

were not sure how to spell. When class proofreading activities are conducted, students learn how to use the dictionary or speller-dictionary to improve spelling in written work. Class time must be taken to teach proofreading skills if children are to develop "spelling consciousness"in their written compositions.

**2.** Opportunities to do wide reading and investigative reading and to be read to.

Extensive reading provides opportunities for students to meet words in meaningful contexts and to develop a sense of the "look" of a word. As children read, they form generalizations about the relationships of speech patterns to sound patterns. These generalizations are used to produce spellings for words that the student is not sure how to spell.

Opportunities to read, investigate, and be read to should be a part of every student's day and not reserved only for those who "get their work done." A wide range of reading materials will be needed for this ongoing activity — reference books, magazines, newspapers, books, and others.

**3.** Opportunities to participate in a wide variety of word study activities.

Word study and vocabulary development experiences can emphasize categorizing, comparing, and contrasting words. Criteria used could include structural patterns, root words, word origins, and others. Commercial games, crossword puzzles, word webs, and so on can be used to heighten interest in word study activities.

As the teacher observes and analyzes writing samples of the children in the class, quick notes can be made about what the children already know about words and what needs they seem to have at present for additional word study strategies.

Finally, let's talk about the role of the teacher when children ask for help in spelling a particular word. Try the following: (1) Encourage the child to try to spell the word first (don't say, "Sound it out"). Many new spellers confuse the letter name with the sound and give up without becoming aware of the many spelling pattern options that may be available for a particular sound. (2) Show the child the correct spelling by writing it next to his attempt. Point out similarities and differences between the correct spelling and the attempted one.

To complete this chapter on teaching spelling in the preschool and primary years, some ideas for enrichment games and activities for the primary children are presented. These games and activities serve more to increase interest in spelling and word study than they serve to teach the spelling of specific words.

## Enrichment — Primary Grades

**Spin and spell.** Use a round paper plate or oak tag circle. Divide the circle into six or eight sections. Glue or draw a picture in each section to illustrate a word from the spelling list. Print the correct spelling for the word on the back of the circle behind the picture. Attach a "spinner" pointer to the center of the circle with a paper fastener. Each team member, in turn, spins and spells the word for the picture illustrated. The team spelling the most words correctly is the winner. Change pictures for new game.

**Hangman.** Draw two gallows on the board and divide the class into teams. Under each gallows the team captain will draw the number of blank spaces for a spelling word. The other team must fill in the blanks by guessing letters until they know what the word is. As each child is called upon, he guesses a letter that may fit. If the letter is correct, it is put in its proper place on the board. If the same letter appears twice in a word, it is put in both places. If the letter named is not in the word, then a head, or a part of the body, is drawn in a noose on the gallows. Alternate teams and words. With each miss, additional parts of the body are added to the man on the gallows until he is officially hanged. The first team to get its man hung is the loser. The number of parts each stick man will have should be established before the game begins.

**Word tower.** Students begin with one letter that forms a word. Underneath they make new words by adding only one letter each time.

> a
> at
> ate
> late
> plate
> plates

**Commercial games.** Scrabble, Jr. Scrabble, Spello, Scribbage, Spill and Spell can be used with small groups of children in a centers-type setting.

**Mnemonic devices.** Help children remember especially difficult spelling by "tricks" such as the following:

> friend — a friend is a friend to the end.
> principal — He is your pal.

**Scrambled words.** Rearrange or scramble the letters in a way that will not represent a misspelled word.

**Picture dictionaries.** Children enjoy making their own and can also get some practice with categorizing words — animals, foods, and so on.

**Synonym cards.** Have children generate good synonyms for overused words like nice, good, big.

**Anagrams.** Rearranging the letters in a word to form new words.

> meat — mate, team
> farm — ram

Crossword puzzles or modified versions of crossword puzzles such as the one illustrated below.

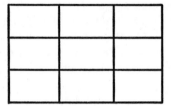

Fill in the squares with any letters to make as many words as possible — one point for each word.

| O | T | W |
|---|---|---|
| W | E | E |
| N | A | B |

6 points

**What am I cards.** Prepare cards with a picture and a word label. Cut the card into three strips. The student must put three strips together to spell the word that names the picture.

**Spelling hunt.** Spelling words are written on pieces of paper or cards and placed in a box. Each student, one at a time, takes a word from the box, looks at it carefully, and hands it to the teacher. The teacher pronounces the word. The student tries to write the word on the board, winning a point if right; if wrong, the child takes the word to study.

**Team spelling.** Class is divided into two teams. Each pupil gets a card with a letter on it from one of the spelling words. As the teacher pronounces the word, the team members arrange themselves to spell the word correctly. The first team to do it gets a point.

**Spelling play.** Pupils take turns dramatizing different spelling words. After a word is dramatized, the student chooses someone to write the word on the board. The one who writes the word correctly takes the next turn at dramatizing.

**Riddles.** Students can write riddles that can be answered with words from the spelling list.

**Rhyming words.** One student stands at the front of the room and says, "I am thinking of a spelling word that rhymes with back." The student can choose someone to write the word on the chalkboard. The student who is correct gets a turn next.

**Make a new word.** Students begin with one word, and by changing only one letter at a time, make a new word

Rule<br>(mule)<br>(mole)<br>(mile)<br>Milk

**Prefix or suffix root wheel.** Prepare two circles, a large one and a smaller one, attached with a brass fastener. Print root words on the larger outer wheel and prefixes on the smaller inner wheel *or* for suffixes, print the root words on the large inner wheel and suffixes on the smaller outer wheel space.

**Code language.** Assign each letter of the alphabet a number. Then develop a message and write it down using the number code. Students translate numbers to letters using the code.

**Beginning and ending chain.** The first person in the game writes any word on the chalkboard, the next person adds a word that begins with the last letter of the first, and so on.

patanamendownewagonowwhen

## RESOURCES FOR TEACHERS

1. Anderson, Paul and Groff, Patrick. *Resource Materials for Teachers of Spelling,* 2d Ed. Minneapolis, Minn.: Burgess Publishing Company, 1968.

2. Applegate, Mauree. *Freeing Children to Write.* New York: Harper and Row, 1963.

3. Botel, Morton. *Multi-Level Speller.* State College, Pa.: Penns Valley Publishers, 1975.

4. Bremer, Neville; Bishop, Katherine; and Stone, Lucile. *Skills in Spelling.* New York: American Book Company, 1976.

5. Farnette, Cherrie; Forte, Imogene; and Loss, Barbara. *Kids' Stuff Reading and Writing Readiness.* Nashville, Tenn.: Incentive Publications, 1975.

6. Fitzgerald, James. *A Basic Life Spelling Vocabulary.* Milwaukee, Wisc.: The Bruce Publishing Company, 1951.

7. Horn, Ernest. *What Research Says to the Teacher, Teaching Spelling,* 2d Ed. Washington, D.C.: American Educational Research Association, 1954.

8. Lundsteen, Sara (Ed.). *Help for the Teacher of Written Composition.* Urbana, Ill.: National Conference on Research in English, 1976.

9. Lutz, Jack. *Expanding Spelling Skills.* Dansville, N.Y.: F. A. Owen Publishing Company, 1963.

10. McCracken, Robert and McCracken, Marlene. *Reading is Only the Tiger's Tail.* San Rafael, Calif.: Leswing Press, 1972.

11. Moffett, James. *A Student-Centered Language Arts Curriculum, Grades K-13: A Handbook for Teachers.* Boston: Houghton Mifflin Company, 1973.

12. Petty, Walter: Petty, Dorothy; and Becking, Marjorie. *Experiences in Language,* 2d Ed. Boston: Allyn and Bacon, 1976.

13. Pilon, A. Barbara. *Teaching Language Arts Creatively in the Elementary Grades.* New York: John Wiley and Sons, 1978.

14. Read, Edwin; Allred, Ruel; and Baird, Louise. *Continuous Progress in Spelling.* Oklahoma City, Okla.: The Economy Company, 1972.

15. Russell, David and Karp, Etta. *Reading Aids Through the Grades,* 2d Ed. New York: Teachers College Press, 1974.

16. Schubert, Delwyn. *Reading Games That Teach: Words, Phrases, Sentences.* Monterey Park, Calif.: Creative Teaching Press, 1966.

17. Sealey, Leonard; Sealey, Nancy; and Millmore, Marcia. *Children's Writing: An Approach for the Primary Grades.* Newark, Del.: International Reading Association, 1979.

18. Smith, E. Brooks; Goodman, Kenneth: and Meredith, Robert. *Language and Thinking in School,* 2d Ed. New York: Holt, Rinehart and Winston, 1976.

19. Stauffer, Russell. *Directing the Reading-Thinking Process.* New York: Harper and Row, 1975.

20. Stoutenburg, Jane. *Word Systems and Signals.* New York: Harper and Row, 1975.

21. Tiedt, Sidney and Tiedt, Iris. *Language Arts Activities for the Classroom.* Boston: Allyn and Bacon, 1978.

22. *Van Allen, Roach. Language Experiences in Communication.* Boston: Houghton Mifflin Company, 1976.

23. Wagner, Guy and Hosier, Max. *Reading Games That Teach.* New York: Teachers Publishing Corporation, 1970.

24. Zavatsky, Bill and Padgett, Ron (Eds.). *The Whole Word Catalogue 2.* New York: McGraw-Hill Paperbacks, 1977.

## REFERENCES

1. Applegate, Mauree. *Freeing Children to Write.* New York: Harper and Row, 1963.

2. Farnette, Cherrie; Forte, Imogene; and Loss, Barbara. *Kids' Stuff Reading and Writing Readiness.* Nashville, Tenn.: Incentive Publications, 1975.

3. Fernald, Grace. *Diagnostic and Remedial Work in the Basic Skills.* New York: McGraw-Hill, 1943.

4. Fitzsimmons, Robert and Loomer, Bradley. "Spelling and Handwriting," in Harold Shane and James Walden, eds., *Classroom Relevant Research in the Language Arts.* Washington, D.C.: Association for Supervision and Curriculum Development, 1978, pp. 119-131.

5. Hodges, Richard and Rudorf, E. Hugh. "Searching Linguistics for Clues for Teaching of Spelling," *Elementary English,* 1965, *42,* 527-533.

6. Horn, Ernest. "Spelling." *Encyclopedia of Educational Research,* 3d Ed. New York: Macmillan Company, 1960.

7. Horn, Ernest. *Spelling Research and Practice.* Iowa City: Iowa State Department of Public Instruction and the University of Iowa, 1977.

8. Horn, Thomas, Ed. *Research on Handwriting and Spelling.* Urbana, Ill. National Council of Teachers of English, 1966.

9. King, Martha; Emans, Robert; and Cianciolo, Patricia, Eds. *The Language Arts in the Elementary School: A Forum for Focus.* Urbana, Ill.: National Council of Teachers of English, 1973.

10. Lundsteen, Sara. *Children Learn to Communicate: Language Arts Through Creative Problem-Solving.* Englewood Cliffs, N.J.: Prentice-Hall, Inc., 1976.

11. Lutz, Jack. *Expanding Spelling Skills.* Dansville, N.Y.: F. A. Owen Publishing Company, 1963.

12. Martin, Bill Jr. *Brown Bear, Brown Bear, What Do You See?* New York: Holt, Rinehart and Winston, 1970.

13. McCracken, Robert and McCracken, Marlene. *Reading Is Only the Tiger's Tail*. San Rafael, Calif.: Leswing Press, 1972.

14. Personke, Carl. "Generalization and Spelling: Boon or Bust?" In Martha King, et al. (eds.), *The Language Arts in the Elementary School: A Forum for Focus*. Urbana, Ill.: National Council of Teachers of English, 1973, pp. 148-158.

15. Personke, Carl and Yee, Albert. *Comprehensive Spelling Instruction: Theory, Research and Application*. Scranton, Pa.: International Textbook Co., 1971.

16. Petty, Walter, Dorothy; and Becking, Marjorie. *Experiences in Language; Tools and Techniques for Language Arts Methods*. Boston: Allyn and Bacon, 1976.

17. Sealey, Leonard; Sealey, Nancy; and Millmore, Marcia. *Children's Writing: An Approach for the Primary Grades*. Newark, Del.: International Reading Association, 1979.

18. Smith, Brooks; Goodman, Kenneth; and Meredith, Robert. *Language and Thinking in School*, 2d Ed. New York: Holt, Rinehart and Winston, 1976.

19. Strickland, Ruth. *The Language Arts in the Elementary School*, 3d Ed. Lexington, Mass.: D. C. Heath Company, 1969.

20. Thomas, Ves. *Teaching Spelling*, Toronto: Gage Educational Publishing Company Limited, 1974.

21. Zutell, Jerry. "Some Psycholinguistic Perspectives on Children's Spelling." *Language Arts*, 1978, *55*, 844-850.

# CHAPTER 7

# IMAGINATIVE PLAY
# AND CREATIVE EXPRESSION:
# CONTRIBUTIONS TO
# THE LANGUAGE ARTS

*Imagination is creative intellect and expression.*

"Jump in my car!" says Shirley to Rogelio as she pushes the wagon in front of him. Rogelio hops into the wagon and exclaims, "Let's get a milkshake and 'fries'!" In unison, they say, "Zoom!" as Shirley pulls the "car" toward the door of the classroom.

In this episode, imaginative play is occurring. Although the themes and stories change, depending on immediate interests, daily experiences, and age of the child, play occurs daily in schools, homes, and neighborhoods across the country. It is natural, very easy, fun, and spontaneous. "The Wicked Witch of the West," "Mommies and Daddies," "Aunt Veronica Visiting the Family," or thousands of other situations are created from a "puff of thin air." The powers of thought and imagination work to create, define, and carry out play in individual and group forms. The powers of communication work to convey meaning of play to the actor, participants, and observers.

Play is the ability of the child to creatively ". . . transform himself . . . to be a person or object other than himself, as indicated by his verbal and/or motoric enactment of his perception of the role." (5) In this sense, play is role taking, thinking, and communicating creatively in both verbal and nonverbal forms. In the act of playing, the children change themselves into other people, objects, or situations, from "Wonder Woman," "Daddy," "cat," or a "tree". The change requires much imaginative thought and creative communication. Just as a "quick-change" artist dashes from role to role, the child in a mental flash transforms himself from a person to another object or situation. In order to show play with objects, people, or situations, youngsters use communication. Using motor and verbal actions in a creative fashion, youngsters show these play transformations to themselves and others.

There are several significant contributions that imaginative play and creative expression make to language learning: (a) growth in imagining, (b) increased recall, (c) discriminative listening, (d) development of novel forms of communication, (e) learning socially appropriate communica-

205

tion, and *(f)* motor actions (38).

The first contribution of imaginative play and creative processes to language is "imagining." It is an intellectual function, the mental capacity to view a person, object, or situation "as if" it is another (20). A youngster who jumps into a cardboard box and pretends he is the "driver" and the cardboard box the "car" is using the mental process of imagining. The mental capacity to imagine "as if" links imaginative or make-believe play with intellectual functions such as language (20). For language growth, the ability to imagine builds conceptual referents basic to receptive and expressive communication (33). In play, the ability to imagine bridges the "change" from the self to another person, object, or situation. ". . . The relationship of play to imagining is . . . the foundation for linking play and languaging" (23). Then too, imagining through make-believe play has the potential to facilitate language growth and recall. Research findings show that youngsters who practice content from children's stories in play have greater intellectual growth and better recall of content than those who are questioned about content (20). In a similar study of the power of play and creative expression to facilitate language, research findings indicated that children who practice content in play show greater growth in language and reading readiness and imaginativeness than those who did not use play to rehearse the same content (30).

Increased recall is the second significant contribution of play and creative processes to language arts. Recall means the ability to remember information about events and situations accurately over short and longer periods of time. Play aids language growth because it provides meaningful opportunities to rehearse and practice situations and event (21). In make-believe episodes such as "Going to Grandmother's" or "Voting for the Mayor," children relive experiences and situations that have happened to them. Children can also contrive imaginative play and creative expression through vicarious experiences even though they have never actually experienced them. By reliving these situations that they have experienced in real or vicarious ways through play, they practice and rehearse for language memory. In turn, the play practice significantly aids recall of language forms, words, thoughts, and actions. Thus, language memory, for example, depends on the amount of play rehearsal used by the youngsters and on their current level of language (6). In addition, research findings show that play rehearsal compared to no rehearsal significantly contributes to the quality and quantity of aural language recall of story content in children ages five through seven (43).

Third, play and creative expression contribute to discriminative listening and seeing. Discriminative listening and seeing, crucial abilities for language arts learning, is the ability to identify and then use relevant auditory and visual cues in imaginative play and creative expression. Perceiving auditory and visual cues enables the player to carry out his role in the episode with thoroughness, meaningful and relevant detail, and accuracy (20). Whether or not the child communicates thoughts and ideas in play depends, in part, on the ability to discriminate auditory and visual cues from other players in the group. Listening and seeing discriminatively enables the child to not only participate more meaningfully in the episode but to show increased attention resulting in expressive and receptive language growth. Since discriminative listening and seeing are linked with the quality of verbal and motor communication used by the child, research results demonstrate that play provides ideal opportunities for children to develop and refine auditory and visual skills (32). In addition, research findings show that those children who displayed low levels of listening and speaking were able to increase their listening and speaking skills significantly through imaginative play from pre- to post-assessment (32).

The fourth contribution of imaginative play and creative processes to language growth is the development and use of novel forms of communication. Imaginative play of young children involves situations that bring a fresh eye to the marvels of language and linguistic sources and symbols (4). In imaginative play, children need to improvise in their roles. The gap between what the child already knows and what the role demands is bridged with new forms and uses of language (10). Imaginative play provides opportunities for children to develop and use novel symbols and figurative properties that convey individual and group meaning. Also, in play, children, ". . . can create verbs from nouns — 'I am blocking!' (i.e., building a tower with blocks) — and he can create nouns from verbs — 'Look! A sweep' (i.e., on discovering a toy broom)" (10). The new uses and forms of language that evolve in imaginative play ". . . have no known models or familiar antecedents" (20:49). Along with the generative power of novel language forms, imaginative play and creative processes facilitate, ". . . originality, spontaneity, verbal fluency, free flow of ideas and flexibility in adapting to new situations . . ." (22:536).

Learning socially appropriate communication is the fifth benefit of imaginative play for language growth. Imaginative play and creative processes provide real-life opportunities for children to learn socially appropriate language by modeling the communication that adults and peers use. Modeling and using language permits children to play ". . . at life and gives them a greater understanding of it . . ." (32:61). Modeling and practicing socially appropriate language also enables the child to identify with adult roles and to try on the roles and language to see how they fit. In the fitting processes through play children behave and think in "as if" form (31). Research findings indicate that those children who use social language in play, ". . . are better prepared and more readily integrated into real-life patterns of their immediate environments at an earlier age than children who do not engage . . . in imaginative play" (32:61).

The sixth contribution of imaginative play to language growth and learning is motor actions. As children play, they use motor movements and actions. The motor actions in play not only develop nonverbal communication but also contribute a conceptual base for effective language learning. As children move their arms, trunks, and bodies in play with or without objects, they use nonverbal language to communicate the meanings of these actions. Young children use a greater number of motor actions than older children; they communicate by physical movements (5).

The conceptual base for all intellectual functions such as language and memory is motor in origin (20). Children first come to know and understand objects and learn lower-order concepts by touching, feeling, grasping, and moving. Imaginative play and creative processes use large and small motor movements that are coordinated and organized into locomotor and nonlocomotor patterns (14). Research results indicate that children who reenact stories using motor (and verbal) actions in imaginative play significantly increase their aural and oral language comprehension on recall of story content more than those who simply listen to content without opportunity for physical action and play (27).

Growth in imagining, increased recall, discriminative listening, development of novel forms of communication, learning socially appropriate communication, and motor actions are the contributions that imaginative play and creative processes make to language learning and growth. These important contributions to communication processes of the young children provide a sound rationale for including and using imaginative play in language arts programs. To help use imaginative play and creative processes in the service of language, diagnosing, evaluating, and then prescribing are prerequisite tools.

## DIAGNOSING AND ASSESSING

Diagnosing and assessing the child's present level or predisposition to imaginative play is an important aspect for all language programs for young and older children. The evaluative processes helps us determine the beginning and ending points of instruction and learning and the growth that each youngster makes compared to himself or to a normed reference group.

For example, assessing whether or not the young child communicates through the medium of objects, such as puppets, helps us use the data for teaching and learning. Communicating through puppets or other play objects tells us that the child projects his language and thought processes beyond himself, shows the ability to coordinate language and movement, and uses verbal and nonverbal expression for individual and group purposes. Having found that the child can communicate through the medium of puppets, we now can plan for appropriate and extended skill learning and concept development in the language arts. During and after instruction, we again assess to determine whether or not the child is learning a particular skill or concept and note the progress between initial and final assessments. For example, after the child has shown the ability to communicate through objects, such as puppets, the educator now plans to increase the amount of oral language the child uses in imaginative play settings or other situations. Through uses of assessment and diagnosis, during and after instruction, the educator determines whether or not the child has learned the skill and accomplished the objective. The child's progress can be compared with himself over time and to a normed reference group. The amount of growth and learning through imaginative play is then estimated.

Evaluating listening, handwriting, or other areas of language arts is similar to assessing, diagnosing, and then prescribing for imaginative play and creative processes. Both formal and informal tools help us evaluate imaginative play processes and prescribe for extended language learning.

## Informal and Formal Measures

There are a number of instruments or evaluative tools that can be used to assess the level of imaginative play and language in young and older children. The instruments can be grouped into informal and formal ones. Informal ones are largely observational in nature and are not generally normed on groups of children. Formal instruments, on the other hand, have been normed on reference groups. Accordingly, scores from an informal measure can be used to compare a child with himself or to his classroom group, and scores from a formal instrument can be used to compare a child to his normed group (as well as with himself and his classroom group) over time.

For the young child at the preschool and kindergarten levels, two informal measures are Parten Social Participation Measure (18) and Yawkey Imaginative Play Checklist (40). For the older child in the primary grades, an effective informal tool for evaluating levels of imaginativeness and creative expression is the Singer Imaginative Play Predisposition Interview (30). For students at the preschool and kindergarten level, two formal measures are the Playfulness Scale (16) and Sociodramatic Play Index (32). For older children, two formal measures are Torrance Tests of Creative Thinking: Verbal and Figural (35), and Preschool Attainment Record (8). Other informal and formal tools useful for assessing creative thought and language in young and older children can be obtained in reference manuals such as Walker's *Socioemotional Measures for Preschool and Kindergarten Children* (36) and Buros's *Seventh Mental Measurement Yearbook* (3).

## Informal Measures

At the preschool-kindergarten level and for childen, age three through five, the Parten Social Participation Scale (18) is a well-known informal tool. Basically used in observational settings, the tool can be used to assess the quantity and quality of imaginative play that youngsters show in spontaneous group-play settings. The Parten Social Participation Scale (18) assesses only 6 given major types of imaginative play actions: unoccupied, solitary, onlooker, parallel, associative, and cooperative creative play actions. Unoccupied play means that the child is simply not involved in creative play and expression. We can also score for solitary (an individual playing creatively alone), onlooker (the child watching others play), and parallel play (two or more pupils sitting side-by-side and appearing to be playing together but not interacting; there is no meaningful dialogue between them). Associative and cooperative play mean the youngsters at minimum are interacting with one another over a play object or over situations. Cooperative play shows the pupils are meaningfully interacting. They pick up on each other's cues, and use their imaginative ideas and language to reach and extend group-generated goals.

The Yawkey Imaginative Play Checklist (40) is an observational tool that essentially assesses the youngster's level of creative thought in either individual or group settings. Similar to the Parten Social Participation Scale (18), you can use the Yawkey Imaginative Play Checklist (40) to rate the pupils on several creative language and thought dimensions. This tool scores both verbal and nonverbal actions that show creative thought. There are four main ideas or dimensions to the instrument, and all items assess the quantity of creative transformation. Imaginative thought transformations are the creative mental processes children use in play to change themselves into other people, objects, and situations (38). In using the instrument, we assess what children say and do in play and thus evaluate the type and quantity of creative mental transformations. Accordingly, the type and quantity of creative transformations of thought and language can be observed and scored by "noting the motor actions children use and how they use them in role play," and "identifying the verbal language they use and how they communicate their ideas in the role" (38:3). The four items of the instrument that assess creative thought and expression are: (1) self-transformation, (2) transformations of objects, (3) transformations of people, and (4) transformation of situations (38). Children's creative thought and language are scored for self transformation when they creatively use their body parts to improvise for make-believe objects, people, and situations (with no concrete and real objects used in the episode). Scoring for transformation of objects and people requires the use of concrete materials in their play. However, through creative thought and language, the children, depending on the theme of the episode, change objects into different ones (such as a cardboad box into a car), and themselves into other people (for example, parents, astronauts, teachers). Transformations of situation, the fourth item, means that their imaginative actions show detail, have a beginning, midpoint, and ending, and are generated and carried out in group settings.

For older children in the primary grades an informal test to use in assessing creative expression and thought is the Singer Imaginative Play Interview (30). Because the test is interview-based, its focus is solely on creative expression rather than both imaginative communication and movements. The Singer Imaginative Play Interview (30) is administered individually, ideal for the older child because of the heavy reliance on verbal answers to complex creative questions, and is individually yet efficiently administered in about fifteen minutes. In the interview, you ask the youngster four questions dealing with personal creative play endeavors and six questions focusing on creative play activities he and his parents do together at home. The first four questions are: (30:278)

1. What is your favorite game? What do you like to play most? (Write verbatim answers. Query if not enough information to score.)
2. What game do you like to play best when you're all alone? What do you like to do best when you're all alone? Do you ever think things up?
3. Do you ever have pictures in your head? Do you ever see make-believe things or pictures in your mind and think about them? What sort of things?
4. Do you have a make-believe friend? Do you have an animal or toy or make-believe person to talk to or take along places with you?

The second set of six questions follows: (30:278)

1. What kinds of things do you do with your parents?
2. Whom do you like best, father or mother, or do you like both the same?
3. What kinds of games do you play with your parents?
4. Do your parents ever read to you or tell you stories? Who? Mother, father, or both?
5. How many children are in the family? Who is the oldest?
6. How much time do you spend watching TV? Favorite programs?

The student's answers to each of the questions in the first set are scored from 1 to 4 with one point awarded to responses with no to little creative thought content and four points given to responses that reflect high imaginative content. The responses to each of the questions in the second set are not rated formally but instead give information useful in explaining the youngster's answers to the first set of questions and in prescribing extended learning opportunities.

At the preschool-kindergarten level the formal measures that can be used as tools for evaluating the student's creative expression and play are Lieberman Playfulness Scale (15;16) and Sociodramatic Play Index (32). The Playfulness Scale provides an assessment of how creatively the child plays and how imaginatively he expresses his thoughts in play. Accordingly, the scale measures quantity and the quality of creative expression based on our observations of the student in spontaneous and adult-guided play activities. Essentially, each item of the Playfulness Scale (15;16) asks the teacher to rate the child along a five-point scale calibrated on the degree that he displays particular creative play and expressive actions. Across twelve questions of the scale, one point is awarded if the pupil rarely demonstrates the action to five points if he repeatedly shows creative expression and play.The twelve items of the Playfulness Scale, Form K, are: (16:153-156)

1. **A.** How often does the child engage in spontaneous physical movement and activity during the play?
   **B.** How is his/her motor coordination during physical activity?
2. **A.** How often does the child show joy in or during his play activities?
   **B.** With what freedom of expression does he show joy?
3. **A.** How often does the child show a sense of humor during play?
   **B.** With what degree of consistency is humor shown?
4. **A.** While playing, how often does the child show flexibility in his interaction with the surrounding group structure?
   **B.** With what degree of ease does the child move?
5. **A.** How often does the child show spontaneity during expressive and dramatic play?
   **B.** What degree of imagination does the child show in his expressive dramatic lay?
6. How bright is the child?
7. How attractive is the child?

The Sociodramatic Play Index (32) is another observational instrument that evaluates the preschool-kindergarten child's level of creative expression and play. Like the Lieberman Playfulness Scale (15:16), the index is used to score the content of the child's language and actions as shown in spontaneous and guided play situations. It is especially useful in assessing language content generated by the children in dramatic and sociodramatic play episodes. Both dramatic and sociodramatic play are forms of group play, and differences between them can be determined by the quality of meaningful interaction of the children at play. Sociodramatic play demonstrates greater meaningful interaction among group members, more attention to detail in play, and greater frequency of group decision making than dramatic play and always occurs in group settings. Additional factors that distinguish sociodramatic from dramatic play are the bases on which the Sociodramatic Play Index is built and used by teachers working with young children. These key factors are: (32:98-99).

1. *Initiative role play.* The child undertakes a make-believe role and expresses it in imitative action and or verbalization.
2. *Make-believe in regard to objects.* Movements or verbal declarations are substituted for real objects.
3. *Make-believe in regard to actions and situations.* Verbal descriptions are substituted for actions and situations.
4. *Persistence.* The child persists in a play episode for at least ten minutes.
5. *Interaction.* There are at least two players interacting in the framework of the play episode.
6. *Verbal communication.* There is some verbal interaction related to the play episode.

Accordingly, the children's creative expression and play actions are scored using one of the four ratings:

1. A  + sign shows this factor was used by the child in dramatic play during one of the periods of observation.
2. A ? symbol indicates this factor was used in the child's dramatic play but only in part or only for a very short time.
3. The O sign shows that the child did not use this factor at all during the observation periods of his dramatic play behavior.
4. The NP symbol indicates that the child did not once engage in dramatic play throughout the observation periods.

Both the Torrance Tests of Creative Thinking: Verbal and Figural (35) and the Preschool Attainment Record (8) are formal instruments to evaluate primary grade children's capacities for imaginative play and expression. The Torrance Tests of Creative Thinking (35) are group-administered, paper-and-pencil tests that are commercially marketed in two forms. Both Form A and B are divided into two sections, "Thinking Creatively with Words" and "Thinking Creatively with Pictures." The verbal section contains "as-and-guess" items, product improvement tasks (where the student is asked to think of new improvements for a toy), and cardboard box activities. The children's answers on the verbal section are scored for the number of possibilities (that is, fluency), development of new ideas (originality), and/or the use of different approaches or strategies (flexibility).

The picture or figural section contains three items. One item or task is a picture construction activity; the second and third involve the completion of pictures and line drawings, respectively. The responses to the items are scored for originality and the quantity of relevant detail added to the stimulus picture and space that encloses it (elaboration). The tasks involving pictures and lines are also scored for fluency and flexibility.

The Preschool Attainment Record (8) is a formal tool used to assess children at primary (as well as lower) grades for various dimensions such as physical, social, and intellectual growth. Specifically, the teacher rates the youngster on eight categories of growth: (1) communication, (2) creativity, (3) information, (4) responsibility, (5) manipulation, (6) ideation, (7) rapport, and (8) ambulation. Each of the eight categories is broken down into subitems and arranged by age, in intervals of six months' growth. The teacher simply observes and checks off the appropriate creative expression and play action that the child shows.

The informal and formal measures of creative language and play actions can be easily used at preschool-kindergarten and primary grade levels. The measures are extremely useful tools, for they provide a partial picture of the child's level of imaginative growth and use of creative expression. In addition, they identify selected areas of creative thought and language that are of particular importance in your work with young children.

## INSTRUCTION

Creative processes used in language and thought as well as in play can be taught to young and older children. Like any skill or concept creative expression and play can be taught and learned. Without systematic teacher attention to creative processes in the language arts, researchers such as Singer (30) conclude that creative language and thought decrease and diminish as the child grows older. With the importance of creative processes and the instruments to assess and diagnose them, the following sections focus on instruction and teacher strategies that can be used to facilitate them with children at preschool-kindergarten and primary grade levels.

### Preschool-Kindergarten: Some Techniques

Young children, ages three through five, are in their formative years of growth and learning. Accordingly, it is particularly important to encourage growth and learning of creative thought and language processes. In order to encourage growth and learning of creative processes and play, several factors are important to accomplishing this objective. They are (1) identifying goals for teaching creative processes, (2) structurally arranging the environment and effectively easing classroom space, (3) selecting and working with creative play materials, (4) developing creative dramatics activities, (5) conducting creative movement experiences, and (6) guiding the growth of "telling stories."

**Developing creative processes.** The necessary ingredients of imagination and creative thought and language are also the three main goals for teaching creative processes to young children (42): control, reality, and motivation. Control is the degree to which a child can exercise his own self-direction in his endeavors. Internal control serves as a vehicle for the development and learning of creative thought and language. In deciding on and carrying out activities they choose, young children nurture the growth of imaginative thought and language. Exercising large amounts of external control over children in play and language situations and always directing them to perform activities that they do not select produce great constraints on internal motivation and on the growth of creative processes in play. To develop creative language and thought processes, a goal of the classroom and the language arts program is to encourage internal rather than external control. Secondly, encouraging creative processes and imaginative play requires the youngsters to suspend external reality in order to "create," to "make-believe," and to "pretend." Freeing the youngsters from the external constraints of reality permits them the opportunity to follow self-guided desires and individual endeavors characteristic of internal reality.

A third goal and necessary ingredient of imagination and creative thought is motivation. Involving the youngsters to become interested in "as if" or "let's pretend" activities motivates them to engage in creative thinking and ultimately to use imaginative expression. The motivation to become involved in these types of activities and ultimately to rehearse, practice, develop, and learn creative expression comes primarily from the child, not the teacher. For creative thought and language to flourish, the young child's activity must be meaningful and relevant to him. The pupils lose themselves in a "sea of words," which defines and refines their creative thought. Motivation to perform this activity rather than that one provides opportune times and serves as a base for the development of creative thought and language processes. The pupil's free expression of creative thought processes is enhanced by their ability to identify and carry out their own actions and decisions. Fostering creative expression and play at the preschool-kindergarten level can only be facilitated when the elements of creative thought become the goals for developing imaginative young children within the language arts curriculum. The degree of control and motivation and amounts of reality form the bricks and mortar of creative thinking and imaginative play in young children.

**Structuring the environment.** A second important factor to consider in encouraging the growth and learning of creative processes and play is structurally arranging the environment and effectively using classroom space. The teacher can survey the classroom environment to see if it says,"Use me in your own way!" Using the classroom in the child's own way becomes challenging and facilitates creative thinking and imaginative play. Bookshelves can become a supermarket food shelf, a work table evolves into a space station, and a classroom is changed into a farm. The classroom is the child's world. Attention can be given to its structure and the materials that facilitate creative processes. Flexibility in structuring and using the environment and in utilizing space maximize the potential for growth of internal control, internal motivation, and inner-directed reality. They facilitate the youngster's creative thought and language. Thus, surveying the environment "with a child's eye" and reorganizing it to say, "Use me in your own way!" provide another approach to reaching your goal of teaching creative processes and play.

**Selecting appropriate classroom materials.** Selecting appropriate classroom materials that facilitate growth and learning of creative thought and language is the third important consideration. Other than flexibility in using the environment, the potential for maximizing creative thought and language rests largely on the quality and quantity of materials within it (9). To insure that the materials and the classroom environment are conducive to creative processes, two questions are important. The questions can be used as criteria to check whether or not the materials have the potential to facilitate imaginative thought and language.

**1.** Are the materials flexible enough for the child to act on them in many ways?
**2.** Are there a number of materials to permit the child many choices?

Observing classroom environments and determining whether or not the materials permit flexibility of actions and a number of choices are two ways the teacher can facilitate creative thinking and play processes.

All the young child's play materials in classrooms can be classified into groups based on the functions that they serve. If the classroom materials are commercially manufactured, carefully examining the objects and reading the directions on the labels will reveal particular purposes, objectives, or functions that they can serve. Based on the manufacturer's purpose for constructing them and not on how the children use them in creative expression and play, the groups are: (1) constructional, (2) instructional, (3) toys, and (4) real play objects.

Constructional materials are made to be used by young children in many ways. Since they have broad rather than specific functions, constructional materials are multipurpose. Building blocks and building sets are the two largest subgroups of constructional materials. Building blocks come in a variety of sizes. Some are made from wood; others are manufactured from cardboard. Large hollow wooden blocks with shallow centers can be carried by the children from place to place. The large hollow cardboard blocks are reinforced with multiple layers of strong cardboard with interlocking surfaces that could support two hundred pounds or more. There are also small building blocks called table blocks; they are smaller in size than the large blocks and are made from wood.

Instructional materials are the second category of material used by the child in creative activities and experiences. However, they are initially designed by the manufacturer to teach particular concepts and skills largely derived from the three ''basic r's'' of reading, arithmetic, and writing. Some of the basic language concepts that could be taught with instructional materials are matching letters; discriminating size, texture, and colors; part-to-whole relationships; and shapes of objects. Instructional materials include puzzles, stacking toys, and nesting toys.

Puzzles are either formboards, or jigsaws. Formboards are the most common type of puzzle for the child at the pre-school level. They have movable parts or pieces with inserts or knobs on them that help children hold and move them about. For advanced preschool-kindergarten children, jigsaws are available. One type of jigsaw requires childen to put together pieces of objects or persons, and the other focuses on relatively simple scenes such as farms, zoos, and others. Another example of instructional materials is stacking toys. They are made from plastic or wood with a base (or platform) and a dowel securely inserted in the middle of the base. The individual pieces have holes bored in the center. The youngsters insert the pieces through the dowel and sequence the pieces by size. Nesting materials, a third example of instructional toys, are made either from wood or plastic and vary by size and shape. The sizes vary from large to small. Examples of shapes include dolls, boxes, chests, eggs, and numerous others. With these materials, the youngster can place one piece inside the other to complete the ordered sequence by fitting them together.

The third group of classroom material is the real play object. Real play objects have specific purposes in the adult world and are largely made for use by adults.They provide tremendous opportunities for children's creative expression and play. The most common examples of real materials are sand, water, wood, clay, and adult clothing. All serve as superb materials for encouraging the young child's creative thinking and expression. Since sand and water take the shape of their containers, numerous kinds of imaginative play become possible. Clay can be patted, pounded, rolled, torn, cut, or squeezed and is an ideal medium for imagination and creative thought. Discarded men's, women's, big sister's, and big brother's clothing is very usable for imaginative and creative play. Other types of adult clothing that have the potential to facilitate creative processes and play are old shoes, both high heels and flats; boots; men's and women's dress-up and work clothing; hats; suits; belts; handbags; and ties.

The fourth category of material used to encourage creative processes is toys. Toys are miniature versions of real objects, people, and animals. They are scaled-down replicas of real materials. Grouped by similarities, toys include: housekeeping toys, transportation materials, and animal toys. Examples of housekeeping toys are dolls, doll clothing and carriages, cots, tables, refrigerators, and ironing boards. Pots, pans, dishes, and silverware are other examples. Transportation toys include toy trucks, trains, ships, airplanes, space vehicles, and 1001 other kinds of vehicles, some of which the children ride. Several examples of these riding toys are wagons, scooters, and tricycles. Examples of animal toys include dogs, cats, tigers, elephants, and others from farm, jungle, mountain, or zoo. Other types of animal toys that depict people in various occupations and life-styles are cowboys, daddies, mommies, soldiers, or monsters.

Selecting and preparing the materials for classroom use is the spice of creative thinking and expression. There should be a number of items from which to choose, permitting the youngsters to use these materials in many ways. Selection and flexibility give children the opportunity to use objects having more than one function, employ them in a number of ways, and encourage their desires to interact with them.

Maintaining a balance among the four types of materials helps to maintain variety among the types of objects. For creative thought and imaginative expression to emerge, the child's world of objects must be balanced. Including a number of play materials from each of the groups in the classroom gives a number of challenges to the children and insures richness and depth of imaginative processes. In addition, a balance of materials among four groups permits young children to pound, dress up, build, color, point, and roll them. Challenge, excitement, and interest are the outcomes of maintaining a balance among groups of play materials that are conducive to facilitating creative processes and play.

**Developing creative dramatics activities.** Creative dramatics is defined as the youngster's ability to improvise and act out feelings, emotions, and attitudes creatively and expressively, using verbal actions and/or motoric movements (24). Expressions, interpretations of concerns, understandings, and desires are ways youngsters create impromptu drama. Youngsters do not creatively develop drama from a formal script. They create characters, actions, and possibly use dialogue as they guide themselves to think, feel, and become involved in the theme or topic. Children develop drama from a story or verse as well as real and vicarious experiences. Such dramatic roles can be performed alone or as a part of a group.

Children receive many benefits from participating in creative dramatics. These benefits are for the most part the contributions of dramatics to creative expression and play processes. As a spontaneous method to test out ideas, creative dramatics help youngsters gain insights into behavior of self and significant others. Secondly, they imitate adults and peers and increase their understanding of those people whom they model. Thirdly, identification of real-life roles offers the child satisfaction when he finds coping with others difficult (12). Dramatics also offers people the opportunity to develop and use creative leadership and express feelings appropriate to real life. Then, too, through reversal of roles, a child can enlarge his concept of himself and simultaneously learn to become a member of a group. By helping to work out problems and creatively experience their solutions, creative dramatics contributes much to the growth and learning of the self and the self in group situations. Finally, creative dramatics simulates intellectual growth by placing the children in situations where they are compelled to behave at levels higher than their chronological ages (32). Thus, dramatics trains young children to create, think, feel, and show empathy.

There are a number of forms or types of creative dramatics (13). They include finger plays, single-action poetry, action games, action songs, dramatic play, sociodramatic play, pantomime, and puppetry. The latter two types of creative dramatics are more characteristic of older primary grade than younger preschool-kindergarten children and therefore are explained in the following section.

Fingerplay as a form of dramatic play includes songs, chants, and rhymes. The youngsters recite them and at the same time they physically act them out. The motoric actions are done with fingers, hands, legs, and body coordinated movements. Examples of common finger plays are "I'm a Little Tea Pot," "The Itsy Bitsy Spider," and "The Wheels on the Bus."

Single-action poetry is another type of creative dramatics for the preschool-kindergarten child. Poems are recited by the children. As they say the words, they act out the poetry by performing actions such as running, hopping, and skipping. The large motor actions can be done "in place" or actually performed, assuming enough movement space for each pupil. Examples include: "A Farmer Went Riding," and "I'm Hiding — I'm Hiding."

The third type of creative dramatics is called action songs. The children sing the song and act out the action words. Action songs are very short and have only a few well-defined movements. Two examples of dramatic action songs which are favorites of preschool-kindergarten youngsters are "Did You Ever See a Lassie?" and "If You're Happy and You Know It." Another kind is called action games. These are group-based games that are neither competitive nor do they have winners or losers. The object of the action game is to make the movement that the adult or child suggests. Some are "Follow the Leader" and "Simon Says."

The fifth type of creative dramatics is action stories. These are rather common short stories that children have heard before. The teacher reads or the child tells the story and then performs the action. As the leader demonstrates the movements, the children follow and perform the same actions. For the preschool-kindergarten child, several examples include "Lion Hunt," "Bear Hunt," and "Brave Little Indian."

Dramatic and sociodramatic play are two more advanced forms of creative dramatics. Dramatic play occurs when the pupil models parents, teachers, peers, and significant others. Since the youngster simply models what the people and peers do and say, dramatic play requires little meaningful interaction with his peers. Sociodramatic play, on the other hand, results when the child is aware and understands that such role modeling involves and requires meaningful interaction with other people. Through sociodramatic play, the student's efforts are aimed at reproducing his world exactly as possible as ". . . he observes it, as he understands, and insofar as he remembers it" (32:71).

In dramatic play youngsters enact immediate sensory impressions, such as acting out mother, father, or baby sister. They use motoric and/or verbal actions to show the role and depict the actions of the model. Experiences in the family and other real activities with family members form the basis for dramatic play attitudes. Vicarious experiences from television heroes and heroines also contribute some story situations and content for dramatic play episodes. This type of creative dramatics like the others can either be initiated by the child or with guidance by the teacher.

Sociodramatic play is a more advanced form of creative dramatics. Involving role play, sociodramatic play is the spontaneous acting out of a problem situation that involves some form of human relations. It is largely social in nature and includes more complex social transactions than dramatic play. Children discuss, decide, plan, and act out the roles in group settings. It involves at least a three-way transaction. Communiction occurs not only between child-players but also between the players and the teacher. Developing creative dramatics with children at preschool-kindergarten levels assists the growth and learning of creative thinking and expression. With the varying forms of creative dramatics, the youngsters' materials and their bodies and minds are the media through which they effectively create and learn.

**Conducting creative movement experiences.** Movement experiences are a form of play and are important to a youngster's creative growth and learning. Students not only respond to stimuli covertly, but young children especially need to respond through overt actions — to move, grasp, touch, and run. Children use movement as a medium of expression and learn the fundamentals of body expression to develop his body and body conditions creatively.

In creative movement, the concern is with self-expression. The self is the focal point of all creative movement learning. The student expresses what he feels, thinks, hears, and sees in his own way through movement. Accordingly, opportunities to show and experience such feelings, thoughts, and expression need to be encouraged and provided.

Developing creative movement in the young child involves three phases or factors (2). They are (1) the child and his creative power, feelings, and imagination; (2) the action or interaction of his experiences; and (3) his outward form of expression.

First of all, in order to facilitate creative movement, the child and his creative powers develop as he learns to explore and discover what his body can and cannot do. The youngsters can discover or the teacher can guide them in mastering various rhythmic movements such as alligator crawl, grasshopper jump, horse gallop, ant crawl. In either guided or spontaneous learning situations, flexibility is important. No standard rhythmic patterns should be continually used. Emphasis should be on providing numerous and varied opportunities to the child to assist growth rather than training Olympic stars in creative rhythmic patterns.

Secondly, creative movement evolves in the child as the product of his actions or interactions of his experiences. Spontaneous and guided movements are natural outlets for teaching creative movement, thought, and feeling. Careful selection of the activities and support provided the child as he performs them facilitate the learning of the creative movements. Creative movement, then, is best learned in mutually interactive settings and situations. For example, in teaching children to express varying movements of animals creatively, the teacher can maximize this objective after the youngsters have returned from a visit to the zoo or circus. Children, having experienced the motor patterns of the animals on a firsthand basis, can learn to model and imitate the movements of the animal's action. Thus, encouraging creative movement in young children is not accomplished in a vacuum but as a product of interactive experiences in the environment. Growth in creative movement is dependent on classroom opportunities as well as on time, space, your supportive attitudes, and the meaningful experiences and urgent needs of the children.

The third factor that contributes to developing creative movement in the young child is his outward form of expression used to enact it. There are a number of basic elements that the child needs to master in order to demonstrate creative movement effectively. These include locomotor movement, body movement, movement combinations, and qualities of movement (2). Locomotor movements are those that help propel the youngster's body through space, that move the child from place to place. They are walking, leaping, running, and hopping. Body movements are nonlocomotor actions begun from a fixed base. Thought of as "what-I-can-do-without-my-body-going-anywhere," the body movements include swinging, bending, stretching, pushing and pulling, twisting, striking, dodging, shaking, and bouncing.

The third motor element that contributes to developing and refining creative movement is movement combinations. Movement actions are locomotor combined with body movements — or just simply putting two or more movements together. Examples include locomotor combinations such as skipping (walk-plus hop) and polka (hop, slide, plus walk), body combinations like bend and stretch or swing and push, and locomotor and body combinations like leap and swing, skip, and bounce. Quality of movement is the fourth element that contributes to outward forms of the expression used in creative movement. This element refers to the mode used by the youngster to execute the movement. The qualities of space and rhythm help students express themselves and define their movements more adequately. Two examples of the characteristics of space are directions and range. The quality of rhythm includes characteristics such as tempo, accent, and intensity.

Through careful and systematic planning, we can facilitate the growth of creative movement in young children. As a base for the motor forms used in creative dramatics and other areas of the language arts, creative movement experiences are vital to imaginative play and creative processes.

**Guiding story telling.** The last factor that is crucial in encouraging growth and learning of creative processes and play is telling stories. For the preschool-kindergarten child, telling stories is a natural, spontaneous, and ideal vehicle for fostering creative expression and thought. Story telling helps to develop such language arts skills as (19):

- Recalling events of a story heard by the children
- Using descriptive statements, sentences, and words
- Speaking clearly and loudly for the youngsters to hear
- Using sentences, gestures, facial expressions, and voice changes
- Speaking easily without being self-conscious

After pupils hear a story, see a favorite television show, return from a field trip, a vacation, or other experiences, the teacher can ask them to recall and repeat the experience. Here, you can informally encourage the child to retell the complete episode, to commence at the beginning, and use as many descriptive words as possible in telling the story. Story telling should also be done informally — perhaps sitting in a circle or on a rug. In retelling the experience, the young child shows enthusiasm in being asked to recount episodes of interest to him. Children listening to the experience are attentive and are willing to volunteer additional information. You should make sure, however, that the story is retold as a cohesive unit. Prompting the pupil at particular points during the playback assists remembering and recalling the events in the story and aids memory processes.

Story telling provides one of the best opportunities to teach creative and imaginative thought and expression as well as numerous other concepts and skills that are crucial to the effective growth and learning of language arts in preschool-kindergarten youngsters.

## Primary Grades: Some Techniques

Older pupils, ages six through eight, can also expand their knowledge and understanding of creative processes and imaginative play actions. Like children at the preschool-kindergarten level, pupils in the primary grades can be encouraged to show creative thinking and language on a systematic basis throughout the week.

Several factors help in facilitating creative processes and learning to speak and think in more creative ways in the older child. Generally speaking, some of the same factors used to enhance the young child's creative thought can be used with the older pupil. These techniques include selecting and working with creative play materials, developing creative dramatic activities, conducting creative movement experiences, and guiding the growth of telling stories.

In addition, there are several other techniques that can be used more effectively with older than with younger students. Specifically, those applicable to older children are guiding pantomime, using puppetry, using directed role play, creating as a language and imaginative experience, and reporting orally. These five techniques require greater conceptual growth, more experiences at living and learning, and higher levels of creative expression and play than those suggested for the preschool and kindergarten children.

**Guiding pantomime.** In pantomime, one of the more advanced forms of creative dramatics, the student expresses himself through gestures and body movements that show his actions and emotions in imitating a person, situation, or object. With pantomime, students use gestures and body movements but may not speak or make sounds in expressing and enacting roles. The actions expressed in pantomime range from the very simple, for instance, stretching and pretending to yawn to more difficult ones, such as climbing a telephone pole or getting lost while climbing a mountain. Pantomime, like the other forms of creative dramatics, is individual and personal. There is no right or wrong expression — only a form of creative communication and play that expresses a particular child's thoughts. If all the ideas that the student shows in pantomime are worthwhile and accepted by the audience and the teacher, he develops self-confidence and a positive self-image in addition to learning creative expression. Therefore an atmosphere of acceptance not rejection, of trust not mistrust, of openness not fearfulness, must be developed between you and student and between the students themselves. The foundation of acceptance, trust, and openness facilitates pantomime. Once these keystones are established, the teaching and learning of pantomime blossom.

There are basically five different types of pantomime (25). Each one is more advanced and requires greater conceptual and creative abilities than the previous one. The types are: (1) narrative, (2) story starter, (3) sensory,

(4) personal, and (5) audience pantomimes (25).

Narrative pantomime is the easiest type to use with children. After the teacher reads the story, the children retell and extend it using pantomime. As they are pantomiming it, the teacher, if needed, can prompt the students with questions and statements to help them remember the sequence, parts, or details of the story. In using pantomime as a "story starter" the teacher begins to read a story that the children have not heard before and stops at a critical point in the narrative. The children's task is to take over and complete the story by creatively developing an ending and showing it through pantomime. Where necessary, prompts and cues can be given by the teacher to assist the expansion of the story.

The third type is called sensory pantomime. This type of pantomime does not use a story as a base or starter for the children's imaginative and imitative gestures. Instead, situations that naturally occur in the classroom are used for pantomime. For example, a stray dog enters the classroom, a child finds a hat on the playground and brings it to the teacher, and a horrible smell breaks out — are also situations for sensory pantomime. These incidental experiences are the bases for this kind of pantomime. In using the personal pantomime, the children are given situations to enact by the teacher or peer group member. Personal pantomime is difficult to perform because it rests on advanced levels of creative expression and conceptual development and requires previous experiences with pantomiming processes. For example, themes such as "a person lost in the post office," or "the first astronaut to land on the planet Mars" are given to the pupils and they, in turn reenact them through pantomime. This type of pantomime has fewer restrictions than the others. The child is free to create and maneuver flexibly and develop his own actions and gestures to fit the theme. Instead of the teacher suggesting the themes for the personal pantomime, the children can develop surprise topics for others to act out.

The final type is called the audience pantomime. Here, the children who pantomime situations perform before an audience. This type of pantomime is actually prepresentational. The audience forces the pupil to communicate his thoughts as clearly as possible to convey his ideas to the observers. The students in the audience cue and prompt the player and use other forms of direction or feedback. Providing feedback to the pantomimist gives the pupil in the audience sound sources to practice in observing and interpreting his actions and gestures.

Pantomime, a form of creative dramatics, is extremely useful and provides much practice in developing and using nonverbal gestures and actions of primary grade children.

**Using puppets.** Puppetry is the last type of creative dramatics that is important to teaching and learning in the language arts. Puppets can either be used with formally prepared and predetermined script or in creative and spontaneous fashion without standardizing the process. Regardless of the procedures followed in using them, puppets are ideal media of expression. Shy children, once able to express themselves, lose their inhibitions and self-consciousness behind the stage or mask. Aggressive students learn to subordinate their actions and reactions behind the mask of a puppet.

Puppetry is ideal for developing imaginative play, creative expression, and language skills. Using puppets motivates the children. They can exchange ideas without fear of failure. They express their imaginations to their fullest potential. The audience, viewing the puppets in action, offers creative suggestions by spontaneously reacting and interjecting ideas to them and the child as the play progresses. Puppets also facilitate reading and writing skills and help children acquire positive social concepts and feelings of belonging, cooperating, and sharing. Outside the objective of using puppets to facilitate imaginative play, they are used to provide therapy to children with handicaps and personality disorders, and they help to control emotional actions by rechanneling outlets for expressions and actions in constructive ways.

Ideas for making puppets can be obtained from pictures, stories, music, holiday themes, and art experiences. They come in a variety of sizes and can be as simple or as complex as you wish to make them. Puppets can be made from many materials — paper plates, straws, bottle caps, hats, socks, or paper bags. The varieties of puppets are just as numerous as the materials from which they can be made, including styrofoam puppets, string puppets, stick puppets, sock, and fist puppets. Since there are so many types of puppets, each having specific purposes and different constructional materials, several handy reference books describing puppets are "musts" for the school, professional, and classroom libraries. Some of the many handy references include Hanford's *Puppets and Puppeteering* (11), Renfro's *Puppets for Play Production* (26), and Tiedt's *Contemporary English in the Elementary School* (34).

Puppets are one of the most useful media for teaching creative expression, thought, and imaginative play to children in primary grades. They are versatile, easy to make and use, and outstanding teachers of language arts skills and concepts.

**Using directed role play.** Once children have had experience in self-guided or spontaneous role play and have learned to define, divide up, and creatively enact imaginative episodes in groups, you can now employ directed role play with primary grade children. Directed role play enables the teacher to guide the imaginative play of older children and use it as a teaching tool for systematic instruction in fostering imaginative play and creative thinking and expression.

In setting the stage for directed role play, you first decide and plan for its educational uses as an integral part of language arts learning and teaching. During the planning stage, the teacher also adjusts the steps in directed role play to fit the grade level, maturity, needs, and age of the pupil. To plan and use directed role play systematically to accomplish specific educational objects for enhancing creative and play processes with older children, there are several steps to examine. The formal steps in role playing are (17):

1. Developing classroom atmosphere
2. Warming up the class
3. Selecting the role players
4. Setting the stage
4. Preparing the audience
6. Role playing the episode
7. Discussing the episode
8. Adding reenactments as necessary (for example, replaying and/or reversing roles, rehearsing following the episode, or simply exploring alternative role planning possibilities)
9. Discussing reenactments where needed
10. Sharing experiences and generalizing

The step of developing classroom atmosphere is the key to developing imaginative role taking and creative expression, for only when teachers and students are perceived as nonthreatening, can role play effectively develop. Accordingly, a positive classroom atmosphere means that the contributions and the needs of both teachers and students are recognized. The second step is called warming up the class. In the warm-up phase, you provide the children with some background on the situation, problem, and story that they are to role play. For example, for the warm-up phase you may decide to read a problem story to the children and stop at the point in the story that poses a dilemma. In order to make the warm-up period more effective and meaningful, the children must first have had experience with a similar problem story from their own experiences. In other words, the students must have some firsthand experiences with similar story themes and problems in order for them to role play them effectively.

The third step in formal directed role play is selecting the role players. In formal role playing, there are a number of ways that roles can be assigned. The teacher can ask the pupils which roles they prefer to play. Sometimes you can select a student to role play a person or situation based on his particular need to identify with it. The students can also be chosen for roles on the basis of whether or not they can identify with them. Setting the stage is the fourth formal set in role play development. After the selection process, the players join together in a group setting to plan broadly what they are going to do in the play. Thus, a broad plan of action is drawn up, and the pupils discuss the consequences of the role play and the roles they are to play.

Preparing the audience is the fourth step. The observers or audience must be prepared to participate actively in the episode. Accordingly, the teacher provides the audience with selected questions to help the observers learn active listening and auditory discrimination skills. The sixth step is role playing the episode. The role play begins with each actor playing the role as he sees it. Discussing the episode, the seventh step, occurs at the end of the entire role play episode. The questions for listening prepared for the audience are now used as discussion points. The most important point of the discussion is to get the pupils to express their opinions and ideas about the content of the enactment, not the student playing the role. They creatively project and explore differing consequences or alternatives to the problems.

Adding reenactments as necessary, the eighth step, depends on your goals for language arts skill and concept development and the student's ideas gathered from the discussion. Also, for educational purposes of reinforcing learning and developing more creative solutions to the questions and problems posed in the discussion, the role play can be reenacted. The ninth step is discussing reenactments. Here, discussion follows the reenactment and is a necessary step in formal role play procedures. With guidance the students analyze and reanalyze the role play situations and at the same time extend creative processes and imaginative play abilities.

The final step is sharing experiences and generalizing. You can use this formal step to evaluate creative language and expression acquired through role play. You may also use the step to provide opportunities to assess the learning of the creative processes as well as identify social problems arising from the imaginative play.

When you use the ten formal steps to directed role play with older children, make sure every effort is made to capitalize on the relationship between learning role taking and developing creative thinking and expressing.

**Creating as a language and imaginative play experience.** The fourth tool to consider in encouraging creative thought and expression in older children is called creating as a language experience (19). A modification of this tool is language and imaginative play experience (41). In creating as a language experience, the teacher can either serve as the writer while the youngsters dictate the story content or have each student write his own story. You may wish to serve as the writer for the group when the children are first introduced to and taught to write stories, need experience in developing written passages from oral discourse, are beginning to master the mechanics of handwriting and spelling, and have all experienced or become involved in the same activity (which is used as a base for their story). Secondly, the teacher may decide to have each child write a story on their experiences when they have sufficiently mastered the mechanics of manuscript or cursive writing and basic spelling words, have learned the basic elements of sentences and paragraph construction, and have experienced an activity that is more appropriate for individual than group expression.

Regardless of which one of the two procedures you choose in the writing, the language experience story helps to develop oral discourse, enriches written language, and serves creative thought and expression. As we pointed out in the chapter on written composition, all direct and vicarious experiences can serve as grist for content of a language experience story. In turn, these direct and vicarious experiences provide a framework for developing the language processes of speaking, listening, and writing as well as reading.

In addition to using field trips, books, favorite television programs, and other group or individual activities and experiences as sources for story content, dramatics are rich sources for creative thought and expression. They are literally reservoirs that can easily be taped for purposes of writing as a language experience. The imaginative content generated by children in play settings is ideally suited for creative language experience because dramatic and sociodramatic play are common experiences shared by all children and occur on a regular basis in all school programs and maximize the contributions of the members of the group and to a group product (1). Children in imaginative play settings share their ideas in the episodes.

In order to take advantage of the children's pretend play as grist for developing creative thought and expression and capitalize on their fullest use of creative communication in dramatic and sociodramatic play, a practical tool called the Language and Imaginative Play Experience Approach (LIPEA) was developed (41). As a modification of the traditional language experience approach, LIPEA contains two fundamental components — observation and creative language development. The observation component is the creative communication and thought shown in the pretend play episode. This component provides the raw data that is used in the creative language development component to develop creative language episodes from children's pretend play.

The observation component has several main elements that are used as guides while you watch the children perform their play episode. These elements are observing, interviewing, and transcribing. In observing, you watch the children in sociodramatic play as they role play themes, such as "On the Farm." Mental or written notes are taken on each child's role in the play. For instance, the teacher notes that Bessie decides to play the farmer's wife; Shanda becomes the farmer; Angelo and Leslie are the farmer's helpers; Sam is the farmer's cow named Henry. Secondly, and as the children perform their parts, you can gather more information about their pretending by listening to their statements and observing their motor actions. In this instance, you can observe and listen for what they say and what actions they use. You can also observe for qualitative characteristics of imaginative play such as how they use verbal statements and motor actions as they communicate to one another in the pretend episode. By carefully observing for the roles the students play and for quantity and quality of statements and motor actions, you prepare yourself for interviewing the children at the end of their creative episode. Gathering information about their uses of language and actions also aids you in transcribing the creative communication that the youngsters used in their sociodramatic play.

In interviewing and transcribing, which are the other two elements in the observation components, the teacher prepares the groundwork for the creative language component of the LIPEA model. Interviewing of the children begins after the pretend play is over. Here, you meet with the children in a group and encourage them to describe the roles played and the statements and actions that they used in the episode. In prompting, the youngsters orally retell the episode. Questions are used, as prompts, to help them recall what they said and did in the imaginative play episode, for example, "What were you playing?" "What parts did each of you plan?" "What did you say or do that showed that you were playing the role of. . .?" and "How did the pretend play begin . . . or end . . .?" In transcribing, the teacher asks the youngsters to retell the story, and she writes what they say on to the chalkboard or large sheet of paper. The transcription is matched closely and in as much detail as possible to the dictation of the students. An example of such a dictation from first grade children playing the episode, "On the Farm," follows:

At the conclusion of the transcribing, the creative language component of LIPEA begins. The three elements of this component are: (1) reading, (2) reviewing, and (3) retyping. Depending on the instructional objectives for developing creative language, the conceptual level, the age of the student, and the level of the child's growth in reading, writing, and spelling, you can decide to use all, none, or one or two of the elements in this second component.

In using the reading element, the teacher reads the story orally to the children after transcribing the dictated story. Each word is pronounced clearly and distinctly as the teacher slides her finger or marker under each word. After the teacher finishes the story, the children are individually asked to read the same selection as she paces them with a marker. If a youngster blocks on a word, the teacher gives the correct pronunciation without comment. The students are asked to read the passage several more times to improve oral fluency. In reviewing, both the youngsters and teacher review the major words selected in the composition. Here you may choose to frame each selected work with your hand as it appears in the story. The youngsters pronounce the words. As a final step, each of the words pronounced are in turn transcribed onto an index card for weekly practice. Each week the teacher and children meet for practice or word study with the index cards containing the new words from the narration.

TABLE 7-10.   ON THE FARM

| Dictation | Teacher observation of roles played and communication processes used in the episode. |
|---|---|
| We're playing farm just like on a real farm. Shanda played the farmer. Angelo and Leslie were the farmer's helpers. Sam was the cow, Henry. Henry was hungry and wanted something to eat. He mooed a lot and moved all around. | Pretend roles and situations |
| Angelo went to get some hay because Henry was hungry and tired of standing all day. Angelo looked in the barn and found some hay. Leslie took the hay and gave it to Henry. | Make-believe objects |
| The farmer's wife said that Henry would get bigger and bigger. Henry munched on the hay and thrashed his head all around. Then, Leslie gave Henry some water from a pail. | Make-believe actions |
| She told Henry not to spill. | Make-believe situations |
| Henry just mooed and drank. | Make believe actions |
| The sun was going down, so it was time to put Henry in the barn. | Make-believe situations |
| The farmer said he was going home to eat. The farmer's wife was going to go too, so we all said, "Goodbye!" | Make-believe situations |

In using the retyping element of the creative language component, the entire imaginative story is typed into more permanent form. The story is reviewed by the children rereading it.

Pretend play using the LIPEA procedures develops and facilitates creative language and thought, provides practice in showing children what a creative story looks like, and helps the children see written symbols for their spoken words. Using the LIPEA method, writing as a language experience story can facilitate creative thought and expression when imaginative play content is used as grist for playback, practice, and rehearsal of the pretend episode.

**Developing mental imagining through gaming.** Developing mental imagining and creative expression through gaming is ideal for the older child who can already distinguish fact from fantasy, has become less egocentric, and has greater control over his thoughts and actions. The techniques of developing mental imagining and creative expression encourage imagination in thought and communication by practicing visual fantasy, requiring the child to fill in details of the pretend image, and asking him to express his pretend image in detail.

In having the child creatively develop and express mental images, there are several important points that the teacher must remember and apply in the instructional or gaming process. First, as the older youngster develops and expresses his mental images, the variety of ideas generated are important and not whether they are right or whether they fit reality! Since children are actively engaged in developing and expressing their imaginative thoughts, have opportunities to generate hypothetical events, and practice productive thinking, all their comments and statements are accepted by the teacher. Accordingly, all the youngsters' comments are right, that is, RIGHTNESS IS NOT IMPORTANT in developing and expressing mental imagining. What is important is the quantity and variety of their expressed thoughts in creatively developing problem solving and inquiry.

Secondly, the teacher must remember that since quantity and variety of the youngsters' thoughts and expressions are her instructional objectives and not whether they are right, she cannot evaluate or judge them. Since the gaming procedures do not emphasize giving facts or judging "rightness" or "wrongness," the youngsters are free to respond and express their imaginative thoughts. Ultimately, as the children gain practice in developing and expressing mental images through instructional gaming, they will learn that they have plenty of room to consider alternatives, state preferences, and independently arrive at conclusions.

In order to develop mental imagining through gaming at least two individuals are needed to play — the teacher and the youngster. The teacher sets the youngster up for the gaming process by first making a reality statement, then a series of fantasy statements about an object, person, or situation. Then you make a series of imperative and interrogative statements to develop mental imagining. These imperative and interrogative statements depart from reality, are fictional — part of the pretend world. The children in turn respond or answer these statements. After the story is over, the teacher ask the youngsters for the name of a title for the game. This question signals the child that the game is over. For example, the teacher says (7:51-53):

The name of this game is BOYS AND GIRLS.

Let us imagine that there is a boy standing in the corner of this room. / Let us give him a hat. What color would you like the hat to be? / Let us give him a jacket. What color jacket shall we give him? / Let us give him some trousers. What color do you want his trousers to be? / Let him have some shoes. What color will you let him have?

Now change the color of his hat. / What color did you change it to? / Change it again. / What color this time? / Change it again. / What color? / Look at his jacket. What color is it? / Change it to another color. / Change it again. /

Change it again. What color are his trousers now? / Change the color of his trousers. / Change them again. / Change them again. / What color are his shoes now/ / Change them to another color. / Change them again. / Change them again. / What color are they now?

Have him stand on one foot and hold his other foot straight out in front of him. / Have him stand on the other foot. / Have him walk over to another corner of the room. / Have him go to another corner. / Have him sing a song. / Have him go to another corner.

Have him lie down and roll across the floor. / Have him run around on his hands and knees. / Have him stand on his hands. / Have him sing a song while he is standing on his hands. / Have him run around the room on his hands.

Have him stand on his feet. / Have him jump up into the air. / Have him jump up higher. / Have him jump up and touch the ceiling. / Have him sit in a chair. / Have the chair float up to the ceiling and stay there. / Have the boy sing something while he sits up there. / Have the chair come down. / Have the boy float up to the ceiling without the chair. / Have him float to a corner of the room up there. / Have him float to another corner. / Have him sing "Three Blind Mice." / Have him float to another corner. / Have him float to another corner.

Have him come down to the floor. / Have him say "Goodbye" and go out the door to visit a friend. / Look into one corner of the room and see that he is not in that corner. / Look into another corner and see that he is not there either. / Look into all the other corners, above and below, and find that he is not in any of them.

Put a girl in one corner of the room. / Give her a red hat. / Give her a blue sweater. / Give her a green skirt. / Give her brown shoes. / Now make her hat blue. / Make her sweater yellow. / Make her skirt purple. / Make her shoes black. / Change them to green. / Change them to yellow. / Change all her clothes to white. / Change them to black. / Change them to purple. / Change them to green.

Have her be in another corner of the room. / Have her be in another corner. / Have her sing a song. / Have her be in another corner.

Have her float up to the ceiling. / Have her turn upside down and stand on the celing. / Have her walk all around the ceiling, looking for the boy who was there before. / Have her look in all the corners up there and find that he is not any of them.

Bring the boy back and put him on the ceiling with the girl. / Have them standing on the ceiling playing ball. / Put another boy and another girl on the ceiling with them, and have all four playing ball. / Put some more boys and girls on the ceiling, and have them all playing ball. / Turn them all right side up, and put them on the roof of the house. / Put them in the play yard at school. / Make twice as many of them, and have them all shouting.

Make a new crowd of boys and girls on the ceiling. / Put them on the roof. / Put them in the school yard. / Have all the children shouting and running around.

Look at the ceiling and see that there are no children there. / Put one boy there. / Put him in the school yard. Put one girl on the ceiling. / Put her in the school yard.

Have no one on the ceiling. / Have it full of boys and girls. / Have it empty again. / Have no one on the roof. / Have it covered with boys and girls. / Have it empty again.

/ Have no one in the school yard. / Have it full of boys and girls. / Have it empty again.

Put one child in the school yard. / Is it a boy or a girl? / What color are his (her) clothes? / What would you like to do with him (her)? / All right, do it.

What is the name of the game we just played? (This question indicates that the game is over and signals a return to reality. If the youngsters do not remember the title of the game, you can give them the name.)

A second example of developing mental imagining through games follows (7:57-58, 62):

This game is called ANIMALS.

We are going to start with one little mouse, and see what we can do.

Let us imagine that there is a little mouse somewhere in the room. Where would you like to put him?/ All right, have him sit up and wave to you. / Have him turn green. / Change his color again. / Change it again. / Have him stand on his hands. Have him run over to the wall. / Have him run up the wall. / Have him sit upright down on the ceiling. / Turn him right side up and put him in a corner up there. / Put another mouse in another corner up there. / Put a mouse in each of the other two corners up there. / Put other mice in the four corners down below. / Are they all there? / Turn them all yellow. / Have them all say "Hello" at the same time. / Have them all say "How are you? / Have them all promise to stay in their corners and watch the rest of the game.

Put a little dog right over there (*Pointing*). / Have him bark. / Have him sit up and laugh. / Give him the name Felix. / Ask him his name and have him answer Felix. / Have him grow bigger. / Have him grow bigger. / Have him grow smaller./ Have him grow much smaller. / Have him grow so small that he is no bigger than a pea. / Have him turn into a cat no bigger than a pea. / Have the cat grow as big as a potato. / Have it grow as big as your head. / Have it grow into a big, fat blue cat. / Have it turn into a horse but stay the same size.

Are the yellow mice all in their places? / Have them clap hands because the cat turned into a little horse. / Have the little horse grow bigger. / Have him grow bigger still. / Have him grow very big. / Have him become little again. / Have him be as big as your head. / Have him be as big as your hand. / Have him be as big as your thumb.

Ask him his name and have him tell you George. / Change his name to Rudolph. / Ask him his name and have him tell you Rudolph. / Change his name to Harry. / Ask him his name and have him tell you Harry. / Take away his name. / Ask him his name and have him shake his head. / Pick a good name for him and give it to him. / Ask him his name and have him tell you that name.

Is he as big as your thumb/? Change him into an elephant but keep him the same size. / Have him grow as big as a pumpkin. / Have him grow as big as your bed. / Have him grow as big as you want him to be. / How big is he?

Have him shrink until he is as small as your thumb. / Have him shrink until he is no bigger than a pea. / Have him be no bigger than a pinhead. / Have him shrink until there is nothing left of him at all.

Look at the place where he was and see that he is not there. / Have the yellow mice clap their hands in admiration. / Put a new elephant there. / Make him as big as a police dog. / Make him as big as a cat. / Make him as big as a mouse. / Make him as big as a pea. / Have him shrink away to nothing.

Look where he was and see that there is nothing there. / Have the yellow mice cheer and wave their arms and legs. / Put a new elephant where the other one was. / Make him as big as you want to make him. / Make him as small as you want to make him. / Have him shrink away to nothing.

Look where he was and see that there is no elephant there. / Have the yellow mice write letters home to their friends to tell what wonderful things you do with elephants.

Put a new elephant there. / Change him to a dog. / Change the dog to a cat. / Change the cat to a mouse. / Change the mouse to a pea. / Change the pea to nothing. / Look and see that there is no pea there.

Put a new pea there./Have it not be there, / Have a dog there. / Have no dog there. / Have a cat there. / Have no cat there. / Have an elephant there. / Have no elephant there.

Have the yellow mice clap their hands. / Have them come to the place where the elephant was. / Have them grow smaller. / Have them grow smaller still. / Have no mice there. / Have some new mice there. / Make them blue. / Have no mice there.

Have one mouse there. / What color do you want it to be? / What do you want to do with it? / All right, do it.

What was the name of the game we just played?

You can make up similar story titles and contents with lead-ins, and a series of imperative and interrogatory statements using the above two narratives as examples.

In using these types of stories with children, there are three other additional instructional procedures that must be used in developing mental imagining: (1) providing the right time and place, (2) setting the pace, and (3) progressing in step-by-step fashion.

Prior to actually reading the story, you can determine the right time and right place to introduce the passage. In order to begin the game and develop mental imagining, the classroom must first be free of distraction (7). Distractions such as loud noises, conversations, playground settings, and others are just not appropriate times for imagining through gaming. Distractions limit the children's attention and concentration on the story setting and teacher statements. The right time and place mean also that the pupils want to play the game. Voluntary participation is a necessary ingredient for developing imagination and creative expression through this form of gaming. The teacher can schedule these games in the classroom on a daily basis or at a minimum once a week. Regardless of the number of times they are played per week, we recommend that the teacher set a time limit for playing. You can also decide the number of games that will be played with the children before they begin.

The second instructional strategy is pacing. The youngsters determine the rate at which they move through the story and respond to the statements. They also signal the teacher when they are ready to move from one teacher statement to another. "Different children will have different ways of signaling. Some will say, 'Okay' or 'Um-m.' Some may not signal at all. Then you will have to ask questions (e.g., 'Are you ready for the next one?') " and ". . . work out a signal that is satisfactory . . ." (7:62). In a group situation, children enjoy hearing and commenting on each other's pretend statements. In these situations, you can allow time for interacting and exchanging ideas. Using the games in group situations, the teacher can also allow "silent sustained imagining," which gives each individual the time to develop mental imagining. Then the teacher can ask for volunteers who want to share by expressing their mental images.

*A slant (/) means that the teacher stops, waits for the child to respond and continues to the next statement after he has signaled to move on.

The final instructional procedure is "progressing in step-by-step fashion." The story content and statements are constructed along a continuum from reality to fantasy, then back to reality. In making up additional stories and statements, the same continuum can be used. This procedure enables the child to begin in reality and end in reality. In progressing in a step-by-step fashion from reality to fantasy and then back to reality, the teacher recognizes that some children may have difficulty in proceeding from reality to fantasy. These children may believe that their imagination must follow the rules of reality, not fantasy. For instance, in the game called BOYS AND GIRLS (7), a youngster may say, "There is no boy standing in the corner of the room!" DeMille (7) offers two alternatives to help free the child from the restraints of reality in this situation. First, the teacher points out ". . . to the child that he does not have to follow the rule of reality when he is imagining things" (7:35). The teacher can say to the child "That there is an imaginary boy" or "that a person could pretend that he is there." The second alternative is used when the youngster continues to insist that the person, object, or situation cannot exist or he (or it) cannot do this or that action. In using this second alternative, DeMille (7:35) assumes that, "for every imaginary event that is difficult to imagine because it contradicts the rules of reality, there is a lesser, similar event that will present little or no difficulty." Thus, "if reality cannot be contradicted all at once, it can be contradicted by degrees" (7:35).

For example, if the child cannot "get" an imaginary boy to appear in the corner of the room, perhaps he can picture his favorite toy he plays with at home to appear. The idea behind the second alternative is to move from reality to fantasy in short easily comprehensible steps and ". . . not to compromise between reality and fantasy but to distinguish them clearly and separate them effectively" (7:35).

Developing mental imagining through gaming is another effective tool that is used to facilitate imaginative thought and creative expression. This strategy like the others is instructional and pleasurable for both you and your children.

**Talking about pretend things.** Many teachers of older children either schedule "talking time" as a part of daily classroom routines or hold it as the felt needs, interests, or occasions arise. Accordingly, in "talking time," children show ideas and discuss items of interest to them. It essentially provides an opportunity for youngsters to share communication and meaningfully interact with one another. At the same time, this spontaneous dialogue on matters of mutual interest provides a time to (1) imitate shared conversation, (2) practice oral language skills, (3) develop listening, (4) focus attention on a topic, (5) practice pronouncing clearly, and (6) practice articulation skills.

"Talking time" can be based on a number of interests and direct and vicarious experiences of the children. These sources include: field trips, an object brought to school by a youngster, a popular story, special events such as birthdays, special holidays of interest to various cultural, religious, and racial groups, favorite television shows, and new ideas and words the children recall from a poem, riddle, or story.

A variation of "talking time" is used to serve the development of imaginative thought and expressive communication. In the variation, the children are asked to talk about pretend things. The types of things used as a source of "talking-about-pretend-things" should be discussed with the children. When pupils are asked to help decide these matters, they are more willing to participate and volunteer their creative thoughts. As "talking-about-pretend-things" is initiated in the classroom, children not only develop and practice communication skills and concepts, but they also develop and practice imaginative thinking and creative expression. By "talking-about-pretend-things," they also are better able to distinguish fact from fantasy, reduce their fears and anxieties about their fantasy world (that adults may not take seriously or do not understand), to receive reinforcement for imagination and to learn that other children have similar creative thoughts. There are numerous sources for "talking-about-pretend-things." Some of these include make-believe companions and what they do and say, the Tooth Fairy, pretend pictures in the children's mind, and dramatic and sociodramatic play themes such as "Mothers and Fathers" or "Going Shopping." There is another source that begins with the statement, "What would happen if. . . ." For example, children could develop and express creative thoughts about the topic, "What would happen if horses could fly?" or ". . . if cats could drive cars?" These situations could focus on objects (for example, animals), people, and situations. These "what if . . ." situations are ideas to spark imaginative thought and develop creative expression.

Many opportunities for "talking-about-pretend-things" arise throughout the day. They occur as the youngsters come in from the playground, as they read stories, perform class duties and special events, and as they go about other normal routines throughout the day. In setting the stage for either "talking time" or its creative variation, "talking-about-pretend-things," the objectives are to develop pupils' imaginative thoughts, practice creative expressions, and develop their spontaneity. The following strategies will help to facilitate group discussion and imaginative thoughts and creative expressions in "talking time" and "talking-about-pretend-things." They include:

1. Sharing ideas with the group rather than with you.
2. Having the youngsters question to find out more about each other's imaginative thoughts.
3. Modeling sound listening habits for the youngsters.
4. Using "circular" or other seating arrangements that develop and

reinforce sound speaking and listening skills.

**5.** Providing the children with the choice of whether or not they wish to share their pretend or real thoughts.

**6.** Praising reluctant or shy children who occasionally share their thoughts.

**7.** Relying upon the youngsters to help make decisions about the topics they wish to discuss.

"Talking-about-pretend-things" and "talking time" are superb strategies to use with older children. They can provide opportunities to help develop and practice imaginative thought and creative expression.

## Some General Teacher Strategies

Whether the young child you teach is three, four, or seven or eight years of age, you strengthen (or weaken) creative imagination and expression in direct and indirect ways throughout the school day. In previous sections of this chapter, we explained specific strategies that can be used with younger and older children to encourage imaginative thought and expression. There are several other strategies that are general in nature. Accordingly, these strategies can be implemented with children regardless of age and in preschools through grade three. These general strategies point out that we, as teachers, can also facilitate creative thought and communication in direct ways, such as through our comments, questions, and statements as well as in direct ways, for example by our facial expressions, body movements, and other nonverbal actions. Through casual statements and nonverbal actions we also have the opportunity of developing and reinforcing creative behaviors in children. The statements and nonverbal actions are actually cues or prompts directed in a planned manner prior to, during, or after they show creative actions. Whether they are direct or indirect, they help children learn to use and apply imaginative and creative actions. These cues also assist pupils in growth and learning when they model or imitate our statements and copy our nonverbal actions in play and work settings. Some of these general teacher strategies that facilitate imaginative thought and creative expression are (1) adult playfulness, (2) oral cues, (3) physical cues, and (4) description.

**Adult playfulness.** Adult playfulness occurs when the teacher acts out, shows, or models a playful person. This general strategy is an indirect but nonetheless a very effective tool. Using this strategy enables children to see and copy your playful actions in their own imaginative and creative activities. Thus, adult playfulness not only provides a creative model for children to imitate but also gives them a sense of security — a good feeling that their actions are accepted. This general technique when used properly is a powerful reinforcer for learning and using imaginative thought and creative expression.

Basically, there are a number of ways of using this strategy of adult playfulness in your work with children and in teaching creative expression and imaginative thought. The teacher models a playful adult through playful gestures and statements made to the youngsters which are used in their imaginative thinking and expression. In playful gestures, the teacher communicates to the pupils in nonverbal ways that reinforce and extend their creative actions. For example, as the children imaginatively express and play their roles in "Eating Dinner," you can use gestures to show eating, drinking, and pleasure. With gestures, the children's imaginative thoughts and expressions are encouraged and reinforced through the strategy of a playful adult.

Secondly, you can also model creative actions for the children through playful statements directed at the pupils' imaginative actions. Depending upon the phrasing, the playful statements may or may not require the children to respond. For instance, you watch the youngster's role play, "Visiting Aunt Bea," and in the episode Aunt Bea becomes ill. You can ask, "What made Aunt Bea ill?" The other type of statement does not require the children to directly respond to your playful statement. For example, the children are engrossed in the creative play theme entitled, "Exploring Mars." One of the "astronauts" says he has just jumped over the mountains on the moon. The teacher, observing their imaginative thought and creative expression, can offer a playful statement such as, "That jump over the mountain was very high . . . .!" It is also supportive of the child's creative expression but does not require a formal response.

**Oral cues.** The strategy of oral cues is direct intervention into the imaginative actions of children through comments and questions. These intervening comments are made sensitively and at an appropriate time in the children's creative thinking and expression and imaginative actions. Accordingly, oral cues present new and novel thoughts into the youngster's creative thinking and increase the quantity and quality of their imaginative thoughts and communication. Thus, the youngsters can incorporate this new and novel information carried in the teacher's oral comments and questions into their creative actions. Since the oral cues are never aimed at the children but at the situations played and objects used in their imaginative activities, they are challenges or prompts and opportunities for additional creative uses of thought and expression.

In using the strategy of oral cues to prompt further creative uses of objects, the teacher, for example, says, "Show in your play how the cardboard box can be used as a bridge for the tiger (instead of its previous use a bed in which it slept)." By incorporating the oral cue and using the cardboard box as a bridge after it was initially used as a bed, the children enrich, expand, and increase their creative thought and expression. Oral cues require the youngsters to determine imaginatively and conceptually and then creatively act out new and novel cues and ideas in the episode.

**Physical cues.** Like oral cues, physical cues or prompts require the teacher to add new and novel bits of information in a sensitive manner and at an appropriate time to enrich, expand, and increase the quality and quantity of the children's creative thoughts and expression. Physical cues add other concrete materials and play objects to the children's creative activities. In seeking to use the new materials in their imaginative activities, the youngsters spontaneously modify and creatively enrich their thoughts and communication within the playful episode. Like oral prompts, physical cues are challenges and creative opportunities to use new and novel objects in addition to the others they are currently using in their play. As the pupils creatively portray "Electing a Mayor," for instance, you carefully observe the play materials used in the episode. At an appropriate time in the episode you introduce, for example, nails, brown paper bags, erasers, or other materials not presently being used in the theme, "Electing a Mayor." Accordingly, the novel objects must be creatively treated and imaginatively used in some form or fashion by the pupils enacting the episode. Physical, like oral, cues are highly useful and successful strategies that serve to enrich, expand, and increase the children's imaginative thinking and creative expression.

**Description.** Similar to the strategy of "adult playfulness," "description" is incidental and more indirect than either oral and physical cuing. Used appropriately and sensitively, the strategy of description focuses solely on the creative language the children use either in their normal daily routines or in their imaginative play. Accordingly, the purpose of employing the descriptive strategy is to extend the child's creative expression and at the same time develop breadth, depth, and richness through its extension. Thus, in applying the descriptive strategy, you first listen for creative communication the youngsters use in their conversations with one another or in their sociodramatic play episodes. The teacher restates the pupil's thought and extends his language statements. In repeating and then extending the statements, the idea is to add words and phrases to the ideas to make the child's communication as descriptive, life-like, and as creative as possible. An example of using the descriptive strategy follows. In their imaginative play, the youngsters may say, "See my house built from blocks!" The statement is creative, and it can be repeated and extended to make it more creative and imaginative. Here, you repeat and extend it to make it more imaginative. For example, you can say:

"See my large brown house built from rectangular blocks!"
"See my house built from blocks which towers high into the sky!"
"See my house built from blocks — it is lean and mean!"

The child's statement is repeated and extended, giving him a model for creative expression. Adding words that clearly form pictures of imaginative thinking vividly communicates what is happening and encourages students to model and thus develop and learn more enriched creative expression.

In addition, you can also use the descriptive strategy through the game called "Guessing the Roles." After the youngsters complete a sociodramatic episode, you describe one of the pupil's roles as vividly and as creatively as possible. Accordingly, the children's task is to guess the name of the role that child was playing. The name elicited by the pupils is the name of the character or role played in the dramatic story, *not* his real name. For instance, the teacher's creative summary of a role is, "Flying around the classroom with a large red cape, the person lightly touched a button on a blue belt hanging from the waist and captured the thief!" Then ask, "What *role* was played?"

The general teacher strategies of adult playfulness, oral cues, physical cues, and description have the potential to encourage imaginative thought and creative expression. By applying them in direct and indirect ways, pupils model and learn imaginative thoughts and creative expression.

## RESOURCES FOR TEACHERS

In previous sections of this chapter, we listed and explained a series of techniques, first at the preschool-kindergarten level and then at the primary grades that could encourage and facilitate imaginative play and creative expression. Examples were given of each of these techniques that could be used, expanded, and modified to fit with specific age and grade levels. In addition there are a number of resources that teachers could readily use to supplement these techniques, including books, journals, records, curriculum packages, and educational materials and objects. Accordingly, the purpose of this section is to acquaint you with current and classical resources for each of the techniques so that you can supplement and extend these ideas to facilitate creative thought and expression of children. Some of these resources can be purchased, while others are available at minimal or no cost. In turn, these resources can become part of your professional, classroom, or school library for immediate and handy use.

### Preschool-Kindergarten Resources

#### Classroom materials.

*Books.*
Croft, Doreen and Hess, Robert, *An Activities Handbook for Teachers of Young Children.* New York: Houghton Mifflin, 1975.

Frost, Joe and, Kissinger, Joan, *The Young Child and the Creative Process.* New York: Holt, Rinehart and Winston, 1976.

Furth, Hans and Wachs, Harry, *Thinking Goes to School.* New York: Oxford, 1974.

Hartley, Ruth; Frank, Lawrence; and Goldenson, Richard, *Understanding Children's Play.* New York: Teachers College Press-Columbia University, 1969.

Hildebrand, Verna, *Introduction to Early Childhood.* New York: Macmillan, 1976.

Lindberg, Lucille and Swedlow, Rita, *Early Childhood Education: A Guide for Observation and Participation.* Boston: Allyn and Bacon, 1979.

Lorton, Mary, *Workjobs: Activity-Centered Learning for Early Childhood Education.* Menlo Park, Calif.: Addison-Wesley, 1972.

Matterson, Elizabeth, *Play and Playthings for the Preschool Child.* Baltimore: Baltimore Penguin, 1971.

Tiedt, Sidney and, Tiedt, Iris, *Language Arts Activities for the Classroom.* Boston: Allyn and Bacon, 1978.

Yawkey, Thomas Daniels and Dank, Herbert, *Play Inside and Out: For Parents and Teachers of Young Children.* Menlo Park, Calif.: Addison-Wesley, in press.

*Journals.*
The 107-page booklet, *Selecting Educational Equipment and Materials,* can be ordered from The Association for Childhood Education International, Publications Division, 3615 Wisconsin Avenue, N.W., Washington, D.C. 20016.

The monthly newsletter, *Today's Child,* offers numerous practical and useful ideas on classroom and home materials for imaginative play and creative expression. Inquiries about the newsletter can be directed to: The Editor, *Today's Child,* 1 School Lane, Roosevelt, New Jersey 08555.

The journal entitled *Theory Into Practice* published a theme issue entitled "The Value of Play" (Volume 13, Number 4), October 1974, and copies of the issue can be ordered by writing the journal offices, The Ohio State University, Columbus, Ohio 43210.

*Materials catalogues.* Commercial classroom materials catalogues are free and available upon request from the following companies at the addresses indicated.

Child Craft Educational Corporation
20 Kilmer Road
Edison, New Jersey 08817

Creative Play Things
The Growing Tree
202 South Allen Street
State College, Pennsylvania 16801

Douglas Company, Inc.
Drawer D
Keene, New Hampshire 03431

Educational Teaching Aids, Inc.
A. Daigger and Company
159 West Kinzie Street
Chicago, Illinois 60610

Fisher-Price Toys
70 Church Street
East Aurora, New York 14052

Galt Educational Materials
63 Whitfield Street
Guilford, Connecticut 06437

Learning Products, Inc.
725 Fee Fee Road
Saint Louis, Missouri 63045

Morrison School Supplies
304 Industrial Way
San Carlos, California 94070

Forest W. Wilcox Associates, Inc.
P.O. Box 23002
Richfield, Minnesota 55423

*Magazines.*
*Instructor Magazine* is available by writing Instructor, 757 Third Avenue, New York, New York 10017

*Childhood Education* can be examined by writing The Association for Childhood Education International, Publications Division, 3615 Wisconsin Avenue, N.W., Washington, D.C. 20016

*Early Years Magazine* can be obtained by writing *Early Years,* 1 Hale Lane, Darien, Connecticut 06820

*Day Care and Early Education* can be purchased from Human Sciences

Press, 72 Fifth Avenue, New York, New York 10011.

*Commercial retailers.* Most hobby and learning stores also provide classroom and home materials for children, three through eight years of age. Teacher supply stores are located in almost every city in the country. They provide a vast array of materials to encourage imaginative play and creative expression.

### Materials for creative dramatics.

*Books.*

Batchhelder, Marjorie, *Puppets and Plays.* New York: Harper and Row, 1956.

Blackie, Paul; Bullough, Barbara; and Nash, Donald, *Drama.* New York: Citation, 1972.

Durland, Frances, *Creative Dramatics for Children.* Yellow Springs, Ohio: The Antioch Press, 1952.

Edwards, Charlotte, *Creative Dramatics.* Dansville, N.Y.: The Instructor Publications, 1972.

Fitzergald, Burdette, *Let's Act the Story.* Palo Alto, Calif.: Fearon, 1957.

Haaga, Agnes and Randles, Patricia, *Supplementary Materials for Use in Creative Dramatics with Younger Children.* Seattle, Wash.: University of Washington Press, 1952.

Hanford, Robert, *Puppets and Puppeteering.* New York: Drake, 1976.

Heinig, Ruth and Stilwell, Lydia, *Creative Dramatics for the Classroom Teacher.* Englewood Cliffs, N.J.: Prentice-Hall, 1974.

Hutson, Natalie, *Stage: A Handbook for Teachers of Creative Dramatics.* Stevensville, Mich.: Educational Services, 1968.

McClaslin, Nellie, *Creative Dramatics in the Classroom.* New York: David McKay, 1968.

Renfro, Nancy, *Puppets for Play Production.* New York: Funk and Wagnalls, 1969.

Tiedt, Iris and Tiedt, Sidney, *Contemporary English in the Elementary School.* Englewood Cliffs, N.J.: Prentice-Hall, 1975.

Ward, Winifred, *Play Making with Children.* New York: Appleton-Century-Crofts, 1957.

Ward, Winifred, *Stories to Dramatize.* Anchorage, Ky.: Children's Theatre Press, 1952.

*Children's stories to dramatize.*

Di Noto, Andrea, *The Star Thief*. New York: Macmillan, 1971.

Freeman, Don, *Corduroy*. New York: Viking Press, 1968.

Piper, Watty, *The Little Engine That Could*. New York: Platt and Munk, 1944.

Sawyer, Ruth, *Johnny Cake Ho!* New York: Viking, 1953.

Sendak, Maurice, *Where the Wild Things Are*. New York: Harper and Row, 1963.

**Materials for creative movement.**

*Books.*

Bartel, Lea, *Movement Awareness and Creativity*. New York: Harper and Row, 1975.

Baylor, Barbara, *Sometimes I Dance Mountains*. New York: Charles Scribner, 1973.

Braley, William, *Daily Sensorimotor Training Activities: A Handbook for Teachers and Parents of Preschool Children*. New York: Educational Activities, Inc., 1968.

Cherry, Charles, *Creative Movement for the Developing Child*. Fearon, Calif.: Palo Alto, 1972.

Davis, Martha, *Understanding Body Movement*. New York: Arno, 1972.

Gallahue, David, *Motor Development and Movement Experiences for Young Children*. New York: John Wiley, 1976.

Latchaw, Marjorie and Egstrom, Glen, *Human Movement with Concepts Applied to Children's Movement Activities*. Englewood Cliffs, N.J.: Prentice-Hall, 1969.

Moran, Joan and Kalakian, Leonard, *Movement Experiences for the Mentally Retarded or Emotionally Disturbed Child,* Minneapolis, Minn.: Burgess, 1977.

Moustakes, Clark, *Creative Life*. New York: Van Nostrand Reinhold, 1977.

Smith, James, *Creative Teaching of Creative Arts in the Elementary School*. Boston: Allyn and Bacon, 1970.

**Materials about story telling.**

*Books.*

Bailey, Carolyn and Lewis, Clara, *For the Children's Hour*. New York: Platt and Munk, 1943.

Chambers, Dewey, *Storytelling and Creative Drama*. Dubuque, Iowa: William C. Brown, 1970.

Colum, Patricia, *Story Telling Old and New*. New York: Macmillan, 1968.

Cook, Elizabeth, *The Ordinary and the Fabulous: An Introduction to Myths, Legends, and Fairy Tales*. New York: Cambridge University Press, 1976.

Gardner, Richard, *Therapeutic Communication with Children*. New York: Science House, 1971.

Krataville, Betty, *Listen My Children and You Shall Hear*. Danville, Ill.: Interstate, 1968.

Moore, Vardine, *Pre-school Story Hour*. Metuchen, N.J.: Scarecrow, 1972.

Sawyer, Dorothy, *The Way of the Storyteller*. New York: Viking, 1969.

Taylor, Loren, *Storytelling and Dramatization*. Minneapolis, Minn.: Burgess, 1965.

Tooze, Ruth, *Storytelling*. Englewood Cliffs, N.J.: Prentice-Hall, 1959.

## Primary Grade Resources

### Pantomime.

*Books.*
Enters, Angna, *On Mime*. Middletown, Conn.: Wesleyan University Press, 1965.

Hunt, Douglas, *Pantomime: The Silent Theatre*. New York: Atheneum, 1964.

Taylor, Loren, *Informal Dramatics for Young Children*. Minneapolis, Minn.: Burgess, 1965.

Taylor, Loren, *Pantomime and Pantomime Games*. Minneapolis, Minn.: Burgess, 1965.

Whitlock, Virginia, *Come and Caper: Creative Rhythms, Pantomimes, and Plays*. New York: G. Schirmer, 1972.

### Puppets.

*Books.*
Binyon, Helen, Puppetry Today. New York: Watson-Guptil, 1966.

Bodor, John, *Creating and Presenting Hand Puppets*. New York: Reinhold, 1967.

Fickley, Bessie, *A Handbook of First Puppets*. New York: Frederick A. Stokes, 1945.

Grossman, Jean, *How to Use Hand Puppets in Group Discussions*. New York: Play Schools Association, 1952.

Hopper, Grizella, *Puppet Making Through the Grades*. Worcester, Mass.: Rand McNally, 1966.

Kampmann, Lothar, *Creating with Puppets*. New York: Van Nostrand Reinhold, 1972.

Stahl, LeRoy and Preston, Effa, *The Master Puppet Book*. Minneapolis, Minn.: T. S. Denison, 1965.

Still, William, *Charming Children With Puppets*. Jacksonville, Fla.: Paramount, 1967.

Suib, Leonard and Broadman, Muriel, *Puppets*. New York: Harper and Row, 1975.

Taylor, Loren, *Puppetry, Marionettes, and Shadow Plays*. Minneapolis, Minn.: Burgess, 1965.

*Children's books.*
Cummings, Richard, *101 Hand Puppets: A Guide for Puppeteers of All Ages*. New York: David McKay, 1972.

Green, Michael, *Space Age Puppets and Masks*. Boston: Plays, Inc., 1969.

Jagendorf, Moritz, *The First Book of Puppets*. New York: Franklin Watts, 1952.

## Directed role play.

*Books.*
Biddle, Bruce and Thomas, Edwin (ed.), *Role Theory: Concepts and Research*. New York: John Wiley, 1966.

Chesler, Mark and Fox, Robert, *Role-playing Methods in the Classroom*. Chicago: Science Research Associates, 1966.

Furness, Pauline, *Role Play in the Elementary School: A Handbook for Teachers*. New York: Hart, 1976.

Gartner, Alan; Kohler, Mary; and Riessman, Frank, *Children Teach Children: Learning by Teaching*. New York: Harper and Row, 1971.

Sarason, Irwin and Sarason, Barbara, *Constructive Classroom Behavior: A Teacher's Guide to Modelling and Roletaking Techniques*. New York: Behavior Publications, 1974.

Shaftel, Fannie and Shaftel, George, *Roleplaying for Social Values: Decision Making in the Social Studies*. Englewood Cliffs, N.J.: Prentice-Hall, 1967.

Sharan, Shlomo, *Small Group Teaching*. Englewood Cliffs, N.J.: Educational Technology, 1976.

**Writing language experience.**

*Books.*

Ashton-Warner, Sylvia, *Teacher*. New York: Simon and Schuster, 1963.

DeBoer, John and Dallman, Martha, *The Teaching of Reading*. New York: Holt, Rinehart, and Winston, 1964.

Heilman, Arthur, *Principles and Practices of Teaching Reading*. Columbus, Ohio: Merrill, 1978.

Holt, John, *How Children Fail*. New York: Harper and Row, 1964.

Lee, Doris and Allen, Roach, *Learning to Read Through Experience*. New York: Appleton-Century-Crofts, 1963.

Moffett, James and Wagner, Betty, *Student-Centered Language Arts and Reading, K-13*. New York: Houghton Mifflin, 1976.

Stauffer, Robert, *The Language Experience Approach to the Teaching of Reading*. New York: Harper and Row, 1970.

Smith, Frank, *Understanding Reading*. New York: Holt, Rinehart, and Winston, 1971.

Tinker, Miles and McCullough, Constance. *Teaching Elementary Reading*. New York: Appleton-Century-Crofts, 1968.

Zintz, Miles, *The Reading Process*. Dubuque, Iowa: William C. Brown, 1972.

**Mental imagining through games.**

*Books.*

Abt, Clark, *Serious Games*. New York: Viking, 1973.

Almy, Milly (ed.), *Early Childhood Play: Selected Readings Related to Cognition and Motivation*. New York: Academic, 1968.

Caplan, Frank and Caplan, Teresa, *The Powers of Play*. New York: Anchor, 1974.

De Mille, Richard, *Put Your Mother on the Ceiling: Children's Imaginative Games.* New York: Viking, 1973.

Piers, Mia, *Play and Development.* New York: W. W. Norton, 1972.

**Talking about pretend things.**

*Books.*

Caplan, Frank and Caplan, Teresa, *The Power of Plan.* New York: Doubleday, 1973.

Klinger, Eric, *Structure and Functions of Fantasy.* New York: Wiley-Interscience, 1971.

Lieberman, J. Nina, *Playfulness: A Relationship to Imagination and Creativity.* New York: Academic, 1977.

Reilly, Mary, *Play as Exploratory Learning.* Beverly Hills, Calif.: Sage, 1974.

Singer, Jerome (ed.), *The Child's World of Make-Believe.* New York: Academic, 1974.

# REFERENCES

1. Allen, Roach, "The Language Experience Approach." In *Teaching Young Children to Read,* ed. William Cutts. Washington, D.C.: United States Department of Education, 1964, pp. 59-67.

2. Andrews, George, *Creative Rhythmic Movement for Children.* Englewood Cliffs, N.J.: Prentice-Hall, 1954.

3. Buros, Oscar (ed.), *The Seventh Mental Measurement Yearbook.* Highland Park, N.J.: Gryphon, 1970.

4. Chukovsky, Kornei, *From Two to Five.* Berkeley, Calif.: The University of California Press, 1963.

5. Curry, Nancy and Arnaud, Sara, "Cognitive Implications in the Children's Spontaneous Role Play," *Theory Into Practice* 1974, *13,* 273-277.

6. Dean, Raymond, and Kulhavy, Raymond, "Effects of Language Facilitation in Learning," *American Educational Research Journal* 1978, *15,* 344-352.

7. De Mille, Richard, *Put Your Mother on the Ceiling.* New York: Viking, 1973, pp. 51-53.

8. Dell, Edgar, *The Measurement of Social Competence: A Manual for the*

*Vineland Social Maturity Scale.* Circle Pines, Minn.: American Guidance Service, 1953.

9. Ellis, Michael, *Why People Play.* Englewood Cliffs, N.J.: Prentice-Hall, 1973.

10. Garvey, Catherine, *Play.* Cambridge, Mass.: Harvard University Press, 1974, p. 60.

11. Hanford, Robert, *Puppets and Puppeteering.* New York: Drake, 1976.

12. Hartley, Ruth; Frank, Lawrence; and Goldenson, Richard, *Understanding Children's Play.* New York: Teacher's College Press-Columbia University, 1969.

13. Heining, Ruth and Stillwell, Lyda, *Creative Dramatics for the Classroom Teacher.* Englewood Cliffs, N.J.: Prentice-Hall, 1974.

14. Hildebrand, Verna, *Guiding Groups of Preschool Children.* New York: Macmillan, 1978.

15. Lieberman, Nina, "Playfulness and Divergent Thinking: An Investigation of Their Relationships at the Kindergarten Level." *Journal of Genetic Psycology,* 1965, *107,* 219-224.

16. Lieberman, Nina, *Playfulness: Its Relationships to Imagination and Creativity.* New York: Academic Press, 1977.

17. Matteoni, Louise; Lane, Wilson; Sucher, Floyd; and Yawkey, Thomas, *The Keytext Program.* Oklahoma City: The Economy Company, 1978.

18. Parten, Mildred and Newhall, Steven, "Social Behavior of Preschool Children," in *Behavior and Development,* ed. Roger Barker, Jacob Kounin, and Harold Wright. New York: McGraw-Hill, 1943, pp. 34-37.

19. Petty, Walter: Petty, Dorothy; and Becking, Marjorie. *Experiences in Language: Tools and Techniques for Language Arts Methods.* Boston: Allyn and Bacon, 1976.

20. Piaget, Jean, *Play, Dreams, and Imitation.* New York: W. W. Norton, 1962.

21. Piaget, Jean and Inhelder, Barbel, *Memory and Intelligence.* New York: Basic Books, 1973.

22. Pulaski, Mary Ann, "Play as a Function of Toy Structure and Fantasy Predispositions," *Child Development* 1970, *41,* 531-536.

23. Pulaski, Mary Ann, *Understanding Piaget.* New York: Harper and Row, 1973.

24. Read, Katherine, *The Nursery School*. Philadelphia: W. B. Saunders, 1966.

25. Rebelsky, Freda and Dorman, Lynn, *Child Development and Behavior*. New York: Alfred A. Knopf, 1974.

26. Renfro, Nancy, *Puppets for Play Production*. New York: Funk and Wagnalls, 1969.

27. Saltz, Eli and Johnson, James, "Training for Thematic-Fantasy Play in Culturally Disadvantaged Children: Preliminary Results," *Journal of Educational Psychology* 1974, 66, 189-194.

28. Saltz, Eli; Dixon, David; and Johnson, James, "Training Disadvantaged Preschoolers on Various Fantasy Activities: Effects on Cognitive Functioning and Impulse Control," *Child Development* 1977, 48, 367-380, 378-392.

29. Singer, Jerome, "Imagination and Make-Believe Play in Early Childhood: Some Educational Implications," *Journal of Mental Imagery* 1977, 1, 127-144.

30. Singer, Jerome, *The Child's World of Make-Believe*. New York: Academic Press, 1974.

31. Singer, Dorothy and Singer, Jerome, *Partners in Play*. New York: Harper and Row, 1977.

32. Smilansky, Sara, *The Effects of Sociodramatic Play on Disadvantaged Preschool Children*. New York: John Wiley, 1968.

33. Smith, Frank, *Understanding Reading*. New York: Holt, Rinehart, Winston, 1971.

34. Tiedt, Iris and Tiedt, Sidney, *Contemporary English in the Elementary School*. Englewood Cliffs, N.J.: Prentice-Hall, 1975.

35. Torrance, Paul, *Torrance Tests of Creative Thinking*. Princeton, N.J.: Personal Press, 1974.

36. Walker, Deborah, *Socioemotional Measures for Preschool and Kindergarten Children*. San Francisco: Jossey-Bass, 1973.

37. Yawkey, Thomas, "Imaginative Play Inside and Out: Assisting the Young Child's Development and Learning Through 'Let's Pretend'," Research Paper Presented at the International Playground Association, Ottawa, Canada, 1978.

38. Yawkey, Thomas, "More on Play as Intelligence," *Journal of Creative Behavior*, 1979, 13(4), 247-256; 262.

39. Yawkey, Thomas, "The Effects of Social Relationships, Curricula, and Sex Differences on Reading and Imaginativeness in Young Children," Research Paper Presented at the meeting of the American Educational Research Association, San Francisco, 1978.

40. Yawkey, Thomas, "Yawkey Imaginative Play Checklist," unpublished manuscript, The Pennsylvania State University, University Park, Pennsylvania, 1979.

41. Yawkey, Thomas and Blohm, Paul, "Imaginative Play: Language and Imaginative Play Experience Approach," in *Piagetian Theory and Its Implications for the Helping Professions,* ed. Robert Weitzmann, Robert Brown, and Patricia Taylor. Los Angeles: The University of Southern California Press, 1978, pp. 315-319.

42. Yawkey, Thomas and Hrncir, Elizabeth, "Using Imaginative Play as a Tool for Oral Language Growth in the Preschool," unpublished manuscript, The Pennsylvania State University, University Park, Pennsylvania, 1980.

43. Yawkey, Thomas and Silvern, Steven, "The Effects of Aural Language Recall in Young Children, Ages Five Through Seven," Research Paper Presented at the meeting of the American Educational Research Association, San Francisco, 1978.

# INDEX